MISSING PINE PARK

A humorous look at the '60s and '70s
from *kick the can* to becoming a man

NEIL R. BELLER, JR.

MAPLE CREEK MEDIA

Hampstead ◊ Maryland ◊ United States

Printed in the United States of America

ISBN-13: 9781942914037
ISBN-10: 1942914032

This book is a work of non-fiction. It is also a memoir, which is to say that the stories contained in this book reflects the author's recollections and interpretations of events. Dialogue has been recreated from memory. In good faith and to protect the privacy of individuals portrayed in this book, the author has changed the names of many characters. The author has also compressed timelines or omitted details in places.

MAPLE CREEK MEDIA
P.O. Box 624
Hampstead, MD 21074
Toll-Free Phone: 1-877-866-8820
Toll-Free Fax: 1-877-778-3756
Email: info@maplecreekmedia.com
Website: www.maplecreekmedia.com

LAURA,
EVEN THOUGH I
AM MUCH OLDER THAN
YOU, I KNOW THIS WILL
BRING BACK MANY MEMORIES.

BEST WISHES!

MISSING PINE PARK

DEDICATION

To all those who dare to take a ride in the ***Way Back Machine***.

ACKNOWLEDGEMENTS

Many thanks to my mother, sisters, brother and neighborhood friends for making my childhood worth remembering; my father for instilling in me the magic of youth and the clarity to carry that magic onward; and to my own family for allowing me to share that magic every night at the dinner table.

CONTENTS

CONTENTS (cont.)

CONTENTS (cont.)

PROLOGUE

I grew up in Carney, Maryland. It is buried in the quiet suburbs of Baltimore County, nestled somewhere between Parkville, Cub Hill and Perry Hall. Carney was named after the original landowners, but years later I find that I constantly have to explain to non-residents that Carney was not a training ground for learning how to bark for the bearded lady at the carnival.

I lived on a dead-end street called Uxbridge Road. It only had houses on one side of the street, as the other side was a small incline that led to a stream and a grove of woods. We lived in the third house, which was originally light green before being painted barn red and eventually adorned with gold aluminum siding with white trim. Next door to us lived the Bells and next to them were the Chadmans. I was at least ten years old before I realized that families didn't live in alphabetical order.

Every time I looked out the front window or ventured from my house to marvel at the wonder of Uxbridge Road, I would see the woods across the street. They looked creepy to me, and I knew that trolls, dwarfs, werewolves and Bigfoot lived in there somewhere. Of course, there were little elves making cookies, too, so that made it worth living near.

Uxbridge Road dissected Appleton Avenue, which was a hilly street. You could say we lived in a valley. When you rode your bike out of the neighborhood, you had to immediately climb a hill in either direction and had your choice of the "little hill" or the "big hill," as the neighborhood kids called them. These names referred to the grade of the hill, and you were considered a genuine neighborhood resident if you could climb the big hill on your bike without stopping. Serpentining back and forth like a cow or traversing the mountainside like a goat were two totally acceptable methods of travel.

The woods were on a plot of land that sat lower than the surrounding streets, so when you looked out at the trees, you were actually staring over their tops or mid-sections to the houses that were speckled up the hill on the other side. I figured it was at least two miles or so to those houses, but in reality they were only about seventy-five yards away.

Every house in our neighborhood averaged 4.72 kids. They varied in age, of course, but in the sixties you played with whomever was around. We had softball games with twenty-six players on a side, and everybody batted. We played in the woods, in backyards, in streets, in streams, and, during a massive game of "freedabox" (translation: "free the box," which was nothing more than a giant game of hide-and-seek), strangers' basements were somewhat allowed. We all got along. The only fight I ever participated in was with the paperboy, and he came from some other neighborhood, so I took him as an invader. After all, this was at the height of the Cold War, and he could have been a Russian spy.

Between Uxbridge Road and the woods there was a stream of running water called Jenny Run. You could jump over it easily, but because of the wild and vicious water animals that I was sure resided there, I never went first. The mouth of the stream was unknown and was thought to have originated as an offshoot of the Thames. As it entered our neighborhood, it went under Appleton Avenue through a huge black pipe that you could walk through standing straight up. We called it "the tunnel," and it was about forty feet long. When you were in the tunnel, light could only be seen directly in front of you or directly behind you. This was designed by the county who had special workers employed in the field of scaring children to death. We referred to their agency as the Department of Cruel and Unusual Punishment or, rather, D-CUP. These elusive employees also invented the playground toy that would spin you around until you puked as well as paper cuts, which made homework dangerous.

I used to get up at 7AM on a Saturday and say, "See you at dinner," as I blew out the front door. I'm sure our parents would check up on us, but it never seemed that way. You ate lunch at whosever house you were visiting, and if you had to go to the bathroom, you just knocked on someone's door and they would let you in. Naturally, to a young boy the world was your urinal, and you got pretty good at writing your name in the snow.

We didn't have sunscreen; we didn't have anti-bacterial spray; we didn't have the ability to see the creepy-crawly microscopic stuff that lived under our fingernails; we didn't have helicopter parents; we didn't have many fences; and we didn't have remote controls or wireless telephones. We had a milk or bread box on the front porch; we had the Good Humor man; we had the world's best snowball stand; we had a gas man that would just walk right into your unlocked basement; we had four channels of television and we loved it.

The adults in our neighborhood were equally cool, and just about every weekend someone was having a cookout. People we didn't even know handed us watermelon, disciplined us, laughed at our antics and told us wondrous stories of their youth, secretly wanting to participate in ours. We had the best trick-or-treating on the planet, and at Christmastime our world became magical. We lived in Carney.

I have always had a great memory. For some reason I have the ability to remember events from my childhood that others think are impossible. And when I say childhood, I mean infancy. I remember sitting in my crib, staring at my parents staring at me. I remember lying on my back, playing with my feet. I remember stretching out across the bottom step of our non-carpeted indoor stairs with my head against the wall, trying, in vain, to make my feet touch the wall on the other side, and I remember chewing the paint off the sill of my bedroom window. Fortunately, I do not remember the stomach pumping that followed.

I don't vaguely remember these things either; I totally remember these things. The way things smelled, the way the sun shone through the blinds in my room, and the way my father walked around jingling the change in his pockets to the sounds of Herb Alpert and the Tijuana Brass are all vivid memories for me. I can clearly see his jet-black hair, white T-shirt, tan khakis, and black belt as he strolled around the house, jingling to every song from *Going Places*.

I used to watch my father a lot, almost like he was a real live movie. He had a James Garner appearance, a smirk like Paul Newman, and a Steve McQueen stare. He developed a peculiar way of sitting in his chair while he watched television. I can still hear him laugh, clear his throat and cough. Since he was a smoker, he made some amazing noises in the bathroom first thing in the morning that I can only equate to as whale sounds.

I always wanted to be him. I remember crying because my feet were too wide to wear penny loafers. I thought his were so cool. He actually put pennies in the slits of the shoes. When I was four years old, our family went to the Bengies drive-in movies to see *Dr. Zhivago*. We got there early, before the sun went down, and had a picnic on the back of the car; then I played on a big swing set.

When the sun finally set, it became a little chilly, so my dad and I put on our matching sweaters. They were white sailing sweaters with blue and red trim and matched perfectly. I was his true Mini-Me. During the movie we had to go to the bathroom, so we walked past other families in their cars to the rest area. I remember thinking how cool we looked walking together and was sure that those watching us were jealous.

It was hot when we walked in, so I removed my button up, Mini-Me sweater and hung it up on the wall. It wasn't until the next day that we discovered it was missing. I had left it there by mistake. My mother called their lost and found, but nobody had turned it in. I was crushed. I wanted them to replace it so bad, but they never did. It left me a little disconnected, and every time I saw him wearing his sweater, I became sad. I can recall images like these at will.

When I talk about these images, I have the ability to relay events with all the detailed specifics intact, placing the listener at the scene. I overheard my brother in law John, once, describing a movie he had just seen to some friends. Suddenly he stopped and said, "No, wait, I didn't see that movie; Neil told me about it."

I have been accused of "creative embellishment" when I bring up these specific details. Their mere mention incites ridicule from my friends. When I re-live a story, I use the **Way Back Machine**. I call it that because there comes a time in our lives as we age, when we forget everything from certain periods of our life, but my memories come roaring back as if they happened minutes ago. It is like I am using a time machine, but everyone knows those don't exist, so I am using a **Way Back Machine**.

It is easy to use, and I don't even have to close my eyes. Right now I am seeing my best friend, Timmy Fitzpatrick, or Fitz, standing on a Flexible Flyer sled, using ropes to steer. He is flying down Appleton Avenue after a snowstorm singing *Bye, Bye, Miss American Pie* at the top of his lungs. As he zips past me, snow from the street flies up and lands on my black combat boots. Seconds later, he hits a patch of bare street where the Sullivans' car used to live and catapults headfirst through a shower of sparks from the rudders of his sled into a nearby hedge. After he sticks, his sled follows him. I still laugh just as hard now, when remembering it, as I did then. The sound of it was hilarious, and his red knit hat became permanently damaged. You have to love the *Way Back Machine.*

THE BLUE BATHROBE

Carney didn't have many restaurants. I remember a small diner in Woolworth's where all the waitresses looked like Flo from the TV show Alice. Most of them were older than the cafeteria lady at my elementary school. We also had a sub shop named Palmisano's where I tasted my first chicken parmesan sub and burned the roof of my mouth from the piping-hot melted cheese. I only ordered cold cuts after that. Then there was the Carney Crab House. The sign had this huge, awesome crab hanging on it, and I always thought it looked menacing. I guess that is why you use a hammer when you eat crabs. Truth be told, we never ate out.

The place where everybody ate was at home. Nobody went out to dinner; there was no point. My mother was a great cook and all my friends' mothers were too. If you needed a change, you could just go over to one of your friend's houses. I had meatloaf at Fitz's house, liver and onions at Buddy's house, and Mrs. Chadman made a killer pot roast. I used to try those meals out at home, and that's how I learned to cook.

Now on every blue moon, we would hit the Gino's on Joppa Road at the top of Perring Parkway for a bucket of Kentucky Fried Chicken. Gino's was owned by Baltimore Colt favorite, Gino Marchetti. He was a beast of a football player and worked out a deal with the Colonel to sell his chicken. Even though a twenty-four-piece picnic tub only cost five dollars, eating out was still was very, very rare for us. There were no Checkers or Taco Bells, and the term "fast food" wasn't even in our vocabulary. We ate slow food.

At the corner of Joppa and Harford roads, sat a diner called Hamburger Junction. When you sat at the counter and ordered your food, it was brought to you on a train. No kidding, a real moving train. It was awesome. The back of the counter had tracks on it, and this small train would come chugging out of the kitchen, pulling flatbed cars, and then your plate would stop right in front of you. The cooks wore engineer garb and everything.

Service had a whole different meaning back then. When you pulled into a gas station, you would ride over an air hose and a bell would go off. Out of nowhere five guys would jump on your car like sumo wrestlers on a box of donuts. One guy would be checking the tires, one cleaning the windshield, one putting in gas, or Ethel Mertz, as they called it, and one guy would be handing drinks to you through the window.

There was even a guy with a red rag hanging out of the back pocket of his clean overalls, passing out S&H Green Stamps or various kitchen implements. We still have a dinner glass with a big dinosaur on it from Sinclair, which later changed their name to British Petroleum, or BP.

I used to love to look out the window and watch them spring into action. Our family car was a 1967 blue Chevrolet Impala, but my dad drove a blue and white Volkswagen van. We referred to it as the "big blue bus," and you could hear it four miles away, limiting his stealth approach. Whenever I see one on the road, I picture my father driving it. The steering wheel was horizontal, so he leaned over when he drove.

When I was eleven years old, the rock group Apollo 100 came out with a great song called "Joy." It was a rock version of "Ode to Joy" by Beethoven, and my father loved it. He would sit at the wheel of the big blue bus and bang his high school ring on the steering wheel while we drove down the road. The song had no lyrics, so he would make noises like he was playing the organ. He wore such a pleasant smile when he was listening to it. Once, during one of his drumming sessions, the stone flew right out of his school ring, so he never wore it again. I think of him every time I hear that song.

On special occasions, my parents would occasionally go out to dinner. It was a very rare treat for them, and I think it was a direct request from some sort of counselor who was helping them deal with their wacky children.

Jan, my older sister, was baby-sitting, which meant she was on the telephone. Karen, my younger sister, was experiencing the joys of diaper rash, and I was playing with matches. That's how it was presented in the incident report, but here is how it really happened…

It was January, and I was under the weather. I never really understood the term "under the weather" until I recently Googled it, so I'll just say I was sick as hell. My bedroom was upstairs, which meant if I opened a window, I would be above the weather. I was stuffed to the rafters and currently on the freezing side of a fever, you know, when one minute you are sweating and the next you are shivering.

Nearing the teeth-rattling portion of my illness, I grabbed my comfy, brand new, blue, nylon cotton-blend, bathrobe and pulled it under the covers to put it on. I had just received it a few weeks earlier for Christmas. Its interior was pure cotton and its exterior was a patchwork of blue, black, and white nylon squares filled with cotton. It resembled a quilt. It had pockets on the front and a real cool tie that almost wrapped around me twice. I had just eased into a peaceful, deathlike slumber. It was darker than usual in my room, but that was only because I was under the covers.

Suddenly, the door swung open and Jan yanked off my comfy covers and told me to come downstairs to help her. I was irrational and mildly insane but crawled out of bed, put on my slippers, squinted at the bright hall light and slowly walked down the stairs. There was no railing at the top of the stairs, so I used the two walls, straight-armed, as support to help me down. Halfway down the stairs, a railing opened up the view to the living room, so I quickly transferred my weight to that. I think my head weighed twenty-seven pounds.

Jan hadn't even told me why she required my assistance. I blindly followed her into the kitchen as she stopped at the oven. She picked up a pack of matches and handed them to me. "Can you light the oven? It scares me."

Had I been of sane mind and proper intelligence, I would have turned and climbed the stairs back to my frozen lair. However, being deliriously lethargic and semi-comatose, I obliged.

By means of the *Way Back Machine*, I have to explain how our oven works. It is a GE brand unit, white, with four burners on top and a pilot light hidden in the middle. The broiler, which lives below the oven, is a flame-thrower for charring meat. To light the oven, I have to open the oven door, light a match, turn on the gas, and drop the match in a small hole where it will slide down a chute to light the burner below. I have seen my mother do it a thousand times. Sometimes I hear it go whoosh when it lights.

MISSING PINE PARK

My sister backed up as I took the matches and bent down towards the hole. I shook my head at her, lit the match and prepared to turn on the gas when I noticed it was already on.

I remember feeling the heat of the fireball as it burned off my eyebrows and evaporated the sweat on my forehead. My crazy sister had turned the gas on before she came to get me. I immediately understood why my parents weren't home. The blast blew me back into an upright position and pinned me against the wall. The good news was that my fever had broken and I was no longer shivering; the bad news was that I was currently on fire.

My sister screamed and started patting me down before realizing my brand new, blue, nylon cotton-blend bathrobe had melted. Through the smoke I could see patches of burnt and matted nylon all over my front. One of my pockets was gone and my cool tie system had totally changed from a solid to a liquid. I was wearing a chemistry project.

Livid with my sister more for destroying my bathrobe than removing my eyebrows, I retreated to my room and crawled back into my bed. I was still smoldering when my parents came home. They were quite upset at the whole blowing up incident, but glad that my fever had evaporated, literally.

Jan practiced the art of being the innocent bystander and claimed that while she was tending to Karen, like the good babysitter she was, I took it upon myself to wander downstairs and stick my head inside the oven. If I had been one of my parents, I would have bought her version too. In a court of law it is called precedence, and unfortunately for me, my parents had many examples of my weird behavior from which to choose.

That was the last time we were allowed to light the oven. In the future when my parents went out, our dinner choices were limited to graham crackers and milk or Jell-O. Both are highly non-combustible.

THE CHRISTMAS GUARD

When I was five years old, I found out what it might have felt like to be an only child. My older sister Jan attended elementary school, so I would sit in front of our television as she would leave every morning, excited that I had the whole house to myself for the morning and entire afternoon. I would watch some of the greatest shows I would ever experience: *Captain Kangaroo, Romper Room, Wonderama and Rocky and Bullwinkle.* My forehead still hurts when I think of those funny, fractured fairytales and their hidden meanings. Even back then I thought Natasha was hot! And Snidely Whiplash ... *I mean, how cool was he?* This is where my creative imagination started to get crisp. I would make up all kinds of imaginary worlds and characters, never leaving the house.

When my mom would vacuum the living room, she would turn the coffee table over onto the couch, and I would crawl in and out of the legs and pretend that I was Dudley Do-Right, trying to rescue Nell. I was a huge fan of *Batman, the TV series*, and spent most days with a bath towel tied around my neck as a cape. I always thought it was cool that there was an actor named Neil Hamilton (another Neil!) who played Commissioner Gordon. I still own Joker pajamas. I used to tour our home wondering where the secret entrances to the hidden rooms were. Inside my second floor bedroom, I eventually found one in the back of the closet.

There was a big, heavy door that pushed inwards and was hinged at the top. It was used for storage, but I knew it held a secret passage to treasure. Once, I crawled in and started moving to the left. At the time I didn't know there was a pull chain light above my head, and so I used the light coming from my room to navigate. All at once, however, I was jolted into complete darkness. It seems that my mother had come into my room to look for me and had turned the light out when she had left.

My father had taught me how to handle fear though. He'd say, "Close your eyes and count to five very slowly and imagine all the horrible things you fear. Then, when you open your eyes, you will see that everything is fine." I had to act quickly because I knew the monsters would come out soon.

It was a well-known fact that monsters were unionized and had a three-minute grace period for all scared children. I closed my eyes, and before I got to the number one, I panicked and started screaming at the top of my lungs. My mother, who had just started back down the stairs, came back up and pulled me from the crawlspace and saved me from a certain gruesome monster-death. *I'll find the hidden room later.*

My fifth birthday party was the biggest birthday party of my young life. I was totally fired up. It was May the fifth, the sun was shining, and I was wearing my bat belt. I looked out the front window all morning, waiting for kids to arrive. My mother told me that if I didn't take a nap, not one person would show up for the party. I drifted off wondering how they would know. *I mean, seriously, were there mothers calling to wonder if I was sleeping? Had spies infiltrated the house relaying coded messages to present-laden kids waiting around the corner? It must be some crazy power that parents have.* Since I was wearing my bat cape, sleep came easy. All superheroes sleep well when they wear their capes.

When I woke up, kids started showing up from every direction with presents. Timmy, Tommy and Brad Bassett, who lived behind us, were climbing the fence into our yard. Some parents were dropping their kids off while other kids were walking up the street, *en masse*. I swear some kids were even parachuting in. It was awesome!

There wasn't a clown or a pony to keep everybody occupied; there were no such things as gymnastic places and Chuck E. Cheese was still in a marijuana haze, waiting to be conceived. It was just the mayhem of a gazillion Carney kids playing together on Uxbridge Road. It was the only birthday party I ever had and the bat cave would never be the same. My cake was multicolored, and it had a tiny train running up the side and across the top. I received a ton of cool toys, including Gumby and Pokey and a Spirograph. Soon, weird geometric circles would be adorning the refrigerator.

The same thing happened for my younger sister, Karen, and my younger brother, David, when they turned five. For Karen's fifth birthday party, my parents covered the whole house in plastic. It sort of looked like they were preparing for a mass extermination of children, but they had just installed wall-to-wall carpet; they were trying to protect it from various vomit volleys. David was born the day after Christmas, so we had his party on June twenty-sixth when he was five and a half, so only half-wits showed up.

My imagination got the best of me on Christmas morning that year. I lay awake half the night, listening for reindeer on the roof or any kind of belly laugh, but the only laughter I heard was from Mrs. Joan Chadman. The Chadmans lived two doors away and were good friends of my parents. They always showed up after we kids went to bed to drink beer, laugh loudly and play cards. Miss Joan had a very distinct laugh, and to this day, my head turns in crowded theaters and bird sanctuaries when I hear the outburst of a loud cackle.

Before babysitters were appropriate and abandoning children was frowned upon, my parents would put us to bed and call the Chadmans on the phone.

Telephones in the *Way Back Machine* are the size of a loaf of bread and are bolted to the wall. Mounted on the front is a circular finger dial where you place your finger in a hole next to the desired number. In a clockwise rotation, you run it all the way around the circle to a small metal stopper and then remove your finger to watch it recoil. You need to repeat this for every number, but never have to dial area codes, unless calling long distance.

All Maryland phone numbers were considered local; the only time we made long distance calls was to our grandmother in Allentown, PA. After driving home from a visit, she always required us to call her so she knew we made it home safely. My father had a great system for saving money on long distance calls. He would dial zero to call the operator and make a person-to-person call to my grandmother's house, but ask for someone who didn't exist. When my grandmother would hear the nonexistent name, she'd know everything was fine and we made it home okay, so she would tell the operator that "the person" wasn't home.

"Sorry, he's not home," she replied.

"Would you like to try again later?" queried the operator to my dad.

"Okay, thanks. We will," he responded. It worked every time.

When my parents wanted to play cards at the Chadmans' they came up with another cool idea. They would call them, then without hanging up the phone, they would wrap the phone cord around the doorknob of the closet in the hallway, which was right outside our bedrooms, and let the receiver hang down. *Voilà!* The very first baby monitor!

They would then go down to the Chadmans' and play cards for hours while someone balanced the other end of the phone on their shoulder, listening for little kids who went bump in the night. It was pretty foolproof, and many times when one of us would get up, there was a parent coming in the front door before we were done peeing.

My mother had a forty-seven-foot phone cord, which was a present from our neighbor, Mr. Herman C Bell III.

We all knew him as Mr. Herman, but my mother always said his full name when speaking of him. The phone cord was her favorite present of all time. She could cook, clean, and go to the bathroom without ever hanging up the phone. That is a normal, everyday occurrence today, but in the sixties that leaned toward miracle status.

They'd always alternate houses, but on Christmas Eve the Chadmans would always show up at our house for *one* reason ... to make sure I'd never fall asleep! I would strain to listen to every muffled conversation, hoping I would eventually hear the front door close. Everyone knows that Santa can't come while people are still awake in the house, especially visitors, so one time I desperately yelled out, "Please go home!"

When my mom came in to see what was going on, I faked a coma until she left. I'm sure she knew it was me and, unfortunately, so did Santa Claus!

The next morning I could hardly wait to get up from my bed. I quickly looked outside the window and saw that it was still dark. I knew there was no way I could go downstairs now without some form of punishment, so I lay back down and waited. I'm guessing that six days had passed until I finally crept out from my room.

I came down the stairs, squinting at the ten thousand watt headlight my dad had on top of his film camera. He was a big movie taker and used to grab footage twenty seconds at a time over the course of a year. I glanced over his white T-shirt, hoping to see the twinkle of colored lights on a tree in the living room. His body was obscuring most of the magic the fat man had left. The blinding light fogged out everything else, so I held my hand up to shade my eyes and walked around my dad.

That is when I first saw it. It was huge! It stood at least five feet tall and looked totally menacing. Sitting in front of the Christmas tree, was a big-ass lion! He was sitting upright, like the Sphinx does in Egypt, and looked down on me with such anger that I stood there and wet my official *Rat Patrol* pajamas. Why Santa Claus would chose to scare the hell out of me with a five-foot stuffed lion, I would never know, but I was pretty sure that at one time he worked for D-CUP.

Turns out, he was my sister Jan's big-ass, scary lion, and,

eventually, he moved to her room to guard her Skippy peanut butter tin can bank, which housed, on a good day, about one dollar and forty-nine cents. After a while he seemed pretty harmless, but during our initial meeting, I saw him as Clarence, the cross-eyed lion from *Daktari* who put the fear of God in me.

That same year I received a GAF View-Master, a cap rifle and an official Baltimore Colts football uniform. I wore the latter almost as much as my bat cape and used to scrimmage against the living room chair. Those cool gifts were all tainted by what later became known as the wet *Rat Patrol* pajama incident. Thanks, Mr. Kringle!

THE HOLE IN THE WALL GANG

One of my favorite things to do was to ride down the indoor stairs on my belly. I would lie on my stomach, facing the top of the stairs, push off and *thump, thump, thump, thump* all the way down. It hurt sometimes, and occasionally I would bang my chin, but it was hilarious. It sounded a little like bowling balls rolling down the stairs at great speed. I used to do it over and over until I would get yelled at to stop.

That was usually my *modus operandi.* I think that during my entire childhood, when I was told to stop doing something, I had to do it three more times before stopping. It was built into my DNA. This included sticking metal things into wall sockets, drinking milk right out of the carton, and pulling all the elastic out of my underwear.

The very last time I rode down the stairs, unbeknownst to me, my father was taking a nap in his room right below me. My mother, who was making chicken potpie, screamed my name and ran from the kitchen because she thought I had fallen. Now being a junior, every time my mother said Neil, my father and I would both answer. Of course, there were questions that naturally fell on the right person like "Neil, did you finish your homework?" or "Neil, where are the sharp knives?" and, "Neil, will you comb the peanut butter out of Karen's hair?"

Anyway, my mother started screaming, "Neil! Neil! Neil!" and ran into the living room to see if I was dead at the bottom of the stairs. My father, who was jarred awake by these same screams and loud thumping, came running out of the bedroom in his boxers, not knowing what had happened. For all he knew, I was tearing out the kitchen cabinets with a crowbar. It has been known to happen.

By the time he cleared the corner from the hallway, my mom had reached the living room and realized that I was only playing. My father was still breathing hard and demanded, "What's the matter? What's the matter?" My mother dismissed him in a nonchalant tone.

"Oh, nothing. Go back to bed." As I watched him, I saw the color physically leave his face, only to be replaced with some sort of plaid.

On a side note, my dad was the only southpaw in the family. As a matter of fact, the only other left-hander I knew was my cousin Randy, unless you count Orioles' Mike Cuellar and Dave McNally, but we weren't really friends.

My mom walked back to the kitchen, but my father stood there for a few seconds, seething in the moment and then... *Bam!* With Muhammad Ali speed, he threw a left hook that caught the living room wall square. It was the fastest thing I had ever seen except for the time Buddy Miller stopped a floor fan with his tongue. My dad pulled his fist out of the plaster and then he retreated to his room in his boxers.

My mom rushed in and said, "What was that?" and then noticed the hole. My father had punched a hole right through the frickin' wall! The plaster dust was still falling to the floor as I stood there marveling at his strength. Holy guacamole, that was awesome!

Unfortunately, my mom didn't think so, and a huge argument ensued. When my parents argued, the decibel level, at times, rivaled a standard KISS concert. My parents yelled at each other often and about everything. Listening once while lying in bed, I heard them argue about if they were to get divorced, who would take custody of which kid. Fortunately for all the kids listening, they both wanted everybody.

This particular argument was about ruining my mother's house, which apparently my father was just visiting. It didn't last long, and soon he was napping, she was cooking, and I was looking for trouble.

Turns out, my father was better at demolition than home repairs. After many plaster applications, my dad finally fixed the wall by covering it with a bookshelf. By removing a few old novels and a blue book about bathroom humor, I could easily show my friends the evidence to corroborate my story.

Four years later, I was standing in my room, holding a pool stick. My dad brought home a second-hand pool table and put it in the basement. I had gathered some skills playing billiards with Joey Orla, who lived at the very bottom of Uxbridge Road. Joey was about four years younger than me but caught my attention one day when he was riding his bike while wearing a football helmet. Keep in mind this was years before any headgear was required to ride a bike; he had the whole facemask thing working and everything. What a trendsetter!

So I'm in my room with four new pool cues and a bag of corresponding tips. My dad just dropped them off and instructed me to put them on. He also told me to make sure they were on tight and to press down on them hard. I always thought they came attached but apparently not. Now this sounds like a simple task, right? Well, I was struggling because they kept falling off. I was using this glue that Elmer made, but it wasn't working. *Maybe I needed some more pressure.*

I couldn't turn the sticks upside down and press down on the floor because of the carpet, so I opted for the next hardest thing: the wall. I held up the stick, glued on the tip and pressed it into the wall. My system seemed to be working pretty well, and I plowed my way through three of the four sticks. The last one was a little more troublesome; I had to glue it twice.

Meanwhile, my mom called us for dinner, and I was hungry, so I took the stick and quickly pressed it into the wall. Before I knew what had happened, four feet of the pool stick protruded on the other side. I had pushed the damn stick right through the wall! *Oh, my God, I am in big trouble now.* To make matters worse, when I pulled the stick out, the tip came off and fell inside the wall. I was now a member of the club; the next day I put up a bookshelf.

BLOODY KNEES AND WILLOW TREES

I don't think there was ever a part of my body that didn't have a scab or a scar or a dried bloodstain on it somewhere. In fact, getting injured while having fun was a rite of passage in Carney. When I was real little, I used to stop my tricycle by dragging my bare feet on the Bells' sidewalk. The tops of my toes were always bleeding, but my nails were beautifully sanded down and all manicured from the concrete.

In addition, all the anti-bacterial foaming soap in the world never would have worked in our neighborhood. More than once, I recreated the thirsty cowboy scene from *Gunsmoke* and drank right out of the side of a mud puddle. Germs? What are germs? I'd eat a germ sandwich for breakfast! The ten-second rule, where if you dropped food on the floor and picked it up before ten seconds were up, never applied to us. We used the ten-minute rule.

I used to get poison ivy so much during the summer that my friends thought I was born with pink legs. One summer I had it so bad between my fingers that I couldn't close them. I'd wake up in the morning and slowly rub the insides of my fingers on the corner of the mattress. I can't describe the wonderful feelings of euphoria before it started hurting. I'm sure there are some masochists out there who get poison ivy every year on purpose. My father taught me the three-red-leaf rule: Leaves of three let it be. Most poison ivy plants have three leaves with a slight red hue. It was deemed a great idea to avoid them at all costs. The rule worked because I found it every year, but I never mastered the avoidance part.

My dad was a lover of nature and possessed a detective's approach to everything he saw. He would have been a good tracker if we ever needed a posse, but no one stole any cattle, so his talents went unnoticed. He taught me how maple leaves turned over right before it rained, how dandelions could be used to make wine and that honey bees kept us alive by pollinating our food. We saw honeybees in a different light and dared each other to step on them with our bare feet. Maybe I killed an okra plant somewhere in Kansas by doing so.

We also played a game called hand-slap. This was where you would hold your hands in front of you, facing up, and someone would hold their hands over yours facing down. As quick as you could, you would pull your hands out and slap the other guy's hands. If they moved before you did, you would get a free slap. I was a master at getting others to flinch. The goal was to bring someone as close to an ambulance ride as possible. We would play until our hands doubled in size and stop when we couldn't write our names.

While attempting to build a fort in their weeping willow tree, Buddy and Tony Miller were regaling me with a little ditty. It seemed that their dad also punched a hole in something, but it wasn't a wall. Unfortunately, before they could tell me what their dad punched a hole in, Tony fell off a branch from the tree and landed right on a board and, you guessed it, a nail went right through the bottom of his foot. His screams simulated a pterodactyl, and the way he was hopping towards his house with a two-by-four attached to his foot, you'd think he was a peg-legged pirate.

I'm pretty sure Tony, the little brother, was extremely concerned with the fact that a nine-penny nail had just gone clear through his new tennis shoe, while Buddy, his older brother, was thinking more about the fallout when his parents found out. The proper train of thought for an older brother was: how would this affect me? In the *Way Back Machine* families run on the principle that you are responsible for all the siblings that are younger than you. Therefore, if they experience an injury, you are ultimately responsible for it.

Fortunately for Buddy, he had plenty of time to get into more trouble in the future so not watching out for his little brother's foot was the least of his worries.

Buddy and Tony were pretty good at pushing the bar when it came to obtaining obscure injuries. On a shelf in their living room sat a small picture frame that displayed a black nickel. I saw it many times before I read the small handwritten caption on the bottom of the frame. I really didn't understand it for years until it was explained to me, and then I never looked at it again. It read: Passed by Tony Miller on March 12, 1967.

Holy Christ, Tony shit a nickel! Apparently, Tony was sucking on a nickel and he accidentally swallowed it. For several days he had to take a dump in a pot or something and then it had to be methodically searched for. I heard about making change but c'mon. *And who found it?* I wonder if they had a giant poop magnet or something. I decided to turn off my vivid imagination at that point.

THE WILD BUNCH

If you climb into the *Way Back Machine,* you find that exterior Christmas illumination is basically medium-based colored light bulbs.

There are no little blinking things and icicle lights, and that inflatable crap is still on the horizon.

Some genius had invented parallel circuits so you can unscrew one bulb and the rest of the string still stays lit. This means that you are able to sneak over to someone's house, unscrew a colored bulb, and hope, from a distance, that no one notices it is missing.

One of the coolest sounds in the world is the sound of a light bulb exploding. The popping noise is very unique, and the higher or harder you throw it in the street, the louder the pop seems.

Stealing and popping Christmas lights became an art. We would stand on a dark street and wing them straight up in the air and then wait for them to hit the street and pop. It was at least six whole seconds of excitement.

Proper protocol demanded you couldn't alter a light display, you couldn't pop a light in front of the house you took it from, nor could you pop a blue bulb because they were harder to purchase. This is where Buddy and Tony excelled. They not only broke all the rules of protocol, they didn't even wait until Christmas.

One hot July afternoon, Buddy went into his basement to get a croquet set, and came back with a string of Christmas lights. He came bouncing outside like he had found Atlantis. We were not impressed, until he busted every one of them, right in his own cellar way, including the blue ones. What *cojones*! He would have gotten away with it too, but the next day his mom was bringing out the laundry barefooted and sliced herself all up. He didn't even clean up the glass. As Bugs Bunny would say, "What a maroon!"

Fitz used to get hurt a lot too, but it was usually in the heat of battle. Taking a softball to the head or running into a low hanging branch was his forte. Once, he tried to jump clear across the stream and fell right in. It was always funny when Fitz went down, due to his over the top reactions. I think that later in life he taught professional soccer players how to flop. I never understood how he wasn't president of the drama club.

While playing hide-and-seek in his basement, I was cleverly hidden under his stairs. He passed by me at least three times before I jumped out and yelled, "Aaaah!" He literally jumped straight up and made a right-hand turn in mid-air and ran right into a door. I fell on the floor laughing. We never knew what to expect with Fitz and his reactions, so when we were trekking through the woods, we always made him go first. While on point, he sure cleared a lot of spider webs for us.

My dad liked my friends and referred to us as The Wild Bunch. I used to think that was an endearment until I saw the Sam Peckinpah movie. My father used to say that if we weren't out looking for trouble, how come we found it so often? He was right, too. Trouble just found us. It was not like call-the-police trouble, but fall-into-a-sticker-bush or get-a-head-stuck-in-the-railing trouble. It was usually our own curiosity that precipitated it.

Once, I found an old empty spray paint can in the Millers' backyard and was dying to find out what was making the rattle inside. I decided to find out. I started banging it with rocks and chewed off the nozzle. There was no paint inside, but something shot into my mouth. It didn't taste good, and I could tell it wasn't supposed to be there. I kept banging the can as long as I could until my imagination had me believing I was slowly dying of poison.

I went home crying to my dad who had his normal response. "What the hell did you do that for?" I had heard that line every day for at least five years but never formulated a proper answer. He followed me to the Millers' to see what kind of can it was. When I showed him the twisted dented can, he just shook his head in disbelief.

I had successfully banged the label clear off the can. We took it home to perform experiments on the can, but in the end he performed an experiment on me.

He made me drink lots and lots of water out of the garden hose, and then he stuck his finger down my throat and forced me to throw up. It was the ol' do-it-yourself stomach pumping.

It worked because I felt better. An hour later on our brick patio, I finally opened the paint can and found the mysterious noisemaker. I had imagined all sorts of interesting things and couldn't wait to see what was in there. When I dumped it out along with some bright metallic red enamel paint and cleaned it off, I was disappointed. It was a quarter-inch hex nut. Are you kidding me? How did that get in there? Somewhere something important like a car engine was missing a quarter-inch hex nut. I knew that whenever the engine fell out of the car, I would get blamed. Well, at least I had something to look forward to.

BLACK-AND-WHITE

My dad taught me to ride a bike in about three minutes. He wasn't a miracle teacher by any means, just effective because he would incorporate pain. I understood the concept but never rode a bike without training wheels and wasn't too interested in doing so.

After taking them off, we walked out to the street, and I climbed on the bike. I remember him saying, "Ready?" and, before I could answer, he pushed me. I wobbled about fifteen feet and fell over in the street. My wrists were scraped and my knees were bleeding. I didn't even have time to cry because he picked me up, put me back on the bike and said, "Don't do that," and pushed me again.

After another fifteen feet, I wobbled and fell again. This time I had small stones embedded in my knees, and he knew I was almost done, so he picked me up and pushed me again. I haven't fallen off since. That was the way he worked: black-and-white... and bloody. He taught me to swim the same way.

His vocabulary of catch phrases was exhaustive, but one of his favorites was simply, "Don't do that."

"Hey, Dad, it hurts when I stick this Popsicle stick in my ear."

"Don't do that."

Once I came down the stairs and turned the corner too tight and wiped out on the floor. He walked in, looked down and said, "Don't do that," and walked away.

As history tends to repeat itself, twenty-five years later I found myself in front of my old house teaching my godson, Johnny, how to ride a bike. He was obviously smarter than I was at his age, and when I went to push him, he held his foot firmly on the brake, so he didn't move. I, however, catapulted into the street. With little stones embedded in my knees, I tried again by pushing harder and soon found myself in a game of tug of war. The harder I pushed, the harder he applied the brake. This went on for about five houses. We had already made a one hundred fifty-seven foot skid mark. I was screaming, "Pedal!" but he didn't want any of it and told me to go home. So I did. Author's note: black-and-white doesn't work with Johnny.

When I was sixteen, Dad taught me how to drive a car the same way. We went behind the E. J. Korvettes, off of Perring Parkway, with my 1971 tan Chevy Vega. He took one pass changing gears while explaining how to use the clutch and then changed seats with me.

I took off in first, popped it into second, and then, for some reason, grabbed the hand parking brake and pulled it. Since airbags hadn't been invented yet, he slammed into the dashboard and bounced off in spectacular fashion.

Fighting laughter, I said I was sorry but was secretly thinking, "Don't do that." The black-and-white method was also used during discipline. An eye for an eye was very common, even amongst threats. My dad often used colorful metaphors when threatening discipline. He also liked to incorporate your crime into the punishment. "If you skip that record, I'll skip your ass across the floor." Now take the time to try and imagine that. If I make the record skip, my father is going to come over to me, pick me up and throw me so hard that my ass will actually skip across the floor. *Damn, that's impressive!*

By the way, before small electronic MP3 files were invented, we listened to things called records.

In the **Way Back Machine** we use a circular piece of thin, black vinyl that comes in a flat, colorful cardboard container called an album. Each record is equipped with a tiny never-ending groove that starts on the outside and ends all the way in the middle of the record. Setting a needle on the groove while it spins at a certain rate per minute, takes patience, but it engages the sound mechanism, and music comes out of the speakers. If you cause the needle to jump, it creates a small gouge in the groove and creates a skip. To this day when I hear old songs on the radio, I can pinpoint exactly where my version would skip.

My all-time favorite line of my father's was "I'll knock you into the middle of next week." He had the capacity to alter the time space continuum and hit you so hard that you would advance through hyperspace and come back on a Tuesday. Needless to say, I was always on my best behavior... Not!

My mother had her own form of discipline, and it revolved around yelling. She could yell very loudly which made her red hair ignite. It was quite comical to see. She also used colorful metaphors but didn't know it. "Hell's bells!" was one of her favorites.

David recently relayed to me a time when he had an explosive diaper that was oozing everywhere, and our mom screamed, "Lord, oh lord!" about twenty times as she was cleaning him. For years he thought that lord meant poop.

Once, in the backyard, I was sitting next to her, playing with a Tonka truck and she said, "Whose damn dog is that?"

I looked up and said, "What damn dog?" Before I knew it, her right arm caught the back of my head, and I tumbled to the ground. "Watch your mouth!" she replied. I didn't even know what I had done.

As we got older, she got bolder and would hit us in the head or shoulders for each word she uttered. "If" right hook, "you" left hook "don't" right hook "clean" left hook "up" right hook "your" left hook "room" right hook "you" left hook "will" right hook "be" left hook "grounded" right hook "for" left hook "a" right hook "week" left hook. I used to feel like a bobble head doll.

When it came to discipline from my dad, he always gave you a choice. It was kind of like Monty Hall in the game show *Let's Make A Deal.* You could go to your room for a week or behind door number two you could just go into the basement and get it over with. I called his bluff once and walked right to the basement steps, went downstairs and lay over the sawhorse.

I'm sure he was shocked, but after a few minutes he came downstairs and spanked my ass. He perfected a way to make his hand flat during the beating to get the maximum effect. He didn't even follow through and just kind of snapped his whole hand like a wet flounder. It hurt like hell, and I cried. Then I went outside and danced and sang under Jan's window, "It only hurt for a min-ute, you have to stay in your ro-om, you should have taken the beat-ing." She was sorry because she opted for the soft discipline behind door number one, which was one week of house arrest, so I kept singing, "he didn't even breathe at me." She knew better next time.

It was a well-known fact that my father was one of the scariest dads in the neighborhood. My friends would recoil at his sight and would never say "Hello, Mr. Beller" in hopes that he wouldn't notice them. My father was a breather. When he was mad, he would just stare at you, and I mean give the most powerful and scary stare imaginable. I would try long and hard not to make eye contact, but soon his tractor beam would lock you in and the staring game would begin.

It was impossible to look away, absolutely impossible. You had to wait for him to make the first move. If your nose was running, you just let it drip because you couldn't move. It was paralyzing. After what seemed like an hour, he would take a very deep breath and exhale it as loud and as long as he possibly could. I swear furniture would move. This was his way of showing you how disgusted he was with you or your actions. After the breath you could look away and move, but never before or during.

All this, of course, was precipitated with a one-line monotone sarcastic statement, spoken slowly, that summarized the entire event. "You don't know how it happened." Now, this was never made in a questionable format, but strictly a statement suggesting that he was in total disbelief at what he was hearing, so his only response would be to repeat what you said. "You didn't shave the cat." Stare. ....Breathe.

THE BACKYARD

Jumping into the *Way Back Machine*, you notice that there aren't that many physical fences where I grew up. Unless you have a dog or a bear, there is just no reason to have a fence. This is what leads to the feeling of openness that we all share. No one's yard is off limits and everybody knows it.

Many kids would walk down the small hill on Appleton and just past the bottom of the Millers' fence, make a sharp right and walk straight through the backyards of the Randalls, the Hudsons, the Bellers, the Bells, the Chadmans, and the Travers before hitting a fence. There were trees and pools and picnic tables but still plenty of room to play ball. Mr. Herman C Bell III had those railroad ties lining his yard, but they were easily traversed while running.

Mr. Herman C Bell III was a funny man. He was about ninety years old, but acted like he was thirty. He would walk all the way around our house to knock on the back door. I never ever remember him knocking on the front door, not even once. He would walk up the street, up our sidewalk and then follow it all the way around to the back door. He used to tell us, "That's what neighbors do."

He would always cut his grass shirtless. He loved my mom and would bring her pit beef sandwiches and soft-shell crabs. He cornered the market on weeding by using pure gasoline. He would pour it on the edges of his sidewalks and railroad ties and the grass would just die. He took weed killing to another level with a hatchet. Some people would use clippers and trimmers; he would use a hand hatchet to sculpt a weed-less edge. With a precise angle, he'd cut a perfect groove all the way around his concrete patio and his fence line. Seriously, it looked beautiful, and I'd be lying if I said I'd never tried it. Still have all my toes.

When I was five years old, he had me clean out some leaves from behind his tall hedges. He gave me a dime for my effort. I remember looking at it in my open hand and thinking it was a million dollars. That was the first time I was ever given money.

He had a bar and an extra bathroom in his basement, which was the envy of the neighborhood. My parents could always be found there, in the bar, not the bathroom.

Knowing all this, you would think he would be kind to me, but if my parents weren't around, and I stepped into his yard, he'd bang on the window like a grumpy old man.   He had a dent in his head from when a series of paint cans fell on him in a Montgomery Ward's storeroom, so he wore a hard hat when he played sports. He ran a softball club called Northside A.C., and until the day that he died, my dad played for him.

They played games every Sunday morning at Carney Elementary, and I attended every one of them. This is where I learned how to play baseball. I was about five and I'd be out there, shagging fly balls, with all these grown men. They taught me everything about the sport like keeping score, making a line-up, and putting a little lemon in the water jug to quench your thirst.

It was an amazing team. A bizarre fact that you will think I totally made up, but I swear on my love for soft-shell clams it's true, is that the third baseman was named John Hancock and the left fielder was named Woodrow Wilson. No kidding! The latter went by Woody...you get the picture.

There were some hilarious men on that team, and the ongoing laughter was proof of that. The catcher was named Larry Drake, and he and my dad got along swimmingly. The Drakes lived on Magledt, which was near the snowball stand. Phil Drake was Karen's age. He and Karen were my first bar buddies! He was at our house once during a cookout when my father came around the corner and let us in on some very bad news. I had been waiting all week with bated breath to learn whether or not Evel Knievel had cleared Snake River Canyon with his X-2 Skycycle. He had his own rocket car! How awesome was that? With a look of extreme disappointment, my father told us that Evel hadn't made it after all. There was no fiery death or wicked carnage though, just a parachute ride to the bottom of the canyon. Later that day, to make our moods even gloomier, President Ford had pardoned Richard Nixon. But he, however, *did* have his own fiery death and wicked carnage.

Northside didn't really have a sponsor, but the Joppa Lounge on Ridgley Avenue was their bar of choice and they were professional patrons. I think a couple of them paid rent there. They had their own nickname for the joint too and endearingly called it the Bucket of Blood.

After every game, everyone would go and spend the afternoon reminiscing about the game they just played. By everyone I mean *everyone*. We kids we even had our own booth.

In the **Way Back Machine** iPods are called jukeboxes and they play three songs for a quarter.

We would sit and drink fountain sodas from glasses, and every now and then some player would put a dime in a table top machine, turn the crank, and drop a handful of bright red pistachios on the table. Every Monday morning during softball season, I had red fingertips. I wonder why pistachios are not red anymore. *It must have been a communist thing.*

I clearly remember watching some kid leaning his head back with a glass over his mouth banging on the bottom to get out the last piece of ice. He was softly tapping and tapping and tapping. The ice was not coming out. We were all watching him, and it was getting old, so David leaned over and whacked the bottom of the glass right into the kid's face. It was funny to see because David was always so laid back, but the glass broke and the side of the kid's mouth was bleeding. Oops!

The Bells had two daughters: Barbara and Kim. Kim was younger and used to babysit us, and I remember her being very tan. She used to lie out in her bathing suit all the time. I mean ALL the time.

In the **Way Back Machine** there is no such substance as sunscreen.

She likes to lather up in baby oil, lie in a big frying pan and almost beg the skin cancer to arrive.

I will never forget looking out of Karen's window once when I saw Kim reach back to untie the top of her bikini while lying on her stomach. That was the closest I had ever come to seeing a woman naked, and you know that is pretty much all that puberty consists of. Coincidentally, it only took me a half hour to figure out how to lob a water balloon over to scare her into jumping up. It worked perfectly.

Other than massive games of "redline" which can be best described as team hide-and-seek, and the occasional episode of brief lawn care, baseball or softball was a twenty-four hour event. If there was no one around to play a game, there was always time for practice. I needed to perfect my pitching and I needed a target, so I took a can of white paint from the basement and painted a circle on the back of our house. I would stand in the backyard and pitch to it for hours. I didn't think painting the wall was a bad idea at the time, and it sure looked nice on our boring cement wall, but my father thought otherwise. I guess he didn't appreciate the shingles I busted when I missed my target either.

The field would sometimes move between yards, but the game never ended. One day, Keith Hudson, my electric guitar playing next door neighbor, wanted to host the game, so we all moved to his yard.

His mother was known as Miss Colleen. She was originally from somewhere in the Deep South; Paula Deen would have nothing on her accent and demeanor. Her hair was white and always up on her head, proving her love of beauty parlors. She could often be found looking out a window of their deep green painted house but rarely seen in the backyard. She helped me when I was having a bad day once. I was pulling my sleigh through the snow to transport my Tonka trucks home from a play date, and I was having a bad time of it. Every time I pulled the sleigh the trucks would roll right off the back. She watched me for a while, struggling and throwing fits, until I was close enough to be schooled. I remember her opening up the window and telling me to turn them upside down. I had them sitting upright so when I pulled them, their wheels did what they were designed to do. I had a huge "Aha" moment, wiped the frozen tears from my cheeks and turned my trucks over. It worked like a champ.

One day, with Keith at bat, Miss Colleen was standing at the glass back door, spectating the game, when the unbelievable happened. It was the very first time I experienced something in slow motion. Keith fouled a Tommy Bassett-pitched ball and pulled it right towards his mother. Her expression changed from observance to awareness to horror as the ball smashed through the plate glass door and struck her square in the head. I say head, but it could have been all hair. The noise was spectacular, and she went down like a rock. We all stood frozen, staring at the empty door until our attention was shifted to Keith who was running in the opposite direction. Obviously, the softball game ended there. Keith never played softball again. And I think they were still removing glass from her hair a week later.

I've been shown home movies of my dad playing football with me in the backyard. The ball was almost as big as I was, but I was always game. He taught me how to kick and throw and tuck the ball, and once I was lucky enough to tackle him. I would tire quickly and want to stop, but he wouldn't let me. He curtly explained to me, "It ain't over till the fat lady sings," and as there were no obese, horn-wearing opera singers in the neighborhood, the game went on. He possessed a sense of empowerment, which was immediately passed on to me.

That trait played out again four months later when I was sledding on the Chadmans' hill. I was so busy having fun that I forgot I was bordering on hypothermia. I'm sure I had wet pants too! I quickly turned purple and just sat down in the snow at the top of the hill. I felt like I was on Mt. McKinley. My mother kept calling out the back door, pleading me to come home, but I was grounded like an airplane in the fog. The pleading and begging turned into hollering and yelling, but still I sat.

I looked across the frozen tundra and into my backyard and imagined a warmer day. A day when grasshoppers lounged and birds rested and I was playing catch with my dad. I stood up, wiped the frozen snot-sickles from my nose and pulled my Flexible Flyer through the snow back home. I felt empowered.

THE MACHINERY

I woke up to a peculiar sound and crawled out of my bed to do some detective work. Across the street from my house were two giant bulldozers. I didn't hear them when they arrived, but their bright yellow paint and the word CAT totally caught my attention. *How did they get there? Why were they here? When can I drive one?* These questions kept echoing through my head as I made my way outside to get a closer look. Machinery had come to Uxbridge Road, and it was heavy machinery too.

Our neighbor Herman C Bell III always had something construction-wise sitting across the street from his house. I say sitting, but I meant abandoned. There were lots of rusty things, like very large old mixing pans, cement mixers, boards with nails in them and buckets from an old steam shovel. I think he was a drywall finisher by trade but collected this junk on the side. Unfortunately for him, he was about fifty years too early for Craigslist.

I was never allowed to go near his collection. Most of it was covered by weeds and high grass and became part of the landscape. It can be seen in the background of our home movies, back-dropped by the green of the woods behind it. However, all that was about to change.

I stood there, comparing the old with the new, when one of the CATs chugged to life. Thick, black and gray smoke billowed out of its stack as it started moving up the street. I ran in the house and changed as quickly as I could. I think I even had my underwear on the outside of my pants when I hit the sidewalk again. It didn't matter; something cool was happening.

Moments later, its twin sprang into action. I had a Tonka dump truck resting in the backyard sandbox, so I ran to get it so I, too, could participate. Machinery was everywhere. They went up the street and turned right on Appleton and visually disappeared, but I could still hear them. Soon, other people were outside watching.

Mr. Hudson was standing there in his unbuttoned, dark green electrician's uniform shirt. He glanced at me as if to say, "Hey, are you seeing this cool stuff happening?" I just nodded in his direction. We understood each other perfectly. Next, I saw Butchie Randall. He lived in the first house on the street. I waved with an excited grin and he waved back. It didn't even matter that yesterday he held me down and spat in my face or that I was wearing my underwear on the outside of my pants; there was something happening and it needed to be shared. It was a shame that my dad was working.

Saturdays were his long day, which meant he worked a "double." When he said double, I would think baseball, but I'm certain he thought scotch. Regardless, I took in every detail so I could regale him later.

The Chadmans were out; even Mr. Herman C Bell III made an appearance. I also saw Ritchie Travers and his dad slowly walking up the street, which was rare because I think they were in the witness protection plan.

Over the tops of the trees, you could see the smoke and, all at once, hear a loud crack followed by a stern *whoosh*. I briefly saw the top of a tree shake violently and suddenly disappear. Then the tree right next to it reacted the same way. It's happening; the machinery is knocking down the creepy woods. Trees started falling at a rapid rate, as the noise of their engines got meaner.

No one ran this by me. I mean how could I have been left off the memo that put into action the tearing down of the woods? Of course, I would have signed off on it. I couldn't imagine vetoing such an important and historical document as to the removal of the creepy woods by heavy machinery. What a great day! Well, maybe it wasn't such a great day for the birds and woodland animals that needed to relocate, but I'm sure they had some government assistance. Somebody from some agency went in and discussed this with all of them, right?

I'm sure the dwarfs will be shipped somewhere near a princess, right Mr. Hudson? Hey Butchie, do you think Bigfoot will run out the other side? Mr. Travers, I know you can't speak to me, but just nod your head if you think the trolls were evacuated properly.

All of a sudden, I had feelings for this small patch of woods. Gone were all the future tree forts; gone were all the spooky walks; gone were all the horrible and painful bouts of poison ivy. Well... that last one was okay but the other stuff ... *I mean, hey Mr. Herman C Bell III, clean up all that crap in front of your house, because with the woods gone, everyone will be able to see it now.*

The whole block came out. Parents and kids stood abreast as the big yellow machinery knocked down the whole woods across the street from us. You could see forever now. It really opened the place up. They went at it all day. I ate lunch sitting in a folding chair right on the front sidewalk. I had never done that before. By the end of the day, it was over. All the trees were knocked down. It felt like a bad Dr. Suess book, except the outcome was different. This was a good thing.

The county was going to turn it into a park. They were going to put in a flagpole; they were going to put in a swing set. There were going to be summer camps, block parties, a manger at Christmastime, and they were even going to put in park toys! *Uh-oh, that means visitors from D-CUP.* Anyway, there was going to be a community park, and it was going to be ours. This was all good.

The very next day, flatbed trucks showed up, and they removed all the trees. A crew of volunteers started whacking down all the little stuff. This was the smaller undergrowth that surrounded the stream on both sides. No water creature could ever get me now, because I could see the stream up and down for hundreds and hundreds of yards. I could see many places to cross that used to be obscured; I think I even saw a frog.

Where the creepy woods used to be were now deep ruts and bulldozer tracks, the perfect breeding ground for mud play of which I was a card-carrying member. From my house I could see tracks that looked like they were made by tanks and other troop transports. Playing army now is going to be easy.

I leaned on the back of the couch and looked out the big picture window. Everything had changed. It was as if our house had moved. The view was totally different, and I could see right into Fitz's backyard. His house was on the other side of the Sullivans'. I could even see right into the tunnel. I couldn't wait to experience the new adventures. People would be coming to Uxbridge Road. Tomorrow every kid will want to be the first one to go exploring. I went to bed that night with thoughts of finding abandoned elf shoes, lost treasure and Bigfoot's tracks.

I was a little bit torn though because I did have at least one good memory of the creepy woods. I was walking down Appleton and I heard, "Hey kid, come here." It was Kevin Sullivan, the oldest kid in the neighborhood, and he was calling me. I looked down the hill into the woods, and there he was beckoning to me, "Come here. Hurry!" I had never blindly followed anybody in my life, but this was Kevin Sullivan, and he had to be at least twelve years older than me, so I ran down the hill after him.

He was running in the opposite direction, weaving back and forth as he went, but he kept turning to make sure I was behind him. "C'mon, faster," he chimed. Something really big was going to happen, and he wanted me to see it. He was leaping as he went, and I was falling back, and then I briefly lost him. He stopped and came back and was about ten feet away when he continued to wave me on. Finally, I took two more steps and fell right through a trap of sticks and leaves into a ditch! When I crawled out, Kevin was rolling on the ground laughing. Was I on *Candid Camera* or something? It was a trap, and for a moment I felt really stupid.

My feeling of stupidity ended ten minutes later, however, when I did the same exact thing to Timmy Fitzpatrick. Hilarious. I was going to miss those woods.

THE DIRTBALL WAR

Tractor ruts still ran every which way, and to a kid, it was like being inside the Grand Canyon. You could crouch down or lie against the side of one of the ruts and be totally hidden to your unsuspecting friends. There was no easy way to walk across the field in a straight line, so your mind took a militaristic approach and your canter soon included diving and rolling. Kids arrived from everywhere, and in my mind they were already wearing uniforms. There were about twenty of us, and our gentle frolicking soon turned rough; before I knew it, I was in the midst of an all-out war.

I don't remember how it started or when, but someone launched a dirtball high into the air, and when it hit the ground, it exploded into a fine cloudy mist. It was the kind of dirt that reminds you of when you slide into home plate and the umpire has to wait for the dust to clear to call the play. It was perfect. To us it looked just like a special effect from the TV show *Combat.*

The ground was littered with golf ball-sized ammo, and before you could double knot your Jack Purcells, they were launched. I dove for cover behind our lines as the dirt grenades rained down. It was awesome! They were landing all around, sending dust and debris high into the air. We didn't even pick teams; we just ended up on the side of whose ditch we dove in. I remember seeing Fitz, Tiny Reece, Paul

Flanagan and Buddy Miller in my ditch. They all had pretty good arms, except for Fitz, but he was the master of evasion. He could change directions in mid-air, and when he dove to the ground, he could roll and get up and dive again in another direction, flawlessly. He certainly wouldn't be killed.

The battle went on for about forty-five minutes with each side exchanging hundreds of volleys. The trenches were long, and because your movements were completely obscured by the high walls, you could sneak thirty feet in either direction. At one point we were all lying at the west end of the ditch, sharing someone's Turkish Taffy, laughing at the continuous barrage landing on our east flank. Returning to the *Way Back Machine* now, and viewing this part in slow motion (Author's note: the *Way Back Machine* sometimes plays things back in slow motion), a projectile comes from the sky and hits Fitz right smack in the middle of the chest. He is dead.

We scrambled for position and returned fire. I peeked out over the top of our bunker and could see the baseball cap-laden heads of our enemies. The barrage slowed down, and it looked like they were running out of ammo. Then it happened...a suicide mission. Gary Brendel, eight years my younger, bounded out of the enemies' hiding place and started picking up dirtballs from the battlefield in front of us. He was running them to his brother Michael, four years my senior. Michael was obviously babysitting his younger brother, therefore making him off limits, but as soon as he became an active soldier again, he landed in our crosshairs. We started lobbing dirt bombs all around him. He was totally oblivious that he was the target of a turkey shoot. I can still see his face as he was trying to hold as many clumps of dirt in his shirt as he could. He was even laughing a little at the sight of the dust clouds popping up all around him. We were laughing, too, as every time he bent over, more fell out than he could pick up.

After a while the fun wore off because nobody could hit him, so we started throwing a little harder. We no longer pretended to pull the grenade pin with our teeth and lob the dirt skyward hoping it would fall on him; we were aiming with pure intent. Without looking, I felt for some ammo at my feet, picked some up and whipped it at Gary. The sound of it striking his head will forever echo in my ears. It didn't explode in a dust storm like all the others; it just went *thud* and Gary dropped like a bag of hammers. His crying was muffled at first, and then when they rolled him over, it became an audible, anxious, agonizing wail.

Obviously, the dirt bomb war was over. We all exited our foxholes and made our way towards the fallen soldier. I saw Michael bending over him. I was waiting for the stop- crying speech that big brothers always give little brothers, but when he looked up in horror ... I saw the blood.

Instantly, Michael picked up his bleeding, screaming brother and started walking him off the battlefield. Someone ripped the bottom of his T-shirt off and handed it to Michael, who held it onto Gary's head. I was sick to my stomach and not because of the blood, but because I had hurt someone. Before leaving, I saw Michael's mad face staring at us as he inquired about who fired the kill shot. He was acting like we were *trying* to draw blood. Instantly, the fun was sucked right out of the air. We all knew the score. I mean, it was war, and we were launching so many missiles in his direction that nobody knew who had hit him, except me. I knew.

I watched my shot the whole way and now I felt terrible. It soon became apparent that someone on our side was going to get in trouble, so it was time for a preventative strike. It was always understood that if you tell your dad before another parent does, you would not get beaten as hard, so I promptly excused myself and headed home. This never would have happened if they hadn't knocked down the creepy woods!

This time my dad didn't get angry, but became very concerned. He grabbed my arm, and we headed out the door and up the small hill towards the Brendels' house. I wasn't sure which house it was, but when we turned the corner onto Summit Avenue, you could see the commotion.

Kids were sitting on bikes in the driveway, and most of the dirtball warriors were there. When we walked up, it was a dead giveaway that I was the one who launched the missile. I was amazed at how fast I had become an outsider. They were looking at me like I was the only one who threw anything. After thinking back, following Fitz's death, nobody else had even gotten wounded. Tony Miller ran right out of his shoes and then tripped trying to get back and landed on a boulder. The ring of spit was visible on the boulder for a while, and he had a swollen lip, but he wasn't injured. Tony was always drooling anyways.

My dad knocked on the door and went in, but I stayed on the porch. I could hear Gary crying and I just couldn't face Michael. Sure I felt bad, but after this blew over, I would become a hunted felon. After a minute, my dad came out and retrieved me. The faces in the house were tense, and it seemed as if in that short period of time, my dad had taught all the grown-ups in the room the breathing trick. Gary was sitting in a dining room chair *zub-zubbing*. In a curious voice, I asked him how he was and what had happened. He mumbled that he had been hurt and was bleeding. To make him feel better, I told him that Fitz was dead. He didn't care.

Then, through the miracle of pre DNA testing, the older brother Michael pulled a dirtball out of his pocket and announced that I had hit him with this. Insert big courtroom gasp here. *Now how on earth, out of the five thousand objects thrown, had he picked up the one that scored a direct hit and knew that I had thrown it?* Then he dropped it on the kitchen table. It was a rock. Somehow in the heat of battle, I reached for the supplied ammo, which were dried dirt balls, and mistakenly found a rock. Throwing a rock in a dirtball fight is totally against the rules. *I'm done.*

Out of nowhere Gary's father stepped forward and pointed out that there was no way to prove that I had done anything wrong and that if Michael had been the proper babysitter, Gary never would have been in a war zone. Acquittal! Then he picked up the rock and said, "Get this off the table!" They thanked us for our concern, and we left the triage area. We started walking down the street as they drove off to the hospital to get stitches. My father walked briskly, and I double-timed to keep up. As we turned the corner onto Uxbridge he said, "Good shot."

OUT AND ABOUT

If you happen to jump into the ***Way Back Machine*** and go food shopping with my mother and me, you find out that I never make it inside the store. There is a long ledge in front of the store, along the windows, and that is where I sit.

Apparently, there were wanted posters with my face on them in the lobby of every grocery store within a thirty-five mile radius of my house. It seems that they frowned upon opened boxes of Cap'n Crunch in the aisles and my incessant bantering with the deli clerk as to what olive loaf really was.

In actuality, sitting outside the store was for my mother's sanity. My father had breathed in my general direction about how crazy I was making her and came up with the ledge idea. I'm sure he briefly thought about leaving me in the car until thoughts of me hotwiring it proved too strong in his mind.

I was well aware of the fact that marketing companies used vibrant colors and funny characters to sell their products, and that they were all at my eye level. So as we walked the aisles, I would casually grab what I wanted and put it in our shopping cart. Most of the time, my mother wouldn't find out until we were already at the register. *Where did these Vienna sausages come from?*

I would also secretly put things in other people's carts. If I couldn't have it, then someone else should. My thought was that they would never notice all the canned soup or feminine hygiene products. I always wondered what they would say to the lady at the register when they saw that tube of Preparation H being put in a brown paper bag. Paper bags were the staple; I can't imagine doing that with a plastic bag. In Baltimore those plastic bags double as the state bird as they always end up in trees.

Once when my baby brother David was shopping with us, I was in charge of pushing him in the cart. In the **Way Back Machine** there are no racing cars attached to the front of a shopping cart; you just drive the big metal-framed basket on wheels.

With him in the shopping cart, I took off on a dead run pushing him. When we got up to a sustained speed, I let go and started running beside him. He was standing in the front of the cart holding on. He looked over at me, laughing as the breeze blew his hair, and then shock set in when he realized that I wasn't holding on anymore. His expression was priceless. I stopped him right before we leveled thirty boxes of Nilla Wafers.

David was oblivious to pretty much everything and everyone. As his family members, it was our responsibility to enlighten him about the world and the variety of people living in it. We failed.

On a Saturday afternoon, my father drove David and me to his work so he could pick up his paycheck. He deposited us in the snack bar, bought us a soda, and went off to the personnel department to get his check. We were seated right in the middle of the fifteen-stool counter, and about seven stools away, sat an elderly black gentleman, drinking a cup of coffee.

I had just taken a big sip through my straw when David asked in an unusually loud voice, "Hey Neil, why is that man's face so black?" I can't even tell you how mortified I was, and not to mention, choked on my soda. The man just started laughing and said "I guess they didn't tell you about us yet." I apologized and prayed for my father to show up immediately, but God wasn't listening.

I gave David an evil stare, and he was quiet for a couple of seconds before demanding, "Well, why is it?" *Death, take me now!* The man left a few minutes later and was still laughing as he patted my back on the way out.

I couldn't be mad at David because he was clueless, and I was very impressed with how the man handled the situation. Once we were back in the car, my father told us that there were many people who made up the world and tried to describe some variations. The next day David asked me where the yellow and red people lived.

The supermarket ledge wasn't my only prison. I was also banned at most department stores. Once when my mother was looking for me in the Montgomery Ward of Eudowood Plaza, I thought we were playing a huge game of hide-and-seek. I found one of those circular clothing racks, crawled inside it and stayed hidden for about an hour.

It was very easy for me to sit and wait as I had lots of practice waiting. My mom was a chit-chatter and was very approachable. It didn't matter if we were in the post office, the bakery or church; my mom would find someone to talk to. I had to come up with ways of making myself busy, and I became pretty good at it.

Once, Fitz and I wanted to go swimming, but we had just eaten lunch, so my mom said we had to wait twenty minutes. I wasn't taught how to tell time yet, but while waiting for her to finish one of her chit-chat sessions one day, I observed the second hand on the store's wall clock; I figured each time it went around was a minute. I told Fitz I'd be right back and ran inside the house. Our clock was in the kitchen, hanging over the window. I stood there and watched the red second hand go around and around, counting each time.

MISSING PINE PARK

When I counted twenty times, I ran back outside and jumped in the pool. My mom yelled at me until I explained that I counted twenty minutes on the clock. I'm sure she wondered how this pants-wetting kid could teach himself how to tell time, but I had.

While hiding in Montgomery Ward, I can remember her running around calling my name, but I wasn't giving in. After a while some other people were calling my name too, but Mom always said, "Don't talk to strangers," so I stayed put.

When I finally came out, I was greeted with tears, three security guards, a store manager and a spanking. My mother was juuuuust a little pissed. I had counted sixty-three minutes on the wall clock and was proud of myself.

I didn't have good luck at Eudowood Plaza anyway and was just getting over the nightmare of climbing the huge stairs to see Santa Claus. I swear it was a scene right out of *A Christmas Story*, minus the boot in the face. I climbed up the big set of stairs, sat on the scary man's lap, told him I wanted a Rat Patrol lunchbox and then cried down the other set of stairs. What a horrible ritual for little kids.

THE EXAMPLE

I never really knew how much I would learn to hate the alphabet. It wasn't the learning part or even that catchy ABC song; it was the way it was used as a sorting tool. I learned very early that life was organized alphabetically.

My belief that people lived in alphabetical order haunted me on many occasions. From seating arrangements to the Dewey Decimal System, I struggled with that concept most of my young life.

On my very first day of elementary school, I was wearing a giant badge with my name on it, along with my bus number and my teacher's name.

You only have one teacher in the **Way Back Machine,** and there is no moving around from classroom to classroom.

I never went to kindergarten, so the first teacher I ever knew was Mrs. Branson. She was your typical wool-dress-wearing first grade teacher, complete with cat-eye glasses hanging around her neck and a mean glance that could melt chalk.

She plucked me out of the gym as I stood around with a hundred other confused, little kids waiting for their teacher and ushered me to the first grade wing of Carney Elementary. I remember passing very tall lockers and a hallway bulletin board covered with a tree and apples with our names on them.

When we finally reached our classroom, we were told to find the desk with our name on it, and I found mine right away, in the front row. To my left was Barry Anton, and to my right was Diane Bowersox, and that was the way it was for four long years. Mrs. Branson learned everybody's name pretty quickly, but when she was stumped for someone to call on, for some reason she chose me. I was always the first kid to come to the front chalkboard to try a math problem. I was also the first kid in gym to try to climb the rope and the first kid to be pulled out of the lunch line if there was a problem. I am most certain that my role in the first grade was to fail so everybody else could learn from my mistakes.

Ironically, in 1997, I was sitting in traffic court and was the very last person called. I couldn't believe it as it had never happened before, so I was pretty excited by the anomaly. Before pleading my case, I explained to the judge that I had always been first in everything, and I thought it oddly strange that I was called last. He laughed and gave me probation before judgment. Mrs. Branson never would have done that.

All of my failures were due to my last name beginning with B; I had to go first. It was impossible for me to learn from others because the only person I could learn from was Barry and he never got called on. He was a good friend though, because he would always give me his bologna sandwich at lunch. He hated bologna, and once when I saw him throw it away, I read him the riot act. I had heard it so many times at home; I had had it memorized, so I launched into the starving-kids-in-China speech. He looked at me, stunned, and he said, "Well then, you eat it," so I did. Lunch was my favorite subject. It still is.

Alphabetically, I was suffering through the first grade, so I acted out. There are no made up syndrome names in the *Way Back Machine* so when you are a hyper kid, the teacher just has to deal with you.

I put Mrs. Branson through the ringer and was told that I would be responsible for sending her to an early grave. One sad day, she snapped and used an entire roll of masking tape to tape me to the chair. She ran around me, still teaching to the class as she circled, and when I wouldn't shut up, she taped my mouth shut. Even to this day when painting trim and I tear the tape with my teeth, the taste takes me right back to Mrs. Branson's first grade classroom.

You would think that incident would stop most kids from acting out but not me. Defiantly, I started rocking back and forth in the chair. Appearing crazed, she got down on her hands and knees and drew circles on the floor around the feet of my chair with chalk and dared me to move it.

In the future, every time I achieved an accomplishment in life that made me proud, my mother would remind me that at her first PTA meeting, she was told I would never ever get out of elementary school. My dad told me she would cry, and he would just laugh and take her to The Rite Spot for lunch. The Rite Spot was a little sandwich joint in Carney for sad and embarrassed parents.

I also remember the day when we were called on to tell the class what our fathers did for a living. I was not prepared, and when Barry was speaking, I panicked because I was next. My father worked at E.J. Korvettes in Catonsville, Maryland. The urban legend was that the store was started by, *eight Jewish Korean War veterans*; hence, the discount store chain was named after them as E.J. Korvettes. It was just a legend.

Korvettes was a great department store and was where everybody bought their 45's. I'm talking about records, not firearms. My father was in charge of many departments, but I didn't know that. I remember hearing him tell my mom once that he had sold thirty-five patio chairs to a local Holiday Inn to put around their pool, but all I had understood was that my dad was a chair salesman. Can you say boring?

All at once, the class was staring at me, waiting for my response. I proceeded to the front of the classroom and faced my peers. With the straightest of faces, I told everybody in Mrs. Branson's class what my father did for a living. It flowed out like butter, and I wasn't as embarrassed as I thought I would be.

That night after dinner, my parents came into my bedroom and said they wanted to talk to me. They asked me if I knew what my father did for a living and wondered if I was embarrassed. I just sat there and played the stupid card.

MISSING PINE PARK

They explained to me that earlier in the day Mrs. Branson had called in an excited voice and asked if my father would come into my classroom and talk to the class about his job. When I asked him if he was going to go, he told me no. When I asked him why, he said because he didn't know anything about being a lion tamer.

STEP BALL

I sat there on the cool cement steps of our front porch, waiting for someone to come to the door and tell me lunch was ready. My mother made the best bologna and cheese sandwiches in the western hemisphere, and I was preparing myself for it. As good as it was at home, it was nowhere near as good as it tasted at school.

I don't mean the kind you buy in the cafeteria (or Cafetorium in my case. I'll address that later). I mean the kind of sandwich that sits for four hours on the top shelf of an eighty-five degree locker and perfectly welds together in a brown paper bag. Each bite was a new adventure in taste bud heaven, and I found myself on many occasions clock watching in the middle of a filmstrip about bee pollination, anticipating that adventure.

While waiting, I decided to finish the step ball game I was currently in the middle of. Unbeknownst to my closest relatives but secretly viewed by the paperboy, I was pitching a no-hitter in the seventh game of the World Series.

I was wearing my favorite baseball uniform at the time. Across the front of my shirt were two birds perched at the opposite end of a stick, which resembled a horizontal baseball bat. The white belted pants led to my black stirrups, and I was sporting my lucky tennis shoes. I called it my Orioles outfit, but since I was only five years old and couldn't read, I didn't know that it was actually a St. Louis Cardinals uniform.

You could throw a stick in my neighborhood and strike a passing child who I knew on a middle name basis, but at this particular moment there was none to be seen or heard. That was a perfect enough reason to partake in a little game of solitaire. I wasn't speaking of a card game, but a derivative of the greatest American pastime. Someone had invented a way to play baseball all by yourself and called it step ball.

With a single set of steps, a hard rubber ball, an official regulation Rawlings baseball glove, and an Orioles hat, pulled down over my eyes to intimidate the concrete, I could play step ball. Brooks Robinson was the greatest third baseman of all time and he played for my home team, the Baltimore Orioles. He was under contract with Rawlings, and I felt I was a better player for even wearing a glove he endorsed. The Orioles had just beaten the Los Angeles Dodgers four straight in the 1966 World Series, and I was still reveling in all their glory. My father and I listened to game one, via Chuck Thompson, on the radio. When Brooks and Frank Robinson hit back-to-back homeruns in the first inning, I was beside myself. I actually left my body and stood beside myself as I jumped up and down in excitement. I looked rather foolish.

Step ball consisted of one player who played both offense and defense. The lineup of the opposing team was usually made up of the best hitters in either league, but it didn't matter with standout Mike Cuellar on the hill. He could hit the corner of any step at will, causing the batter to pop up a can of corn or hit a frozen rope directly at the stellar defensive team I had assembled. I always thought that baseball had the coolest sayings. A frozen rope was of course a line drive and a can of corn...well, that was just corn in a can.

So, here we were: two outs, bottom of the ninth, three and two on the spunky Joe Morgan. He's got his twitch going pretty good as Mike winds up. The leg is raised, the arm draws back and... the door opens. "Lunch is ready!" called Mom. I had never dropped a baseball glove in my life, but the thought of a bologna and cheese sandwich can make a major leaguer do silly things.

I called time out for a fifteen-minute mound conference and sprinted into the house. When I sat down at the dining room table, for some reason I looked up. On the ceiling was a ladybug. Ladybugs are considered good luck and I was going to need that with Joe Morgan. I sat there at the table, thinking about who was coming up in the next inning. I think it was Roberto Clemente, and he scared me too.

The last time I faced him, something terrible had happened. It was starting to drizzle when he came to the plate, and my dad was standing at the door watching me pitch to this future Hall of Famer. I threw a screwball, low and outside, and it skipped backward off the corner of the step and slammed into the glass door my father was standing behind. My father taught me everything I knew about baseball. Until that very second, I was proud that he was watching.

The door shook violently, and I thought it was going to shatter glass all over him, which would have ended the game immediately and, of course, my life. Bottom line, I hate pitching to Roberto Clemente when it is raining and when my father is watching. He also decided it was my job to start putting in the screens. I learned that when the glass broke so would my consecutive-day record for going without spankings.

My mom sat down a cold glass of milk in front of me because every ball player loves cold milk. Years later many professional players would adorn a milk moustache in print advertisements. I started that trend.

With a smile my mother placed a paper plate in front of me with a napkin perched majestically on top. I smiled at her, scooted in, and removed the napkin to reveal a tuna fish sandwich.

What? Did this really happen? There was a pitching change about to happen, and I'm eating tuna fish? Where is the bologna and cheese? The mayo? The kind of lunch that grows champions? The kind of lunch that when your father makes it and forgets to take the plastic edging off of the bologna, you eat it anyway? I mean, what was happening here? I sunk in my chair, dejected, and reached for the solace I would find in my cold glass of milk. I took a sip and quickly spit something out into my hand. It was a ladybug.

THE CRITTER

We heard they were coming to put some toys in Missing Pine Park. Kids were still cruising by on their bicycles, checking the area out, wondering what was going to happen there. *They just built the Reliant Astrodome in Houston, Texas; maybe they will put one of those suckers here.* We used to think big in Carney.

Grass was slowly growing in after they smoothed out the tank ruts, and it looked like nature might be coming back. For the longest time it resembled a construction site, but now it was shaping into a park. I sat on the steps and imagined all the fun we would have.

Occasionally, you would see a deer pass by, and birds would land to peck at the grass seed. Nature never got in our way, but I still wondered where Bigfoot was living now. I walked down the grassy hill into the area, which later became known as home plate. In the future I would spend a lot of time there.

I was just looking around when something caught my eye. I saw some movement over by the bushes that divided the park from the Sullivans' yard. I say bushes, but mean briars and a tangled mess of thorny thickets. There were crawling paths all through the thickets from the kids that had been visiting. Rabbits could be seen from time to time, and it looked like a great place for the Easter Bunny to reside. To us it was uncharted territory, like the Yukon, or say, Nebraska.

I inched a few steps closer, waiting for the movement again, and it hopped. A toad! *How cool! A toad!* Catching your first wild animal is a rite of passage to a little boy. I needed to check this off of my bucket list.

I bet I was funny to watch because I walked bent over with my hands cupped in front of me for about twenty minutes before I realized he didn't want to be caught. I tried coaxing him with toad speech, but he wasn't listening.

I really thought saying *redeep* over and over to this little guy would make him stop hopping and hold a conversation with me. I concluded that I must have had an accent. He could be a northern toad and had issue with my southern drawl. I tried again, *ridip.*

A few years earlier, our family went camping at Shad Landing. It is somewhere on the Pocomoke River in Snow Hill, Maryland. After a brief rain, my dad and I went on a walk and saw all these mini-toads having a party. They were so tiny and seemed so happy. They occupied their own little world.

My dad picked one up and placed it on my thumb. We watched it crawl around, exploring my landscape. It was my first real glance at wildlife. We put it down and stood watching for a few minutes; then my father asked in all seriousness, "How many of them do you think it would take to make a stew?" *Funny guy my dad.*

I had danced with this little guy long enough, so I finally performed the diving double step and had him pinned under my outstretched hands. I scooped him up and pulled myself into a seated position to admire my catch. He was dark brown and had weird, rough, bumpy skin. You could see his heart beating throughout his whole body, and he had two big eyes that seemed to say, "Take me home and keep me in a shoebox with some grass in it." He was cool, and I immediately fell in love with him.

We never had any wild animals as pets, and the closest we came to owning one was when a box turtle came wandering through our backyard. I fashioned a shoebox and filled it with some lettuce and hoped he would call it home. My parents, however, thought he should be set free to roam the world as turtles do and assigned me the painful task of setting him free.

I was really heartbroken until my father came up with a great idea. He told me that turtles are creatures of habit, therefore, he was sure he would pass this way again. Since all turtles look alike, we decided to paint a big number 1 on his back and set him free. Sure enough, for three straight years, a turtle with a number 1 painted on his shell made his way through our yard. My sister Karen sat on the back steps waiting for the number "2" turtle. He never showed up, and she just assumed that he must have been visiting another yard.

I was pretty sure my mother wouldn't want my new toad in my room, but my father would totally understand and welcome him like a true member of the family. Just then, the Millers drove by the front of the park and headed up the small hill to their house on the corner. Buddy and Tony were finally home. They had been away all day, and when I knocked on their door earlier, their uncle told me he didn't know when they were coming back. I had to show them my new pet.

They would know I was a true hunter, which would aid me as a leader of my team in any game of army that we would ever play. I started towards the Millers' in hopes of naming my new friend on the way.

By the time I got to their backdoor, Tippy and I were the best of friends. I think he peed in my hands, which of course meant I should have warts by dinnertime, but I didn't even care. Through the glass door, I could see the whole Miller family: Mr. and Mrs. Miller, their grandmother, their Aunt Clara, their Uncle Joe and Buddy and Tony, all sitting at the table.

Their backdoor led right into the dining room with the kitchen on the immediate left. They waved me in, but I couldn't use my hands because I was cupping the wild animal I had just caught. He was tame now, of course, and would listen to any command I would throw out there. I tried to open the door with my elbow, but it didn't work.

Finally, someone opened the door and I stepped inside. Everyone could tell by the look on my face that I had something cool in my hands. I was sure they all wanted to hear the story of how I beat the odds of nature and captured a wild animal.

I knelt down between the kitchen and dining room with everyone standing over me, and I placed Tippy on the floor. The gasps were outstanding, and I could tell they were in awe. A wild animal! And I caught it!

I started answering a flurry of questions and regaled them with my hunt. I was so happy and felt a satisfaction like I had never known. I reached out with my index finger and touched his little behind and said, "Jump, Tippy, jump." He followed my command immediately and leapt high into the air. Yells and cheers were heard as he slowly flew higher. I saw all of this in slow motion as I planned on recalling it many times in the future, and I wanted to remember every detail.

However, in a blinding flash, the Millers' German Shepherd burst through the crowd and snatched Tippy while in mid-air. He didn't even hit the ground. My former wild animal best friend was now in the belly of a black German Shepherd named Shep. Shep sat there and licked his lips and looked around as if to say "thank you." The Millers were speechless and all retreated to their places at the table. I stood up to leave without my wild animal. It happened so fast I didn't even have time to cry. I left their house, dejected and friendless, and headed home to deal with my warts.

SECOND BASE

The park across the street from my house was now completely covered with grass. No longer was it a creepy patch of woods or a lot filled with muddy tractor ruts. It was a nice field in the middle of nowhere, but it was ours. We would hang out and play rundown all day long.

Rundown is a game that is played with two bases, two fielders and at least one runner. The two fielders play catch until the runner takes off from one base and tries to get to the other base without being tagged out. If a fielder throws the ball to the other fielder before the runner arrives, then the runner changes direction and a rundown is created. When tagged out, the runner switches places with the fielder who tagged him and a new game starts.

We would play with twenty-five runners. It would resemble a jailbreak. The bases would get larger and then there would just be bare spots on the ground. We couldn't wait for the grass to come in, and then when it did, we promptly wore it away. "You're out" and "you missed me" could be heard over and over as instant replay hadn't been invented yet. I still love that game.

One day on my way home from school, after passing the Sullivans' house, I stopped next to the lone tree and glared into the park. When they knocked down the woods, they left one pine tree at the top of the small hill that led down into the park. To the immediate right of the tree, they sank railroad ties into the side of the hill to make steps. They were laid three-deep and consisted of seven tiers. I stepped down the first step and couldn't believe my eyes. Right smack in the middle of the park was a thirty-foot flagpole. There was an American flag waving and everything.

Holy cow! I knew we lived in America and I should have been proud as punch, but I wasn't. I saw Paul Flanagan of the Flanagan clan and called him over. At least I thought it was Paul. The Flanagans lived in a four-bedroom colonial that resembled ours, yet they had about twenty -seven kids. Okay, I'm exaggerating; they had twenty-five kids. I used to think that their home had three subterranean floors to house everybody. It is a well-known fact that a Flanagan graduated from Parkville Senior High School every year for thirty-seven consecutive years. It's a state record. Look it up!

Anyway, it wasn't Paul; it was Michael. He walked down the street, passed the tree, and stopped next to me on the steps. "Hey, what the hell is that flagpole doing there?" he remarked. *Exactly!*

Apparently, while we were at school, the county stopped by and planted a flagpole. There was no doubt in my mind; that flagpole was planted by the good people of D-CUP. The fact that they never asked our opinion was unnerving, because they put it right in the middle of second base. I thought we were the planning committee.

After dinner that night, the word spread and kids came from

everywhere to see the new second base. It was white and tall and a flag flapped in the wind while the metal clips that held the flag in place would swing into the pole, making a clanking type noise.

As dusk approached, we were sitting on the steps in a herd when a car stopped right behind us. A Boy Scout in full uniform got out of the car, walked down the park and unceremoniously took down the flag, folded it and left as quickly as he arrived. The next morning at 6AM, he came back and put the flag up again. *What the heck was going on here? How can we play baseball with a giant pole at second base? How can we play football when someone doing a down and out might really be down and out? Boy Scouts? Really?*

In hindsight, the flagpole was a true blessing. It just so happened that it was placed right on the fifty-yard line, so it made playing football easier. I remember only a couple of times when the ball actually hit the pole in mid-flight, which was pretty cool and would stop the game with a moment of awe. The flagpole also became a tremendous second base. You could push off from the base with your foot to get a great jump, slap it with your hand as you were sprinting by, and sliding into it was the perfect cup check.

In late fall of that year, right across the street from our house, they put in a telephone pole. For a long time they didn't attach anything to it, so we all tried to climb it without spikes on our shoes. Can you say huge crotch splinters?

In November, they finally ran electric to it from the pole in our front yard. I remember hearing rumblings in the house to the tune that we might solely be paying for the electric because our next-door neighbor Mr. Hudson, who was an electrician, had climbed the pole in the dead of night. We could never prove that he rewired anything, but every time his central air conditioner kicked on, somehow our lights dimmed. Of course, this was merely an unsubstantiated rumor.

In December, someone erected a manger right next to the flagpole, complete with hay, Mary, Joseph, and a big ol' baby Jesus. He was kind of pudgy. From the new telephone pole, they ran electric down to the manger, and before you knew it, we had illuminated religion. It was actually nice to drive or walk past it and see the manger all lit up at night.

Remember that lone pine tree that was spared at the top of the hill? Well, the neighborhood got together and decorated that bad boy.

They even ran an extension cord from the Sullivans' house to power it up. We had ourselves a community Christmas tree! It was so pretty and really got the neighborhood excited for Christmas. We didn't even mind having a fat baby Jesus.

Santa stopped by it once and sat in a big red chair that was dropped off near the tree so all the local kids could come and sit on his lap. I remember Fitz saying he was going to put water balloons under the seat cushion but thought wiser about it. About a week out, it snowed briefly and remained cold, so there was snow around in patches. It's a well-known fact that a white Christmas is better than most, so all was perfect in Carney as Christmas grew closer.

On Christmas morning, Jan and I woke up, pre-dawn as usual, only to be told to go back to bed and wait a few more hours. I think the sound of my parents finally shutting their bedroom door is what jarred me awake. The go-back-to-bed-before-I-end-you face was a game changer. To say I was disciplined by fear was like saying marshmallow was sticky.

To a kid, waiting a few hours felt like a millennium, so I decided to take in a Christmas morning scene and look out my window towards the community tree. It wasn't there! The lights that I saw every evening were non-existent, and through the gray morning, all I could see was a stump. We learned later that on Christmas Eve, someone in a pickup truck stopped at the top of the park and cut down our fully decorated Christmas tree and drove off with it. *What the hell is wrong with people? Don't they know we have a community thing going on here? I mean, damn!*

As you can imagine, it was the talk of the town. The one tree left when they knocked down the scary woods was stolen on Christmas Eve. There is not even a device invented now that could measure the level of shock I was experiencing. Of course, the shock turned into laughter later that spring when the Christmas Eve caper would be forever chiseled in the stone legacy of Carney.

In early spring, we were hanging off the second base flagpole when a truck stopped by. Five county workers erected a big three-paneled wooden sign to the right of the hill leading down into the park, right over the tunnel. It instantly became a Kodak photo spot. Baltimore County, in all its wisdom, finally named our play area Missing Pine Park. *Brilliant!*

THE MAN BOX

One day in June of 1969, strangers started showing up to Missing Pine Park. Curiosity got the better of me, so I went down there to get a better look. I mean, after all, they could have been members of D-CUP. They were running all around, marking and measuring things; they even put a cinder block right on third base. *What the hell was going on? If that was some kind of new sadistic ride, I was going to report somebody!*

Pickup trucks began arriving, and more strangers were unloading things and setting them up right on the street. I saw signage describing cool treats and pictures of halved lemons with candy cane straws in them. I just love those lemons with the candy canes. They were thicker candy canes with a small hole all the way through. When you sucked the lemon juice through them, you were greeted with a minty lemon treat.

I looked up the little hill and then up the big hill and noticed that they were blocked off to traffic. There were wooden carnival stands going up everywhere in the park.

I walked up the little hill towards Buddy and Tony's house, gathering other concerned kids along the way. Fitz was at my side, followed closely by Bobby Flanagan, Jimmy Grayson, and one of the Hudson girls.

When we passed the fifteen-mile an hour speed limit sign, it meant we were halfway up the hill. At the bottom of the sign it said, "Checked by Radar," and I had always wondered if it had anything to do with the corporal on M*A*S*H.

When you reached the sign, you could look right into the Millers' backyard through the slats in their dark wooden fence. Most houses didn't have fences, but the Millers had a big, scary, frog-eating dog, so they put up one. They didn't have a chain-linked fence but a plank fence, which had three horizontal panels, inches apart, nailed to vertical posts. Each panel was about six to eight inches wide, and the color was very dark brown but looked black. I spent a lot of time standing on the bottom plank and peering into their yard. I never scaled their fence because of Shep and never went into their yard uninvited.

We all stood on the bottom plank and looked over the fence. Jimmy couldn't see that high, so he bent down to look between the slats. The Millers' yard had all kinds of activity going on too. I saw a man carrying bowling pins and another guy laying down some carpet. I saw Buddy coming down his stairs, carrying five baseballs, so I called him over. He was the oldest one of my closest friends, and I usually took his word as law.

He told us there was going to be a block party! They closed off Appleton at both ends and were setting up games and food stands all over the place. In the Millers' yard there was a stand where you threw baseballs at bowling pins and another game where you had to jump through hoops. I didn't try that one but should have because years later when I was applying to own a business, I had to jump through all kinds of hoops and could have used the practice.

The block party was going to follow the big Flag Day parade. It was going to start at Alda Drive, hit Summit Avenue and then snake around the block to Appleton and stop at the top of the park. They were going to have the Balladettes, a baton and drum corps, perform and even feature some psychedelic musical group called White Lightning. It was going to be a great day!

As I walked back down the hill, I spied more and more people showing up, and before I knew it, everything had opened up. There were clowns walking around, music was playing and carnival food was being offered all up and down Appleton. The park had other games too, the kind that required skill, so, naturally, I hung out there. One game specifically caught my eye; I was quickly drawn to it. It was a simple putting green that was about twenty-feet long with a slight dogleg left. The prize was a set of baby blue glass Zonker balls, and I wanted them.

Zonker balls were all the rage. They were glass balls connected by a string that was dissected by a small plastic hoop. When you held the ring in your thumb and forefinger and slowly rocked your hand up and down, the balls would start banging together making a loud clicking noise. Each time they met, they bounced further away from each other. The faster you moved, the harder they hit until they were not only meeting at the bottom but flying apart and hitting each other at the top, forming a complete circle. The noise was fantastic.

I ran home and talked my mom into giving me a dollar in change so I could try all the games, but secretly I had planned on hanging out at the putting green. My idea was to spend ten cents on the golf game and then zonker my way over to the lemon with the candy cane straw stand, where I would look cool and have a cool treat simultaneously.

When I got back, there were already other kids standing in line, so I had to wait and watch their awful skill sets as they tried to perform this simple task. I never knew there were so many untalented kids in Carney, but they were gathering in Missing Pine Park.

When it finally came to my turn, I handed over a quarter, took back fifteen cents and stepped up to the green. The next two minutes were a blur, and before I knew it, I was out a whole dollar. *What the hell? I know I am better than these knuckleheads, and now they have infected me.* I walked around a little, pretending to have fun, but I was seething on the inside. I made my way back home and searched for some more change.

My mom walked by me while I proceeded to dig through the couch cushions and said she would be back in about a half hour. She grabbed her keys and left. I still don't know how she got our car out. I totally struck out with the furniture and started cruising the house. I looked everywhere and found all kinds of lost things, plus I found my intolerance for not finding any loose change!

I'm not sure how, but I ended up in my parents' room which was completely off limits. I knew there were hidden traps everywhere designed to catch me, but I was jonesing like a heroin addict, so I entered, cautiously.

I was drawn to a brown box on my dad's dresser. It was kind of like a jewelry box, but since men don't wear jewelry, it was just a man box. It hinged on both sides and opened like a tackle box to reveal other cool compartments with watches, cuff links and trinkets. I found a coin that had a head on each side and another coin with a naked lady. I visited that coin many times in the future.

In one compartment I finally hit the jackpot: an entire roll of dimes. *Perfect!* The roll appeared opened, and a couple had fallen out, so I quickly picked up the loose dimes and headed back to the park.

I repeated this disappointing trip four or five times until my mother came home. During my horrible losing streak, I had burned through about three dollars in dimes. Finally, with twenty cents to spare, I sunk the stupid golf ball and was rewarded with my baby blue glass Zonker balls. My life, for the moment, was complete. I zonkered my way up the park, making sure everybody within earshot heard me banging my balls. I was a first-class ball banger.

The block party went on for two days, and everybody seemed to enjoy themselves. About an hour after the last vendor packed up and left, my father came out of his room looking a little distraught. I saw him address my mother in a whisper. *Maybe he was out of underwear or something.* When I heard him yell my name, I knew instantly that I had set off some secret tracking device or pressure pad and was going to be questioned.

Punishment was far from my mind, because I had replaced the dimes with loose change from Jan's Skippy peanut butter coin bank and left everything the way it was. I soon found out how wrong I was.

I played thirty-two games of putt-putt with my dad's rare 1947 solid silver Roosevelt dimes. According to today's exchange rate, my baby blue glass Zonker balls cost him seventy-three dollars and sixty cents. I couldn't sit for a week, and, to this very day, I am reminded of it every time I grab my putter.

YACK

I threw up a lot as a kid. I didn't have the flu, and I wasn't under the influence of anything. I just had a very weak stomach. It pretty much was an everyday occurrence in elementary school, and my friends were entertained by the outcome.

I inherited a gag reflex from Dad. I watched him change David's diaper once, and he was making noises and facial expressions that I had never seen or heard before. His eyes were watering, and he sounded like a cow retching into a fifty-gallon drum. It was funny to see such a strong man gagging.

I, on the other hand, had a severe problem with gross things. The first time I remember losing it was in the first grade at lunch. This kid, Billy Whitman, was talking to me and at the same time he was eating a turkey salad sandwich. He was talking with food in his mouth, and I felt drawn to watching every motion like a moth to a bright light. He was telling me a story about a motorcycle, and, like most kids who tell stories with sound, stuck his tongue out and made a giant raspberry sound. Instantly, my face was peppered with little chunks of spat-out turkey salad. I sat there, frozen, and could feel each, individual, little, wet chunk on my face. He didn't even stop talking.

I was holding half a bologna and cheese sandwich, which was in the line of fire too. The thought of finishing it was more than I could handle, so I opted for paybacks and ralphed right into Billy Whitman's face. It was a clean hit, and nobody else was a recipient. He was still talking when I coated him, so I'm pretty sure I scored a mouth shot.

I was sent to the school nurse, who called my mother, and I went home. Apparently, it was against school policy to barf into people's mouths at Carney Elementary.

I know this because I was sent home many, many, many times. In the third grade, I was in a reading group in the back of the room, sitting next to Robert Shaffer. Robert had very blonde hair, which almost appeared white when he wore a red shirt. He was sitting there in a comatose state, staring blankly at the bulletin board. He seemed a little pale.

I looked at the board to see what had his attention, and all I saw was the state's name Arkansas. The whole map of the United States was there, but I fixated on Arkansas. I looked at it for a few seconds, and then I had a cool learning moment. I noticed that the state of Kansas was actually stuck inside the state of Arkansas. It was truly a magical moment, and I wondered if anybody else in the world had figured that out. *No way! I was a genius.* From that moment on, I referred to that state as Ar Kansas.

I was excited at my discovery; however, my glee had vanished quickly when Robert decided to blow chunks on my shoes. They were my hard shoes, too. If you jump in the **Way Back Machine** and go to Carney Elementary, you only see kids wearing hard shoes because tennis shoes are strictly used for gym.

I had a white pair of Jack Purcells in my locker for such an occasion and a blue pair at home. Heaven forbid if I ever wore the white pair at home. "Heads will roll." That was one of my father's favorite sayings.

I hated hard shoes, especially with throw up all over them. The only day I remember liking hard shoes was when our class went to the library. There was a big fluffy rug on the floor behind the couch, and when Todd Arnold walked on it and touched somebody, we all saw sparks. He created static electricity, and we all wanted to be like Thomas Edison and experiment with direct current.

The static charges even doubled if someone was wearing a sweater. I think I *pinged* about ten people on their ear. It was great fun. I would stand in place and slide my shoes back and forth on the carpet as long as I could. It seemed the longer you did that the higher the charge. Then when I was at full capacity, I would find some unsuspecting ear for discharge purposes. The emitted scream and miniature lightning bolt would let you know that you were successful with your science experiment. A similar stunt could be done with a balloon and a full head of hair.

My brother David had the very best head of curly hair to rub with a balloon. We used to rub balloons on his head and then stick them to his back and watch him walk in circles, trying to get them off. Pure entertainment. I always felt bad for bald men because they couldn't enjoy the rub-and-stick routine.

About ten seconds after Robert Shaffer barfed, I followed suit. I wasn't sick at all; I felt great. I just couldn't handle the noise and smell of someone else's vomit cookie. While sitting next to him in the nurse's office, I determined that he was really sick because he threw up again. I quickly grabbed a trashcan and performed the jersey yodel. The school nurse knew my work pretty well. She saw me at least once a week as I was often there with some ailment or injury. I would split the crotch out of my pants, have a ballpoint pen explode in my pocket, or even bite the side of my mouth. *Damn, that hurts.*

Even with rotary phones the nurse had my mom on speed dial. She knew the routine and was most likely sitting next to the phone, waiting for it to ring. A week later I threw up on Martha Tippet. It was picture day, and she was all gussied up in a pretty yellow dress with white lace around the neck. I felt pretty badly, but this time it wasn't my fault.

Some of my good friends thought it was hilarious that they could make me throw up. When I say good friends, I mean my best school friends. David Thomas and Kenny Brandt would hock loogies in a plastic sandwich bag and show it to me or pick their nose and smear it on my math book. Real classy stuff. They treated me like a circus act, and I never disappointed.

MISSING PINE PARK

The only way to get back at the loogie spreaders was on the Greek dodge court, and I was all about the illegal headshot. Greek dodge was just like regular dodge ball except when you were out, you stood behind the opposing team, sandwiching them, and could get back in the game if you hit one of them with the ball. Gladiators had an easier time killing each other than we did while playing Greek dodge. We would go at it the whole recess period. The game would end up with two people, often Harry Dillon and me, fighting it out while the rest of the class watched from the sidelines.

You were considered a wuss if you intentionally threw at someone's feet. I played with a lot of wusses. Whenever that would happen, I aimed at their shoulder so the ball would take a wicked bounce onto their head.

If I ever hurt someone, I could easily repair the relationship with a trip to the school store. It seems that in the **Way Back Machine** little erasers shaped like Jack Purcell tennis shoes are on everybody's want list. They come in many different colors and are strictly for show because they can't erase a thing. They are too rubbery and soft to work properly, so most kids place them on their pencils and then chew on them. I only tried that one time and I threw up. *Who would have thought?*

THE BREAD BOX

In the **Way Back Machine** you have to cover all of your schoolbooks. I don't know why. I guess it is because you have to return them at the end of the year, and they don't want them to be covered with some snotty kid's DNA.

The best way to remove snot and DNA was with a brown paper grocery bag. You could write all kinds of things on the outside and doodle on them all day long. If it became too busy with graffiti, it was easy to change.

Little girls would write their first name and the last name of their boyfriend on their covers. This is the genesis of the wedding fantasy that most adult women have. Since the dawn of time, when the first girl carved Eve Smith in an apple tree, it was a lock that she was going to marry Adam.

It was always a challenge to obtain a "smart book." Every kid had to write his name on the inside cover so you could chart who had it last. If the kid was smart, their books were considered a premium. The dumb people's books were the last to go. I am pretty sure my books are still sitting on a shelf somewhere.

The only thing better than getting a smart book was being the first in your class to get a penny with the new year stamped on it. It only happened once for me, and that was in 1968. I discovered it in my milk money, which was four cents at the time. When I saw it, all new and shiny, I immediately checked the date and was so excited. I was the hero that day, as everyone wanted to see it. Kids crowded around just to see the year 1968. When a new 1968-penny was found, it was usually around the same time that you had finally stopped erroneously writing 1967 on all your papers with those big-ass Lincoln Log pencils.

When I wasn't the school hero, I was the school patient. I got hurt a lot at home, too, and always in a freaky kind of way. Once, during a very windy Sunday, my sister Jan went outside to get the newspaper from the mailbox. I was standing at the glass storm door, watching her hair blowing in the stiff wind, when my mom asked me to bring in the milk.

In the *Way Back Machine* most houses have a breadbox on the front porch. Ours is silver with the words Cloverland Green Spring Dairy painted on it. Every single day the milkman stops by and drops off fresh milk and bread and takes the empty bottles with him.

One special day, he let me look inside his truck. Milk bottles were in crates stacked up on shelves. I could've sworn there would have been a cow back there.

When I started to open the glass front door, the wind grabbed it and whipped me right out the door. The force catapulted me into the air, down the stairs, over the metal railing and right onto the edging material around our hedges. Unfortunately for me, there were bricks placed in the ground pointing straight up, and I smashed my head right on one of them.

I landed on the spot right above my right eye. My head exploded open. I sat there in shock, my sister screamed and my mother raced down the stairs calling my name, in horror. When I stood up, I couldn't see out of my right eye because of the blood and thought I had gone blind. It was a real bleeder, and not until years later after watching Rocky get cut in the corner by his trainer did I know what I must have looked like.

My mom came charging towards me, wearing a white Mickey Mouse sweatshirt, and when she hugged me, the blood transferred to her. When she pulled away, I saw how bloody she was, and I started crying. A leaf had been stuck to my eye by the blood, which would explain my temporary blindness. She was a mess now too, but at least I could see. I had always wanted to fly but wasn't thrilled with my first attempt. *This would have never happened to Batman.*

My parents kept staring at me funny and decided I needed to get some proper medical attention. My dad took me to the brand new Franklin Square Hospital, and for my troubles I was given five stitches above my right eye. My mom had given me a baggie of Cap'n Crunch, and I wore my pajama top to the hospital.

My father stood next to me, gagging as they stitched my eyelid. The numbing needle didn't work too well, and I can vividly remember kicking my shoes off as they stitched me up. They were hard shoes too. Amazing, all that blood and I didn't even throw up. Ask me about my scar.

When it was time for the stitches to be removed, my dad taught me one of his life's lessons. Speed rules. I was sitting on the couch, trying to peel off the Band-Aid that was covering my eyebrow. I was taking it very, very slowly, thinking that slower was better. Much like listening to someone in a movie theater open a piece of cellophane-wrapped candy, slow was actually more painful.

My dad leaned in, grabbed a corner of the Band-Aid and swiftly ripped it off. Four of the stitches and a good portion of my eyebrow went along for the ride. I screamed at the shock of it, but there was no pain. He was a genius. Lesson learned.

THE JOLLY GREEN GIANT

Television was my best friend growing up. Well, next to Timmy Fitzpatrick, I guess, but a very close second. We had a little Magnavox television, complete with rabbit ears and aluminum foil. It sat on a cart in the living room. One morning I noticed that it was void of color. My dad used to tell this story about when I was five and came running into their bedroom a little before 6AM, all upset that the television was broken. The television worked fine; it just wasn't on yet, but I didn't know that. The programming didn't start until 6AM, and it stopped at midnight with its demise preceded by the national anthem. For six hours there was an absence of television programming. It was replaced with signal absence, or, as most people called it, snow.

Snow has a horrible static sound and its very mention conjures up visions from the movie *Poltergeist*. Sometimes before it would come back to life, the television would have odd-looking test patterns with numbers and Indians and other non-specific hieroglyphics. I used to watch and wonder for hours what the hell all those patterns meant and why not a cowboy?

The signs of television had saturated my childhood. Everybody had antennas on the roofs of their houses, and they were all different. When you looked out over the neighborhood, you would see oddly shaped metal attachments with arms and various appendages sticking out all over the place. Some looked like chicken wire, some like tire spokes and others like empty signposts. They must have been a pain in the ass for Santa Claus to get past.

I bet his reindeer were running into them everywhere and were probably very instrumental in the invention of cable. Our antenna looked like a satellite with arms sticking off in all kinds of directions. You would have thought we could pick up transmissions from the Apollo space program, but we only received three channels, sometimes four if you walked by the television wearing metal pants.

Commercials are very interesting in the **Way Back Machine** and seem to contain a lot of people smoking. Even if the commercial isn't about selling cigarettes the spokesperson has one in his or her hand or one is nearby, smoldering in an ashtray.

I just assumed everybody smoked and figured my parents would eventually pack them in my lunchbox.

There were an assortment of car commercials, Colgate toothpaste ads, and who could forget the Cracker Jack commercial? I can see it now with the little boy and girl on the boardwalk running to the Cracker Jack stand, dumping everything out of his pockets, looking for the proper change to buy a box.

He even gives the clerk a marble; then they run hand in hand across the pier to sit down on the steps and eat the tasty snack while the song plays in the background "Lip-smacking, Whipcrackin, Paddywhackin, Olagazackin, Infolackin, Alliganackin, Crackerjackin, Cracker Jack! Candy-coated popcorn, peanuts, and a prize ... That's what you get in Cracker Jack!" Everybody remembers that, right?

However, aside from the crying Indian littering spot that totally gutted me in the early seventies, the one commercial that really affected me as a kid was the Jolly Green Giant. "From the Valley of the Jolly, Ho, Ho, Ho, Green Giant." How cool was it that this big-ass giant had a whole valley of little animated people working for him and he was jolly? I am thinking this was the first gay character on television. I loved the kitchen cut green beans he made, and it had nothing to do with the bacon grease my mother put in them. I found out that if you ate enough cans you could send in the labels and get a Jolly Green Giant kite. Nobody in my neighborhood had one of those, so I woofed down green beans by the case, and sure enough, after a couple of tense weeks, it showed up. It was huge. It stood taller than me and the tail was about a block long. I was going to need Jesse Owens to get this baby up.

When you are a kid and you have a kite, all you want to do is get it airborne. You never take into consideration things like room to run, trees, breeze, wind, air, you know, the essentials for proper kite flying. If I lived smack dab in the middle of a forest, I would still try to fly a kite. *How can I make this happen?* I came up with a plan and waited. At 7AM my father dressed in his polyester brown slacks, white shirt and a tie and prepared for a twelve-hour workday. As he was walking out the front door, I presented him with my plan. Five minutes later he was running back and forth in our backyard in his penny loafers, trying to get the Jolly Green Giant off the ground. The wind was blowing at a steady zero miles per hour, and it was already eighty degrees outside. I watched from the back patio with great anxiety, waiting for him to hand me the reins. After about fifteen minutes he walked his sweaty body over to me and sadly told me he had to go to work. There would be no kite flying today.

I took my green friend into the basement, but only because I couldn't get it back inside the house, and went outside to watch the weather. It didn't move. Have you ever noticed how slow time moves when you want it to move fast? I still didn't officially learn how to tell time, but I could tell it was moving backwards. I watched every tree in our yard and not one leaf swayed, twitched or even breathed. I was sitting on our brick patio and decided I had enough and rose to go inside. My hair felt it first, and then I heard the trees moving. I spun around just in time to see the wind enter my yard. It had arrived and the trees woke up.

Maybe if I called my dad he could come home from work early and help me again. Why did he have to work anyway? Then I started thinking about doing it myself. It was time to stop relying on others for my own fun. I could fly the kite. The Jolly Green Giant had nothing on me. I removed him from the basement and walked him over to lean on the Hudsons' newly installed fence. I let out some string and started running to the other side of the yard.

I looked over my shoulder and he was up. It was brilliant. He was backlit by the sun and cast an awesome shadow over the yard. It looked just like the commercial with him towering over everything. The wind started whipping now, so I let out some more string and he rose higher. His tail was fluttering around like a snake, and it made the sound sheets make when hanging on the clothesline. I was standing on one of Mr. Herman C Bell III's railroad ties, and Mr. Jolly was at the opposite end of the yard. I had hoped someone was watching me. I had hoped kids all around my neighborhood were looking up to see the giant on my kite. After all, my whole intestinal track had been changed forever by eating a skid of kitchen cut green beans, so someone had better be witnessing this event.

He was slowly losing height, so I climbed over the twine fence Mr. Bell had invented and walked backwards through their yard. I had never been over here. Our house looked completely different from this angle. I was almost nearing the Chadmans' fence when the wind shifted. The trees near the back of our yard were calling the giant, but I wasn't going to let that happen, so I started walking towards the Bells' house, and the kite followed. I can still remember how wonderful it looked hovering over our house. What a great day!

When my father got home from work, I was alone in my room sitting on my bed. I had been crying for hours and hours. My eyes were puffy and red, and my nose had completely run out of snot. He walked in my room and stood over me. He had a slight smirk on his face, like he had some knowledge I wasn't aware of, and he asked, "Why is there a Jolly Green Giant wrapped around my television antenna?" *Damn reindeer were right.*

THE OPERATOR

Our phone hung on the wall right inside the back door. When the door was open, it was completely covered up. It was rectangular, black and had a rotary dial in the middle. The receiver hung on a horseshoe-shaped metal hook that stuck out of the front top of the box. When you hung the receiver on the hook, the metal piece would lower down and disconnect the call. That is where the term "hang up" actually came from. I don't know how people hang up phones today.

My mother would use her thirty-five-foot phone cord and stroll all over the house. There were days when I would walk in the back door and follow the cord from the dining room wall, through the kitchen, down the hall and under the bathroom door. I had no idea what was going on in there but doubted she was on an advice hotline.

It was quite a novelty to be outside while talking on the phone. Can you imagine talking on the phone outside? If you jump into the **Way Back Machine,** you often hear other people talking on your phone. It is called a party line. My guess is that if there is a whole bunch of people on the phone at the same time, it feels like a party. In actuality, it means we are sharing the phone line with another family somewhere.

You can pick up the phone to make a call and hear other people on the line and the people aren't even in your own home. It makes it easy to eavesdrop or scare the hell out of people with the "I'm in the house" line that will later be monopolized in every slasher-horror movie, with the exception of *Friday the 13th* because Jason can't talk.

My sister Jan was on the phone about twenty-three and a half hours a day. I think I answered the phone about a hundred times a week, and it was always for Jan. The following conversation happened every six minutes:

Ring,ring.

"Hello."

"Jan there?"

"Yes."

"Can I talk to her?"

"JAAAAAN!" Usually the yelling would take place right into the receiver.

Once I placed the receiver on the side of the box and forgot to call Jan. About an hour later, I was walking by and heard someone yelling, "HELLO!" Apparently you could not hang up and get a new dial tone with an open line somewhere in the house. Silly me.

By the way, if you have to Google "dial tone," then you should purchase an urban dictionary and take copious notes while reading this book. I was hardly ever on the phone because I found it unrewarding. I would usually stand by the back door next to the phone and play with any one of the thousand rubber bands that could be found on the back door knob. That was rewarding.

Most houses had a bazillion, red-rubber bands on the back doorknob. In our house we had rubber bands on every doorknob. They were collected, of course, from the newspapers, which came twice a day. When bored, I would set up all my army men at one end of the room and then shoot rubber bands at them from across the room.

Another reason I hated talking on the phone was for fear of the operator. I'm not talking about the operator that you'd call to find out information, like the number for Perring Plaza Cinema, but the operator who cut in on your call to tell you to hang up because your father was trying to call you. Oh, my god, that was the scariest thing in the world.

My father absolutely hated hearing busy signals. He hated them so much he would call the operator and have her break in on the phone call and let us know that we needed to hang up for an important phone call. Jan would immediately burst into tears and beg me to answer the phone when it rang and to tell our dad, through all his deep breaths, that I was on the phone. And, for some stupid reason, I would.

It really only happened to me personally once. I was talking to Fitz about playing with our Matchbox cars when I heard a funny series of noises followed by a female voice. I thought Fitz's mother had taken the phone from him and was about to laugh when the female voice stated, "I have an emergency call from Mr. Neil Beller. He is requesting that you hang up and take his call." I immediately started shaking. I hung up on Fitz and prepared to sprint from the house.

He knew the score. You couldn't pull anything on my dad, so me telling him that I wasn't on the phone held no water. I mean this was the same guy who could climb the steps up to my room without making a single noise. Our steps were the squeakiest stairs on the planet, and he knew exactly where to step and how much weight to place on each foot in order to avoid squeaking. He was the inventor of stealth.

So, the phone is ringing and Jan is begging me to answer it. You would think that this would be the exact time for me to spin my magic and blackmail her, but I hadn't wised up yet.

The phone call was short and not sweet at all. In a monotone voice, he wanted to know what was going on, who was on the phone, where everybody was, and who had gone into his room to look for "the treasure."

After a while, I learned how to handle that call. I told him that a magazine, addressed to him, had shown up in a brown cover, and I put it on the shelf in the living room. It took me about three years before I realized that it was *Playboy*. It was an immediate conversation ender.

SEWER HOLE

I'm not exactly sure what my mother put in our dinner when I was a kid, but I'm pretty sure it was laced with time-released crack. No matter what we ate or how much we ate, approximately twelve minutes later we were doing cartwheels in the living room.

Most people settle down and rest after a meal, but not us. We would take every cushion in the living room and lay them out in a row and wait for someone to yell "Let the tumbling begin!" If you started on the couch, you could dive onto the cushions and somersault at least three times before hitting the hardwood floor. That would last for about a half hour before the cushions were folded into a nice-sized fort.

Mom was definitely the unsung hero of the house. She cooked

every meal, washed every piece of clothing, and made sure we did our homework. She used to crochet afghans, so we would throw one over top of four cushion walls, sporting the latest in kid hiding places.

It was always a fun game to sit in there and wait for a parent to come looking for you. They would be calling your name out loud and pretending not to see the pile of sofa parts in the middle of the floor. When they would get closer, I would kick one of the sides out and scare them. Oh, the hilarity! That would work with my mom, but not with my dad. He would kick in the side and scare the hell out of me!

I guess I had an attraction with hiding or crawling into things because it became progressively worse. At the top of the park right underneath Appleton Avenue was the tunnel. The first time I had ever walked through it alone was scary. It was becoming dark outside, which made it appear even darker inside. *I'm definitely going to wet my pants.* I mean by accident of course, because I was somehow always wetting my pants. I might as well address this now, as the topic will surely recur.

They say, for boys, the world is our urinal. I think I was fifteen before I learned that peeing in public was frowned upon. I always thought that running home to pee was a sign of weakness, and I swore that as soon as I left to do so, I would miss something. Therefore, I usually just peed wherever I was. I don't mean in someone's living room, but if we were in the woods, there were many options.

Most boys peed in the woods. There were streams and trees and a variable, never-ending supply of bushes to be aimed at. Sometimes, however, like right in the middle of a football game, when the urge hit me, I would try to hold it in as long as possible until I failed. This outside activity coincided with my inside action as I never wanted to get up out of my nice, warm bed to go to the bathroom. That is why I slept on plastic sheets. That is also how my brother learned to swim at a very early age. We shared a double bed, so he also wet the bed, by default.

Okay, back to the tunnel… There was always water trickling through it, so you had to serpentine back and forth, jumping over it as you walked. Halfway through was a smaller tunnel, about shoulder-high, going off in a perpendicular direction. At the other end of the smaller tunnel was the "bus stop sewer hole."

We called it that because it was right at the top of Uxbridge Road, the perfect place for the bus to stop. We would stand on top of it waiting for the bus, and I often jumped down to the street to peer down into the black sewer wondering what was down there. The long opening at street level was ten feet long and only about five inches high. On each end, a small opening would filter the rainwater into the deep pit. The water would run through the opening into the small tunnel, then into the big tunnel, eventually running all the way to the Nile River.

Once after a nice rainstorm, we all peered inside the big tunnel and saw the water shooting out of the little tunnel, landing on the other side with a loud roar. In my neighborhood after a big rain, every kid would run over and look at the stream to see how fast the water was moving. It was a requirement.

You could hear it long before you could see it, so you just followed the noise. Then, of course, you ran and dove through every puddle you could find in the yard, all the while looking for a rainbow. Puddle diving was an Olympic sport in Carney, and I was a medal winner.

My dad and Mr. Herman C Bell III taught me how to slide into a base properly, so I knew all about sliding. It took about three hours of constantly doing it before I perfected my technique. They started teaching me on Mr. Herman's hill, and when I got better, they moved me to flat ground. You had to get low to the ground and throw your weight forward so you didn't stick up like a lawn dart. Some boys would jump too high, so all the inertia would be directed downward, and soon enough they would land on their balls. Check into it. Every summer some kid somewhere would drown in a mud puddle because he jumped too high and landed on his balls.

Rainbows were the only natural occurrence that could make an errant puddle-jumper feel a little better. They were rare, and I never understood why they didn't come out during the day. It seemed that they only came out around dinnertime and always over at the Hudsons' house. My father finally sat me down one day and explained light refraction and how the sun's rays would skip off the wet ground or through a rain sprinkle and be broken up into the seven colors that make up a rainbow.

In order for it to work, the sun had to be low to the ground so the angle would enable the light to skip. It is kind of the same thing as jumping in a mud puddle and landing on your balls, right?

Roy G. Biv was the name of rainbow man. My father taught me about acronyms so I could learn all the necessary codes. Acronyms saved me in school as I used them to remember everything. Take the rainbow: red, orange, yellow, green, blue, indigo and violet, or Roy G. Biv. He also taught me how to remember the Great Lakes as HOMES: Huron, Ontario, Michigan, Erie and Superior. Even the ZIP code stands for Zone Improvement Plan, and who could forget ALOB, or Accidentally Landing On Balls?

One day we were standing by the bus stop sewer hole when someone dared me to go into the big tunnel and crawl through the small tunnel and then into the sewer hole. It was a dare, so I had to do it. There was no water trickling out of the small tunnel, so I reluctantly hoisted myself up by standing on a piece of wood and started crawling through the tunnel.

I saw some light in the distance, and I could've sworn it was nine miles away. I crawled through spider webs, wet grass chunks, and some unrecognizable things, only stopping once to look behind me on my way to the sewer. The light was getting brighter in the front and fainter in the back, so I couldn't turn around.

There was no room to turn around anyway, so I continued on. I could hear the others talking and their voices were getting louder. Finally, a small puddle sat at the threshold of the basement of the sewer. I crawled through it and stood up under the manhole cover. I had done it! I had crawled at least as far as that guy in the *Shawshank Redemption*, and now I could look up through the manhole cover at the feet of everybody standing in the street. "I'm here!" I shouted.

"What took so long?" were the harsh words directed back at me.

I didn't care; it was a major achievement for me because I knew that none of my friends would have done it, and secretly they now respected me. I was very proud of myself.

My pride didn't last long, however, and was quickly replaced with sheer panic. It had started to drizzle while I was making my way through, and some of the bigger kids started talking about a massive thunderstorm making its way towards Carney.

My first thought was that as I was still underground, I wouldn't get wet, but then it hit me. All the rainwater would be headed in my direction. I totally panicked and immediately wet my pants. The guys were really on me now and said it was raining harder. I was convinced that at any minute I would be floating in the Nile River, so I started crying.

The guys were all telling me to go back. They were telling me to crawl through the small tunnel, but I knew I could never out crawl through the impending deluge, so I just stood there bawling. I could see it was getting darker up at street level and just assumed it was the approaching storm.

Timmy Fitzpatrick panicked as well and did what he thought was best; he ran to my house to tell my mother that I was stuck in the sewer. "Oh, good God!" was all I could hear as my mother ran towards the sewer. I was crying. She was crying. Fitz was crying. It was an ugly scene. My mother was trying to figure out how I got in there and barking all kinds of questions at me, but I couldn't hear anything clearly.

I was trying to resolve whether or not I could crawl out any of the openings, but I couldn't reach them. My mom was getting hysterical and flagged down a passing motorist. He pulled a crowbar out of his trunk and pried off the manhole cover.

The whole sewer lit up, and feeling relieved, I saw a menagerie of heads staring down at me. I was free! I reached up as high as I could, and a couple different people reached down and grabbed my hands, pulling me out of the sewer, wet pants and all.

My mother rapidly ushered me home, scolding me the whole time. I turned around briefly to take in the scene, and I swear there were a hundred spectators. And what a spectacle it was! It never did rain. It was a humiliating end to a glorious day, and to make matters worse, I tripped going into the house and fell on my balls.

OPERATION NUTS AND BOLTS

Army was a popular game for us, and sometimes there were twelve kids on each side. We never picked teams; they just formed based on our political ideologies. Are you kidding me? We had no idea what was going on in the world. Aside from the occasional air raid drills we had at Carney Elementary, where we would go out and put our hands over our heads at the foot of our lockers, there were no foreign or domestic enemies that we knew of. Well, unless you counted the Perry Hall kids. Perry Hall was the next town over and our rivals.

By the way, it is common knowledge that leaning over in a crouched position with your hands over your neck will absolutely save your life in the event that a fifty ton thermonuclear hydrogen bomb were to land on you.

I did know that the Vietnam War was happening, but not because I saw it on TV every night, I had an up and close connection. One time, while the whole class was taking a bathroom break outside of the Cafetorium, I was reminded of it.

The Cafetorium was a unique room at Carney Elementary. It was a combination of a cafeteria and an auditorium. It was where we ate lunch, but it also had a stage with a big blue curtain. We had a janitor named Mr. Sweepman. I swear it! His name was Mr. Sweepman, and he always pushed around a giant broom with sawdust in front of it to clean the floors. He had a bazillion keys hanging off of him and always wore gray. I think he lived in a room beneath the Cafetorium.

Right across the hall stood the bathrooms. We always went as a class and in groups of five. Somehow we all aligned our pee to be programmed for release at the same time. While in there with my group of five, I stepped on a small bolt with my hard shoes. Remember... in the *Way Back Machine* you are not allowed to wear tennis shoes, or jeans for that matter, to public school. For gym class you bring out your Jack Purcells, but during the day you always wear hard shoes.

I wondered what I had stepped on when Harry Dillon stepped on something else. He found a nut, and I had a bolt. We noticed that there was another set on the floor and realized that they had both come out of the dividing wall between the toilets. A dividing wall was a piece of metal that was about ten inches from the floor and extended six feet in the air. In order to see over it, you had to stand on the toilet. Don't ask me how I knew that.

We both knelt down to put the hardware back in. I put the bolt through the hole, and he was turning the nut on the other end when, suddenly, the teacher was upon us. I was completely shocked that a female teacher was inside the boys' room, and before I could say Gloria Steinem, she was dragging us to the vice principal's office.

Apparently someone went out and told the teacher that we were taking the bolts out, not putting them back in. It was clearly a case of not knowing righty-tighty versus lefty-loosey.

Minutes later, I was sitting in Vice Principal Darrin's office. He was obviously a man who used fear to control his students because he was scaring the hell out of me, and he wasn't even breathing in my direction. I remember him asking me why I was removing the bolts, and before I could answer, he slammed his hand down on his desk so hard that the sound made my ears pop.

He bent down towards the chair I was sitting in and pointed deep into my face and yelled, "There are young men dying every day in Vietnam, and here you are pulling nuts and bolts out of bathroom stalls!" I had to sit and think about why that was significant, but I could find no correlation in his argument. I am pretty sure Harry received the same retort because they sent us back to our classroom, and we never looked at Vietnam the same way again. To this day whenever I see a quarter inch bolt, I am instantly reminded of the Da Nang Peninsula.

When we played army, we had bases, hospitals with nurses, battle plans and even tanks if you count Tonya Chadman's wagon. In the summer we would camp out in someone's backyard, and once we even took part in a surprise night attack. This particular night attack actually introduced me to beer as we found three bottles of warm Natty Boh in a cooler in the Millers' backyard. We had our bivouacs there. When we stumbled upon the forgotten cooler, the fighting stopped for a while. As I recall, I slept pretty well that night but had a huge craving for a 7-11, microwaveable burrito. By the way, Natty Boh is short for National Bohemian, which is a beer originally brewed in Baltimore.

Missing Pine Park was a theater of war. You could transgress through the tunnel, down the stream and sneak up on the enemy with pinpoint accuracy. We used to bus soldiers in, so we had plenty of reserves. We were pretty good at shooting each other, and we all had our own distinct machine gun sounds. By rolling your tongue a certain way, you could emulate just about any automatic weapon.

I think I held the record for most times getting killed in one day with something like forty-two times. I used to like being shot when I was running up a hill so I could fall backwards and roll down the hill in slow motion.

I always played army in slow motion. I also ran the bases that way, but not on purpose. I even took a shower that way. What can I say? I used to watch a lot of Breck commercials. The best hill to die on was The Chadmans' hill, because it was covered in the kind of thatch that turned yellow, like hay, and was easy to slide down. The second best hill was in the park.

About a year after the park opened, the members of D-CUP visited and put in some toys. At the bottom end of the park, they planted monkey bars, this thing we called a pretzel and one of those spinning things that made everybody spray colorful vomit.

About forty yards deeper into the park they cemented in a huge swing set. It was the professional grade kind with the big black rubber seats. When you sat in them, they would close and smash your thighs and contort your sides together like a sausage press. It also had one baby swing that looked like a mechanical diaper.

The previous winter Tiny Reece, Buddy, Tony Miller and I went on a pilgrimage looking for a better sleigh-riding hill. We checked every hill we saw and then ventured to the bottom of the park. This part hadn't been developed yet.

We found this hill, which had grass sticking up a foot out of the snow, and I suggested we try it. Buddy bent down and made a grass-laden snowball and claimed that he would eat it if I could get enough speed to pass his position on my sleigh.

I promptly climbed to the top and rode my sleigh down the hill, all the way to the stream and came back just in time to see him finish the snowball. From that point on, whenever anybody went sleigh-riding, it was down that hill.

I laughed my ass off on that hill many times. Once I saw a kid go down the hill sitting up on his Flexible Flyer, heading right towards the swings. Someone yelled, "Watch out!" but it was too late. The kid raised his arms to protect his face and his elbows caught the inside of one of those belt swings. The momentum thrust him forward, and he shot off the sled, being supported by his elbows while his sled flew into the stream. He went back and forth at least five times by his elbows until his ass dragged him to a stop. What a vision!

Another time, Chuckie Shepard, who weighed about twenty pounds, jumped on our big orange saucer and flew down the hill like a Japanese bullet train. When he hit the stream, a big splash went up, and we all applauded. Moments later, he turned purple, and since he lived all the way up on Summit Avenue, I took him to my house and put him inside our dryer.

The only way to get into the park was to walk down the steps at the top of Appleton or to slide down a hill and jump the stream along Uxbridge Road. This became a nuisance and semi-dangerous, especially for the little kids.

I was a stream jumper from the get-go. My father even jumped the stream on occasion just to play catch. We used to play catch all the time. Sometimes it would last for an hour, but that was totally under my control. When I was ready to stop, I had to complete a predetermined ritual called the "big three." I needed to catch one ground ball, one pop fly and one fastball. If I missed one, we had to start over again.

It was a well-known fact that my father could throw a ball 2.3 miles into the air. Airplanes needed to change their flight patterns, and I had to run forty to fifty yards looking straight up in order to catch one of his pop ups. The grounders were pretty easy, but that fastball was a game changer.

On more than one occasion I had caught one in my gut and fell to the ground, gasping for air. In any kid's pain tolerance chart, having the wind knocked out of you is second only to being kicked in the dangly parts by a wayward mule. In this case, second place was good enough, and I went down like a sack of potatoes.

My father would just calmly walk over and pick me up by my belt and tell me to breathe. *Oh, is that all I'm supposed to do, breathe? Right now I'm trying to determine if my lungs are actually attached. He might have to snake the bicycle pump down my throat and jumpstart those puppies. I wouldn't mind if he would do calisthenics on my breastplate to get some air in there.* Eventually, some oxygen had snuck back inside, and I slowly came back to life. Catch was over for the time being, so I headed home to check on my will. On the way back over the stream, my father slipped and went in. *Splash!*

I could hear his wet shoes squeaking as we walked home. It was now obvious to even my dad that we required another entrance to Missing Pine Park. We were pretty sure that the members of D-CUP would show up and add some crazy spiked and deadly alternative entrance and we wanted none of that.

MISSING PINE PARK

Taking matters into his own hands, literally, Mr. Chadman built a bridge to traverse Jenny Run. We all called it Missing Pine Stream, but the official map name was Jennifer Run. It was built of wood and held together with nuts and bolts, and it was majestic. To us it looked like the structure from the *Bridge over River Kwai*, although this one was not slated for pyrotechnic demolition like the one in the movie.

It was super sturdy and had railings and everything. He dug it in to the side of each bank, right across the street from his house. He lived in the fifth house on Uxbridge, so it was basically right in the middle of the street and enabled us easy access to the park. You could even ride your bikes over it. It dumped you out right in front of the toys, so if you ever wanted to puke, you didn't have very far. You could simply cross the stream and spin around until you would barf in a timely fashion. Mr. Chadman was now a neighborhood hero. *I wonder if he had learned how to build bridges in Vietnam.*

DORCAS

I once saw Mel Brooks and Carl Reiner doing a comedy routine on TV called the "2000 Year Old Man." Carl was playing a reporter and asked the two thousand year-old-man what the greatest invention he had ever seen was. The possibilities were endless, and I was immediately thinking he would say telephones or airplanes or nuclear weapons, but the answer he gave was Saran Wrap. "It clings and you can see through it." He did have a good point.

I have always been intrigued by what people find value in. I'm not talking about hoarders and their sixty-four cases of spent Spam containers. I'm talking about what triggers their best memories. Psychologists say that scent is a powerful memory trigger; for me it has always been movies.

Whenever I watched a movie for the first time, the surrounding memories were permanently etched in my mind. When I see the same movie again, the **Way Back Machine** takes me right back to my first time seeing it.

To this very day whenever I watch Clint Eastwood and Shirley MacLaine in *Two Mules for Sister Sara,* I have the desire to eat Vienna sausages. Doesn't everybody? My dad pulled out a couple cans of those and some Saltines the first time we viewed it, and that trend stuck. It is a great movie by the way, with or without Vienna sausages.

Clint Eastwood might be more responsible for my bad eating habits than any other person. *I wonder if he knows that. The Good, the Bad and the Ugly* is one of my all-time favorite movies. For three years in a row, it came on TV the week of my birthday, so I always associate chocolate cake with that movie and have been known to sneak away from my birthday get-togethers to find a television.

That movie is one hundred and sixty-one minutes of awesomeness and has become my reference to wasted time. For example, if I am ever stuck at a bad recital or in a traffic jam that lasts over two hours, my thought process is that I wasted enough time that I could've watched the first two thirds of *The Good, the Bad and the Ugly*... And then eaten cake.

Through Clint, I became a big fan of director Sergio Leone and musical genius Ennio Morricone. Ennio is responsible for those drama filled trumpet sagas and tense music box concertos. *A Fist Full of Dollars* and *For a Few Dollars More* still remain classics among those movies with catchy music and horrible audio dubbing.

I'm sure that somewhere a true fan, the theme to *The Good, the Bad and the Ugly* helped escort a bride and a groom out of a reception. *I mean, who hasn't whistled that?*

Sergio Leone is responsible for those extreme eye close ups that jump off the screen and stay with us for days. He helped bring out the cool in many scenes and enabled me to act them out on the hill in Missing Pine Park.

Contrary to popular thinking and nomenclature, I do not crave spaghetti when watching a western.

My father adored westerns. He didn't sit around wearing a Stetson, but if a cowboy was on the television, we were watching him and having a hoedown. I mean, we downed a lot of Ho Hos.

Westworld, starring Yul Brynner, Richard Benjamin and James Brolin, was a fake western, but a great movie. It dealt with a bunch of modern day people who went on vacation to an adult amusement park. Life-like robots would simulate life in an authentic western town and guests would assume characters like a sheriff, bank robbers, and townees.

At first it was difficult to decipher the guests from the robots. However, after a computer malfunction, the robots went rogue and started killing all the guests. My father pointed out that they most likely didn't have many repeat customers. He loved Yul Brynner and used to regale me with his early work in *The Ten Commandments, The King and I* and of course *The Magnificent Seven*. I was more intrigued with the anti-smoking ads he did on television that didn't air until after he died of cancer in 1985. He died the same day as Orson Welles.

My dad was a night owl. He would wait until our mom went to bed and then he would wake up Karen and me to watch TV with him. He enjoyed the company, but even more I think he liked to share the programs he liked with us. There were late night shows we never heard of like *Don Kirshner's Rock Concert*. My dad was a head-banging rocker! Who'd have known?

To us it was special to hang out with him because that was also when the secret junk food came out. He served chips, pretzels, lunchmeat, and canned corned beef. Food and TV go together so well, especially with my father and a movie.

When Clint introduced me to *Dirty Harry,* he also taught me how to properly apply condiments. "Nobody, I mean nobody, puts ketchup on a hot dog." When I heard Clint say that to a fellow cop eating a hot dog at a crime scene, I instantly vowed to never do that, not because I didn't like ketchup, but because I was afraid of what he'd do if he found out. "A man's got to know his limitations!"

Last week I heard someone whistle in a way that put me right smack in the middle of *West Side Story*. I could feel the heat of the city as I paused. I thought about concrete, spray paint, busy overpasses and Officer Krupke. I always thought that the guy who played Riff was the same guy who played Dano on *Hawaii Five-0*. I was wrong. I still bend over snapping my fingers while walking through parking garages. I know the security guards monitoring the cameras enjoy it.

My father also turned me into a Paul Newman fan. *Cool Hand Luke* was a staple in my house, so much so that before issuing a severe spanking, my father would say, "What we've got here is a failure to communicate." He was a world-shaker. (See the movie and you will understand all of this. If you haven't...shame on you!) When *Cool Hand Luke* comes on now, I have to watch it while sitting on a pillow, just a little subliminal ass protection.

Butch Cassidy and the Sundance Kid was another great Paul Newman movie and turned me on to George Roy Hill, the director. He also directed *The Sting, The World According to Garp* and *Slap Shot*, three of my all-time favorite movies.

Butch Cassidy set the precedent for his directorial style and he even mixed in a top forty hit, one of the first directors to do so. Burt Bacharach wrote "Raindrops Keep Falling on My Head," which had absolutely nothing to do with the movie. However, it was a popular song and even Brenda Bowman sang it on the stage at Carney Elementary in a school play.

That movie also reminds me of the television show *The Addams Family.* The tall dude who played Lurch in that show, plays a member of Butch's gang. The actor's name was Ted Cassidy and during a knife fight, he gets kicked in the balls by Paul Newman. Classic. You guessed it... I like to eat nuts while watching that scene. You see the pattern here?

There is not one man on the planet that can channel surf past *The Dirty Dozen*. It is an extreme impossibility, and it is not in our DNA. The same goes for *The Great Escape* and *The Magnificent Seven*, unless for the latter it isn't actually the movie, but the Elmer Bernstein's epic theme song being used in a beef commercial. When I hear Sam Elliott say, "Beef, it's what's for dinner," I am seeing Yul Brynner and Steve McQueen shooting it out with Eli Wallach in an out-of-the-way Mexican town.

As cool as Clint was, my favorite cowboy was Terence Hill. He starred in *My Name is Nobody*, *They Call Me Trinity* and *Trinity Is Still My Name*. I saw the first Trinity movie with Timmy Fitzpatrick at the Senator Theater, and we pretended to be him for weeks afterwards. He easily eats two pounds of baked beans in every movie. He wasn't just cool, he was ultra cool! Even Quentin Tarantino borrowed music from Terrance Hill's movies to use in his award-winning epic *Django Unchained*.

Not too long ago I drove past a barn under construction. In an instant, I was in *Seven Brides for Seven Brothers*. I often think about that movie when I see a bearded man wearing a brightly colored buttoned down shirt or when I'm snowed in with fourteen strangers.

If you haven't seen the movie, it is about these seven red-haired brothers who are rugged mountain men that can sing and dance like

Gene Kelly. The older one goes to town and comes back with a bride. She finds out the hard way that he has six unattached brothers. Not to be outdone, they go to town and kidnap six women. Hilarity ensues, and they all fall in love. Sounds like a fine Disney movie, doesn't it? My favorite character was a woman named Dorcas.

Who the hell names their daughter Dorcas? Actually, Dorcas was played by Julie Newmar, who later played Cat Woman in the much-acclaimed TV series *Batman*, so I gave her a get out of jail free card.

One afternoon after watching *Seven Brides*, I went outside and skipped right into Buddy Miller. Immediately my candor changed when he questioned my jovial mood. He wondered what I had just watched on TV; I had to lie and tell him *Patton*, another great movie. I am pretty certain there was no singing or dancing in it. Buddy was none the wiser.

My adolescence was filled with wonderful movie memories. My puberty years were filled with fear. Oh, sure, my face was breaking out, my voice was cracking and my hormones were in business for themselves, but that wasn't the source.

It was Hollywood. They decided to cheer up my uncertainty with *The Towering Inferno, Earthquake, The Poseidon Adventure, Airport* and *Jaws*. I couldn't swim, go on a boat, fly in a plane, enter a building or walk the earth. *What the hell?* At least I could still take my pretty mouth and go hiking in the woods. Nope, spoke too soon, *Deliverance*.

I also realized that Ned Beatty and Neil Beller possessed the same initials. My parents went to see that movie on a date. The next morning my dad told me about the awesome dueling banjo scene, with joy in his eyes. Then he made pork chops for breakfast.

ORGANIZED NATURE

I remember it like it was yesterday. It was 1970, and I was standing in the slightly wooded area below the playground at Carney Elementary. Standing next to a nearby picnic table with a sour look on her face was Deanna Shock, and sitting on top of the picnic table holding their knees were Diane Sadowski and Therese Cromwell. I loved these girls ever since they wrote me a chalk love letter in the first grade. They could do no wrong in my eyes. I still think of Therese and her pretty smile every time I pass that area of Carney Elementary School.

I always liked to show off in front of them, or anybody for that matter, but there was no need because nature was showing off that day. Something strange had crawled right out of the ground, and I was poking at it with a stick. Moments later another one showed up, and before you knew it, they were everywhere, and I mean everywhere. The girls screamed as Miss Erickson came over and excitedly exclaimed, "They're here!"

They were cicadas and for a few weeks they took over my world. I was sure they were from the Jurassic Period or perhaps outer space, but I was wrong. They were just drunk insects that would crawl from the ground every seventeen years, gross everybody out, fly into a wall or windshield, then die. The sound they created was amazing which made the trees sound as if they were haunted, right in the middle of the day.

I studied them as much as I could because I had figured out they wouldn't return until I was twenty-six, and that was close to ninety years away! Most of the boys were catching them and throwing them into some girl's hair to make them lose their mind. Mark Slater had a different way to gross them out and just started eating them. He was always a standout when it came to raising the bar.

I became friends with Mark when I made him cry in the very first week of elementary school. We were all in the gym, and there were several people leaning against the wall, including Mark. I saw Buddy Ferguson kick out someone's feet, and they slid down the wall in a slow, funny manner, which made me laugh out loud.

I had to get in on this, so I kicked out Mark's feet. Unfortunately, he slid down very fast and banged the back of his head on the cinderblock wall and started to cry. I had not anticipated that happening, and when someone went and got Mr. Kuzemchak, I knew I was a goner. This was the very first time I was in trouble at school and this incident became the front-runner for many more years of principal visits. Needless to say, we were on a first name basis.

Prior to living on Alda Drive, which was about half a mile from my front door, Mark's family rented an apartment on top of Len Dees. Len Dees was the neighborhood store at the corner of Joppa Road and Oak

Summit. Besides the snowball stand, it was the only place to walk to get a special treat. It was a community store, a deli, and a candy shop, and if you were in a bind, Mr. Len or Mr. Dee would deliver stuff right to your house in a brown paneled van. They knew every kid in the neighborhood and called you by name when you entered their store. You could even go in there with a note from your parents asking them to sell you cigarettes. What an establishment!

The entrance to Mark's apartment was in the back and immediately led you up a flight of stairs to their home. Right over the entrance hung a stuffed fish that his dad had caught. I remember looking at it and thinking they have a dead fish hanging on their wall and wondering if it smelled on hot days.

I was allowed to walk all the way to Mark's house and hang out with him when I wanted. This was a big step for me because I could go on my own without parent supervision. It seemed that Mark lived about five miles away, but it was really about a half a mile.

One day after a snack of his mom's famous mock apple pie, we were taking turns reading *See Dick Run*. I came across a word I thought I could pronounce and threw it out there. It was a two-syllable word, and to me it rhymed with scratch. The word was stomach, but I read it as sto-match. Mark fell out of the chair, laughing at me.

He told me the proper pronunciation, but I totally disagreed with him because there was not a "k" in the word. He got his mother who corroborated with him and then laughed even harder at me. I left in a huff and walked home, thinking that I should have kicked his feet out harder.

Years later, Mark, who had become a well-qualified wordsmith, saved my bacon at the neighborhood bar called The Barn. The Barn was at the corner of Joppa and Harford roads and is where most of us paid rent. When two knuckleheads had an issue with my presence, Mark intervened. He held up his hands in a weird manner and said, "Hey, I know haiku!" The two looked at him for a few seconds and then thinking he was going to do some wipe on wipe off action they turned away. I've always wondered if they *had* challenged him, would he have actually launched into a haiku and recited a seventeen-syllable poem to them.

Mark was usually in my group when we went on field trips. He always had great lunches. The Smithsonian Institute was a class favorite. We took for granted that we lived so close to Washington, DC, or, as the locals say, "Warshintin."

To see the Hope Diamond, the original Star-Spangled Banner and the giant wooly mammoth was an awesome experience. There were so many cool things to see and learn about, but my favorite thing was the pendulum. I loved to watch it swing back and forth and knock over the little pegs. I wanted to ride it.

I sat in utter amazement and watched it for an hour. I could have thought about the earth's rotation, which kept it going, or the changing of seasons that was slowly happening outside, or the fact that this two hundred forty pound brass ball hanging fifty-four feet in the air was actually stationary. By the way, the ball wasn't actually moving; the earth was moving beneath it. Unfortunately, my thought process went a little deeper, and I wondered who was responsible for setting the little pegs back up once they were knocked over. Now *this* was organized nature. I knew it had to be a qualified scientist or an ingenious mathematician. When Connie Evan's mom finally moved our group along, out of the corner of my eye, I saw the janitor set them back up. It was still a great field trip, minus the singing of "One Thousand Bottles of Beer on the Wall." I hated that song.

When we were in the fifth grade, we, as a class, went on another field trip. We didn't go to a museum nor did we visit the zoo. We went to the original EPCOT. EPCOT is an acronym which stands for the Ecological Prototype City Of Tomorrow. No, we didn't visit Florida; we went to beautiful Columbia, Maryland.

Columbia was the first planned community in the state of Maryland and was built and designed by real estate developer James Rouse, who later built Harborplace.

Harborplace consisted of two waterfront pavilions full of shops and restaurants. It was opened in 1980 as the center of the Inner Harbor revitalization project. Prior to that, a small beach and lots of industry ran the area. I actually took a sail boating class one Saturday morning on that beach and on Saturday afternoon I sunk my boat. I was told to never return.

I was never banned from Columbia, but there's still time. The whole fifth grade class gathered in front of the Columbian man-made lake, called Kittamaqundi, and learned about how this community was designed to eliminate racial, religious, and class segregation. As we gazed up at the big metal People Tree, we hoped our future would experience that kind of world.

Years later, whenever I retell the story to friends who live in Columbia that I visited there on a field trip, they all laugh. In 2010, Columbia and Ellicott City were ranked number two in the top one hundred best places to live in the United States, according to *Money Magazine*.

However, in the ***Way Back Machine***, they have nothing on Carney. We don't have anything silly like a metal tree. We have a six-thousand-pound elevated moving truck on Harford Road, right off of the beltway, exit 31.

We drove by it for years and years. My father told me that some guy accidentally drove it up there. I never even questioned him but instead was amazed at the driver's skill.

There was a Republic Van Lines moving company there, and to advertise, they hoisted up one of their trucks and mounted it on two poles. Nothing says welcome to Carney like an elevated moving van!

COOL LIGHTS

My dad loved to usher in a thunderstorm. We would sit on the front porch and watch for brilliant lightning flashes and then count the seconds it would take until the boom of the thunder would hit. He loved the power of nature and never feared the fact that it had deadly consequences.

He didn't walk around carrying curtain rods or hold onto car antennas, but you could tell he was daring the Big Guy. It was always exciting as the storm got closer and the counting became less and less until you heard the rain approach. I enjoyed the thunderstorm bond we shared.

Recently, I was looking into the distance at a thunderstorm wreaking havoc somewhere close by, and when I said out loud, "Somebody is getting nailed over there," I immediately heard my father's voice. He said that once when I was a kid as we watched a storm go by, and I guess it resonated with me.

When the storm would be on top of us, we would listen as the raindrops first entered the neighborhood. They would literally come right down the street. You would hear them hitting the Randalls' awning, and then a few moments later they'd be dropping on the Hudsons' cars and then, finally, they would fall at our house.

We never came in until we started getting wet. Our house was in a low-lying area and our sump pump would start running when it heard the weather report on TV. It would run non-stop during the storm and sometimes for three weeks after the rain stopped. Most of our neighbors would grow grass, but we grew rice. Get the picture? Our yard was wet.

In 1972, a crazy female blew into Carney. She ruined everything everywhere she went and totally wreaked havoc on our home. Her name was Agnes, Hurricane Agnes. In mid-June of that year, it started raining, and it rained for three straight days. Ever since I was four years old, I would run through the sprinklers and scream with joy as the cascading water sprinkled down on me lightly. Running through this torrent, though, was like getting a seventy-five mile an hour enema.

Prior to her visit, when a heavy rain would start, we would sit on the couch and look out the living room picture window. The front yard had some low lying areas that filled with water, creating puddles that quickly turned portions of the front yard into islands.

I remember when we had a big winter snowstorm that melted into puddles and then froze. I can still picture Karen wearing her white ice skates, doing her best Peggy Fleming right in the front yard.

A couple of times we were allowed to run outside and sneak a peek at Missing Pine Park's stream. That baby was thundering along, and all the tall grass on the bank was facing the same way, having been swept up with the extreme flow of water. It was too dangerous to stay there, so we retreated to our homes. Our picture window rattled, due to the frequency of rain, and sometimes you couldn't even see out.

The trees were all blowing sideways and debris was falling to the ground, along with all the things we had lost over the years. Frisbees, kites, balloons and even a plastic whiffle ball bat that I had completely forgotten about fell to the ground. Then, in an instant, everything went dark.

My dad had been in the basement for hours already watching the sump pump chug along at an accelerated rate and praying that the power would hold out. Not! I heard him cuss as soon as the house went dark. "Son of a bitch!"

At the time I didn't know the severity of what was happening, but soon found out. My dad came up from the basement and instructed everyone to round up flashlights. We had approximately seventy-three flashlights in the house. There was one in every drawer in the kitchen and randomly strewn about the house in various places, but when one needed to be had, they had all disappeared, every single one.

The one that was finally found had two D-cell batteries inside that had started a random, chemical experiment, months earlier, and had to be destroyed. "Jumping Jesus Christ!" That was the colorful metaphor that my dad yelled when he found out we would be operating in the dark. "Holy guacamole!" was what I yelled when he instructed me to strip down to my underwear and find a bucket.

The sump pump was located on one side of the basement and the laundry tub was on the other side. A path was cleared between the two, and for several hours we would lean over, fill up buckets of water from the sump pump and walk them over to the laundry tub to dump them. At first we were winning the race but fatigue quickly took over. Our basement had a cellar way that had a drain that also emptied into the sump pump, and I think there was also a direct feed from Niagara.

The water started coming out of the sump pump, faster than we could empty the buckets, and we were running headlong into each other. With a stroke of genius, my dad remembered that he had these things called Cool Lights. Nowadays, they are pretty common and called Glow Sticks, but in 1972 they were still a novelty. Basically, nobody had ever seen one. Their brand name was Cool Lights, and they were a gift to my dad from a salesman at work.

I was amazed that you could bend this tube, hear a snapping sound inside it, and watch your whole hand glow lime green as a result. They were going to be selling them at his store. He brought them home thinking we would eventually use them in the backyard to lure in lightning bugs so we could spread their glowing gel on our faces, but those plans had now changed. We had about five of them hanging in the basement, and the whole room looked something like a nuclear event. I loved them.

The water started flowing out of the sump pump with greater enthusiasm, and soon there was about two inches of water covering the basement floor. My mother was crying, my dad was bailing and I, in my underwear, was marveling at how cool the basement ceiling looked as it shimmered in the cool green reflection of the water. It was quite beautiful actually; however, my parents were not enjoying the moment quite like I was.

At one point during the deluge, someone had banged on the front door, but Karen and David didn't answer it because of the "stranger danger" rule. I remember my father being particularly upset by this because even a complete stranger could carry a bucket from the sump pump to the laundry tub in the cool green basement. The water was coming in faster and faster and soon boxes and toys started floating around. My mother noticed that the row of houses behind us had power. She could see lights through the torrents but didn't know how they could help. I don't know who came up with the idea, but, before I knew it, a plan was launched: change my wet underwear and then run an extension cord up to the neighbor's house behind us.

The Gunthers lived behind us, and all their kids were grown up and out of the house. Mr. Gunther was nice enough but was a loner. The only time I remember any interaction between us was several years earlier when his daughter's boyfriend was cutting the grass. He was definitely a product of the sixties, and had Jesus hair that flowed wildly in the wind as he pushed the mower. The Randalls had moved out and a policeman had moved in. He was having a cookout with some other policemen in attendance; they were drinking heavily when one of them adorned a dry mop on his head and went over and tapped the hippie on his shoulder. He didn't take too kindly to the joke and a screaming match ensued. That was the only time I heard Mr. Gunther speak.

So, now I began snaking a series of extension cords up to his house to see if he would plug it in for us. My dad went outside as well and took the filter right out of the pool, hoses and all. By the time I got back, he had the pool filter sitting in the basement with one of the hoses shooting water right out the basement window. It wasn't green anymore, but it was still awesome! It ran for two days.

When Agnes finally packed up and moved on, it was the perfect time to go exploring. The first place I checked out was the stream. Kids were gathering on top of the tunnel and looking down at the river that had developed. The water that was flying out of the tunnel was like nothing I had ever seen; it was like a dam had burst. It dug a giant hole as it shot out, and our cute, little, quiet stream was currently a weapon. It destroyed everything in its path, including the wooden bridge that Mr. Chadman had built. It was still a bridge, but it was now located two miles away.

We had to throw away a whole mess of stuff from the basement, and my mother still talks about how all the baby books got wet. On a positive note, I did find my whiffle ball bat.

SHOW-AND-TELL

My brother David was born on the day after Christmas, 1968, when I was seven. I remember the first time I laid eyes upon him; my mom was standing next to the Christmas tree, holding him. He was small and wrinkly and looked perfect in my mother's arms. Karen and I had been shipped off to our grandparents' in Pasadena on Christmas night and we stayed there for two days until the hospital released him to our asylum. To hear our grandfather tell the story, we had stayed with them for two months.

We gave Grandpa a run for his money and tested his patience. Because grandpa decided to quit smoking, cold turkey, as homage to our new brother, his threshold for nonsense was nil. He was the most easygoing man I had ever known. He taught me to how drive a car. I have very fond memories of sitting on his lap with my hand on the wheel while he drove around the neighborhood. However, on this particular occasion, nicotine aliens took over his calm demeanor and turned him into a crazy old man.

Apparently, he didn't take into consideration that Karen would order three different things for breakfast, only to change her mind after he finished making each one.

We're not talking bowls of cereal here; we are talking eggs Benedict, Belgian waffles and a spinach omelet with fresh truffles. He also didn't take into consideration that I would destroy the spring in the gas cap of his 1967 baby blue Ford Mustang and break all the points on his graphing pencils. Silly Grandpa.

David was the fourth child in our family and evened out the boy:girl count to two apiece. Before he popped out, I was flanked by females, had to share the bathroom, and was made to help Jan wash and dry the dishes every night. After he popped out, I was flanked by females, had to share the bathroom, and was made to help Jan wash and dry the dishes every night, and I had to share my room. *What?*

My room was upstairs on the right, which, coincidentally, was where all the heat in the house resided. Our home was a colonial, so the ceiling was pitched on both sides of my room. To make upstairs more appealing for me, my dad placed NFL team helmet emblems along the pitch. Walking from one end of my room to the other was like walking through an NFL gauntlet. He also hung up a poster of Brooks and Frank Robinson. No, they weren't brothers.

Along the wall on the right, a chest of drawers was counter sunk into the wall. It was pretty cool because there was no dresser in view, just drawer fronts so I had more room for my Hot Wheels track.

I had a routine, enjoyed my own space and sometimes didn't mind getting punished to my room, but now all that had changed. My single bed was positioned up against the window, so I had the privilege of remaining awake all night by the Hudsons' central air-conditioner. They were the first ones in the neighborhood to get central air. Before that happened I could lie in bed at night, listen to crickets and sweat. Afterwards I could lie in bed at night, listen to a loud-ass compressor kick on and sweat.

I used to hate the upstairs room because of the laundry hanging out of the window. Let me explain. I noticed this kind of décor a lot in other homes back in the day. If you were to jump into the **Way Back Machine**, you find things called clotheslines. These ingenious inventions are placed in backyards and are easy to use.

Follow along: Wash your clothes. Carry them outside. Hang them on the clothesline. Brilliant. Nature itself dries them with a nice, cool breeze. As an added bonus, you have the opportunity to see all of your neighbors' underwear. Okay, depending on your neighbor, not really a bonus.

The sheets always smelled clean and fresh, and that is why I felt bad after wetting the bed every night. To my chagrin, my mother would occasionally skip the clothesline portion of the program and hang them right out the window. To me it was like unfurling a flag of failure for all the neighborhood kids to see. Years later, Michael Landon made a movie called *The Loneliest Runner* which addressed the same issue. So, go and rent that and you'll understand.

When you walked through the doorway, immediately on the right sat David's crib. It looked out of place among my sports paraphernalia, so my parents moved all of it to the basement. I opted to move David, but they weren't having any of that. I now became responsible for someone else.

My father told me that sharing a room with my brother was a privilege. He shared a room with all three of his brothers, and they were pretty close, so I saw it as an opportunity. He explained that little brothers were special and since he was the oldest in his family and had three in that category, I should heed his advice. I figured I could secretly make him become a fan of rock music and baseball and eventually teach him to swim. I felt excited because I finally had a brother.

I learned to un-crib him and bring him downstairs and put him in for his nap. It wasn't too bad because David was pretty user-friendly. He didn't cry much, seemed to like me, and looked pretty cool when he was sleeping.

When he was a little older, he had this awesome way of rocking himself to sleep. He would get on his hands and knees, lean forward and rock backwards over and over letting his big-diapered butt strike the mattress. He would do this until he got tired and then he would just crash. Later on, as he continued this unconventional self-rocking, he learned this action could literally move his crib around the bedroom.

One morning I woke up facing the window. I rolled over and there was David, inches away from my face. This tiny prisoner hunched down, looking through the bars of his cell, waiting for me to wake up. He had rocked his crib the whole way across the room until it was pinned against my bed. I was trapped. Unbelievable!

Additionally, he liked to have imaginary conversations with the wall. I remember him walking back and forth in the crib looking up in the air and saying some gobbledygook and then walking to the other side and saying some more gibberish. Since he was the last to use the crib, the mattress sagged in the middle, so as he walked back and forth, he was also tasked with toddling uphill and downhill.

When he wanted to get out, he would hold his arms out and smile at you. He didn't learn to talk because he didn't have to. We all knew his code.

"Ehh."

"Oh, you want to get out?"

"Ehh."

"Oh, you need a cookie?"

"Ehh."

"Oh, you want us to start you a 401K?"

When I was in the fifth grade at Carney Elementary, my favorite teacher of all-time, Mrs. Forster, taught us. To find out more about her students' favorite things, she implemented a show-and-tell program where each kid brought in something they thought was cool to share with the class. When it was my turn, I brought in my baby brother. I had kept him a secret until it was my turn to address the class.

My mom had him all dressed up, and when I went out into the hallway to get him, he gave me a big smile and pointed at me. That was his sign of affection. I opened and shut my locker, for effect, and then walked in, holding his hand, to the sounds of "Wow!" He had long, blonde, curly hair, and was wearing a pair of denim overalls. The class was in awe. They just stared at him, and he stared right back. I remember a classmate inquiring, "What does he do?" and another asking, "You kept him in your locker?" Mrs. Forster told me it was the best show-and-tell ever.

SNOWMAGEDDON

I was twenty-two years old when I first saw Orson Welles's classic movie *Citizen Kane,* and if I had seen it eighteen years earlier, I certainly would have secured a lawyer and sued Orson Welles for theft. I, too, idolized my Flexible Flyer but never went as far as naming it Rosebud.

After all, little Ritchie Petrie of Dick Van Dyke fame already had Rosebud for a middle name, so I never would use that. I was original in my monikers, so it was simply known as "my sled."

Excellently honed and perfectly suited for my lumpy body, my sled would come when I whistled for it, like a trained horse. Even the old rope that threaded through the sled handles and allowed me to pull it back up a conquered hill was the perfect length.

You know how clumps of frozen snow would get stuck to your mittens and you would suck on them until you got wool in your mouth? Well, I would suck the frozen chunks of snow right off of the sled's rope, just like a candy necklace.

Uxbridge Road was very secluded, and when we would get a substantial snowfall, which was more than three inches, it would be days before the snowplow would find us. In 1966, we had the first blizzard that I can recall. It was a dry snow and so windy that when it had ended we had snowdrifts up to the second floor of the house.

The back of my house resembled the hotel in *The Shining* when the little kid went out the bathroom window and slid down the snow to go hide in the maze. The snow had piled up in a drift all the way across the back of the house.

My dad used his best groundhog skills and made a series of tunnels that winded throughout the drift. I spent hours crawling in and out until I got to the other side. It was awesome! I think the snow finally melted in May.

On New Year's Eve in 1971, it started snowing, the snowstorm lasting two whole days. I remember how cool it was ringing in the new year that way. My parents let me stay up to watch Dick Clark rock in the new year for the first time.

I was totally confused at the dropping of a big ball. *I mean, who thought of that? Why a ball? Why not a giant fat baby or something exciting?* Anyway, I sat there on the floor next to my dad's chair and watched all those knuckleheads in Times Square jumping up and down, cheering while wearing all kinds of silly things.

My dad asked me what my New Year's resolution would be. "What's a resolution?" I responded. He told me that on New Year's Eve people think of things they want to change about themselves or they make new goals and announce them to others. "Do you mean like eating more donuts?" I inquired in earnest.

"Yeah, something like that; they're usually positive things to make your life better."

"Do you mean like quitting smoking?" My father stared at me for a second before turning his head and answered, "Yes, just like that."

My father smoked Lucky Strike cigarettes. Cartons of them had their own space on a shelf in the kitchen. I'd seen him wake up and before his feet would even touch the floor he'd reach for a cigarette. He would run off of the softball field and light one up on the bench. Cigarettes were more than a part of his life; they *were* his life.

As a matter of fact, it seemed that all the adults smoked. All his friends smoked and all our neighbors smoked. They were always borrowing or bumming or exchanging cigarettes, and lighters were abounding. There were ashtrays on every table in the house. I used to suck the dead soldiers right into the vacuum.

My father's initials had been engraved on his lighter. The can of lighter fluid lived on the kitchen shelf; I watched him use it many times. He could open his lighter, fire it up, light a cigarette and close it, all with one hand. He taught me how to do that too, but I knew I would never start smoking and I had wished he would stop.

We had learned about the dangers of smoking in school and how it caused cancer. The pictures were terrible. I secretly made a New Year's resolution that I would try to get my father to stop smoking.

It was raining in New York, but snowing like a pig in Carney. The Millers had their floodlights on; I loved how the illuminated snow appeared almost angelic as it floated down. I opened up the back door to get a closer look. The snowflakes kissed the ground as they landed. Their kisses resembled whispers and seemed alive.

We were still watching Dick at 12:30 when we heard a bang at the front door. *Who the hell could that be?* I had never stayed up that late before, and I couldn't even believe that someone would be out in a blizzard, much less have the nerve to knock on our door at that hour.

My dad jumped up from his chair and opened the door, and there, on the front porch, standing in a foot and a half of snow, waited Buddy Miller holding a football. He wanted me to come out and play. I couldn't believe it and excitedly asked my dad for permission. The look he gave me certainly meant no, so I waved goodbye to Buddy and goodnight to my dad. I retreated to my room to watch their game out my window.

More lights were on and lit the backyard, so it looked like Memorial Stadium. Tony made his way outside and slowly walked into their backyard. It was still snowing and it was already knee deep. I watched as they tried to scrimmage; they lost the ball after the first tackle. Running was impossible, so Buddy just jumped on his younger brother for a while and then they trudged back inside.

A couple of years later and after a nice wet snow, Karen and I spent all day making an igloo. It was not difficult because our blood contained Eskimo DNA. Instead of carving blocks of ice and stacking them neatly, we just piled all the snow we could find into a big mound, patted it down, and hollowed it out.

It was really cool inside our igloo. We carved little shelves to hold candles and laid a blanket on the floor. There was practically no sound inside; it made a warm and comfy fort. Those Eskimos were really smart. The only difference was that we used candles and they burned whale blubber.

Oh, and we didn't have seal meat hanging from the ceiling, only bologna sandwiches. To this day, I am not sure exactly what set the next step into motion, but we decided we needed to sleep in it. I was even more shocked when our parents agreed. Maybe the Eskimo DNA had stopped with them because we had frozen our little asses off. Karen was a real trooper and lasted until 3AM. We used sleeping bags, blankets and even an EZ Bake oven to generate heat, but we still froze. The next day, when the sun peered out of the clouds, our igloo melted in record time.

I loved playing in the snow and wouldn't come in until I was a lovely shade of purple. I used to make little snowmen and place them on the fence posts of Mr. Herman C Bell III's Beverly Hillbilly fence. Mr. Herman had fenced in his yard with railroad ties and two by fours connected together with two rows of twine. *House Beautiful* wasn't interested and neither were the Clampets.

I would pretend I was a pitcher and try to knock all the snowmen off from a reasonable distance. Some days, I would pitch a complete double header with snowballs. That took some real work because nobody was throwing them back, so each pitch had to be made individually.

Sledding down Appleton was spectacular. We would climb to the top of the Beachs' hill. Karen Beach lived at the corner of Appleton and Oakdale and her front yard was an enormous hill. *I mean, how do they cut that grass with a push mower?* I used to think that they must bring goats out at night.

We would come down her hill, make a quick right-hand turn and fly down Appleton. If you were going fast enough, another extreme left would take you down a hill into the park. The best run of the day would take you right past the flagpole. You were really "the man" if you could pass the manger and considered a sledding god if you reached the monkey bars. The only thing left was that ten-minute walk back up the big hill.

Being part of a sled train was fun and only slightly more dangerous than transporting nitroglycerin. You never wanted to be the caboose because chances were good that you would be catapulted into a hedge or kiss the bumper of a nearby station wagon. In the *Way Back Machine* bumpers are made out of actual metal, and if your mouth is open when you smash into one, a really cool *thunk* noise is emitted.

To make a train, you would lie down on your sled and put your feet into the two square holes of the sled behind you. When ten or more cars joined, you would start heading down the hill. After picking up speed, the engineer would start snaking left and right while hastily heading down the street. When the momentum was sufficient, he would make a very sharp turn. That's when the real fun would happen.

This action would cause the end of the train to immediately wreck or make it swing around and whack the middle of the train, sending kids spinning out of control in various directions. It was pure street fun.

When the plows showed up, we had to migrate to the hill in the park, which caused things to calm down a bit due to the existence of the stream and the swing set at the bottom of the hill. When you started to throw in swing set poles and running water, sleigh riding became an Olympic sport. During this time sleds were slowly being replaced by saucers, toboggans and on one occasion the hood of a '63 Plymouth Fury. I'm not kidding either. Three guys standing on the upside down hood of a car, picture it!

One night after dinner Karen and I became neighborhood heroes at the hill. The snack bar had recently closed, for good, at the store where our dad worked so he brought home all the supplies for the popcorn machine. We had canisters of kernels, oil and this crazy stuff in milk cartons called Flavacol. Flavacol was basically butter and salt flavoring in a powder form that could be sprinkled on the popcorn.

MISSING PINE PARK

The coolest part of the booty included a giant green hefty bag filled with popped popcorn. He emptied the whole machine into a giant garbage bag, and we took it to the park. That night about thirty kids sat at the top of the hill and ate popcorn until a powdery butter-flavored substance oozed out of their earmuffs.

THE HOLIDAY BREAKDOWN

Our house was a great place to be on any holiday. My parents always made them special, and I really think this is one area where my dad cornered the market. There were four tiers of holidays and their breakdown was fairly easy to comprehend.

Tier one consisted of the big two, Christmas and Easter. These were only two of the three holidays which involved outside helpers. The third occasion wasn't technically a holiday, but a financial windfall. The three helpers were known as S. Claus, E. Bunny and T. Fairy, and I think they were all related, like cousins or something. One wrote a note to us, one received a note from us and the third one would just leave coinage. I referred to them as the "Initial Gang" because that is how they signed their names.

Tier two contained birthdays and anniversaries. These days were special on an individual basis and aren't really considered holidays either, but in our house they felt that way. Tier three included Halloween, New Year's Eve, St. Patrick's Day, Fourth of July and Valentine's Day, which my dad pronounced as "Valumtimes Day."

These special days usually centered on food and candy, especially for Halloween. Its booty was based on individual merit, endurance and performance and what you could secretly swipe from your siblings.

In the final tier belonged the throwaway holidays like Presidents' Day, Flag Day, Veterans' Day, Arbor Day and Columbus Day, the latter being when we celebrated the discovery of Ohio. They were all special, in their own way, but unless a gift or candy was received, they didn't prove to be *that* important in a kid's eye.

Each holiday was yearned for as soon as the previous one ended; we would start preparing for the next one immediately. I'm not saying we were limited in things to look forward to because we were not. There was always something looming on the horizon.

There are no DVRs in the *Way Back Machine*, so each moment is lived to the fullest. If you blink your eye, you can miss something, and we all know it, so nothing is taken for granted.

Truth be told, each holiday was actually a huge letdown when it was officially over. To this day, my two least favorite things to do in life are taking down the Christmas tree and covering the pool. It signifies that things have come to an end. However, when one ends, I do start thinking about beginning the other. *What is that old saying? When one door closes, a swimming pool opens or something like that...*

Christmas was truly magical at our house, and I can't think of one memory about it without smiling. A lot of our neighbors put up their tree early because of family traditions. Some even did it Thanksgiving night, so by Christmas they were tired of looking at it. Personally, I can't imagine the smell of turkey and pine at the same time. In reality, I'd probably be too busy fighting a tryptophan coma to put up and decorate a tree.

In our world, S. Claus brought our tree when he stopped by, so we kept it up until February. One year, we even hung paper hearts on its cold, shriveled and decaying carcass. My parents were up until 4AM decorating everything, which shows you how much they wanted us to experience the Christmas magic. One year the sound of them finally shutting their door and turning in woke me up. It was 4:45 in the morning. I rushed downstairs and witnessed that Santa had come. The living room was a marvel of colored wrapping paper, the smell of newness and a six-foot sparkling tree.

I went into my parents' room to inform them that he had arrived. As bad as I was that year, he still came. My exhausted parents declined my invitation to get up and told me to go back to bed.

What? Go back to bed? Are you kidding me? Santa came! I'm sure there are presents for everybody, but you have to get out of bed first. C'mon, let me help you.

I pulled my father's feet off the bed until they reached the floor. I started grabbing his muscular arm to pull him up.

"You have to see the living room; you have to see what he did." In my loud excitement I woke Jan and Karen, so there was no turning back. That year, Christmas was celebrated, in all its splendor, at five o'clock in the morning.

I remember peering out the living room window and spotting the lights on at the Flanagans' house. They, too, must have been having an early morning Christmas. The rest of the neighborhood was pitch-dark. After every gift had been opened, my parents made us all go back to bed until eight. It seemed like an eternity. By 8:30 I was wearing my brand new official Baltimore Colts uniform and knee deep in a game of Battling Tops. A few hours later, I went with my dad to give some gifts to the Bells and to show Herman C Bell III my awesome outfit.

The Bells had a silver tree that had colored lights shining on it to make it appear like a real spectacle. Their tree also had those lights that looked like little candles with moving bubbles inside of them. Mrs. Dorothy showed me her happy dance in front of it. They didn't know it at the time, but they created the dance phenomenon called disco.

They were very impressed with my uniform and asked me what position I played. I sadly informed them that I wasn't a real player, just a huge fan. They seemed disappointed. I wasn't though, because it was Christmas, the second best day of the whole entire year!

Another favorite holiday was Fourth of July. We would have a bike parade in the morning and then head to the Chadmans' house to eat meat on a spit all day. Red, white, and blue streamers were methodically run in and out of the spokes of our wheels, every inch of the bike with a patriotic flair, including baskets, handgrip streamers, balloons, fancy hats, and the whole shebang. Little kids were pulled in wagons, and everybody waved flags. This is what it felt like to be an American.

I couldn't wait to decorate my bike because it was the only time my parents would let me put baseball cards in the spokes. By using clothespins to attach baseball cards to the forks of my bike, this great Harley Davidson-chopper sound would ring out. I was told it could weaken the spokes, but who cared when it sounded like a hog. Heaven forbid you accidentally attached an Orioles baseball card; you would have been shunned from the neighborhood. It made for a good morning as we slowly drove around the neighborhood going td-td-td-td-td-td-td-td-td.

I had a pretty cool bike too. Orange with a banana seat and one hand brake, my bike was my second home during the summer. My baseball glove slid over the left handlebar, and as I pedaled, it would tap against my knee. It really made me work up an appetite. I'm sure the cavemen who invented the wheel had something in the spokes to make noise and then afterwards ate meat over fire.

The Chadmans put on a great party. I can still hear the rotisserie as it made that high-pitched, spinning and humming noise. When too much meat was sliced from one side, it would be off-center, so the roast would slowly turn upward and then fall heavily down the other side. Like anything else, there was an art to the carving, and Mr. Ed Chadman was the master at it. He had a very sharp knife and a keen eye for tenderness. Whatever he cut was crispy and flavorful and tasted awesome on rye bread with mustard, horseradish and onions.

Weather permitting was never a requirement because Mr. Ed would just move the grill into his shed. I can remember one Fourth of July when it was pouring and Mr. Ed and my dad remained in the shed, drinking and grilling all day long. The way the smoke billowed out, you would have thought they had elected a new pope, but it was just a brisket.

In 1972 I was given the job of being the runner. I was the unfortunate person who would dodge the raindrops carrying two pieces of mustard-buttered rye bread and thinly sliced onions on a paper plate and deliver it to some hungry person in the house. Mr. Ed had built the shed himself; it had two thick French doors, which opened to reveal my dad sitting on a bicycle and Mr. Ed in a blue fold out chair. There were plenty of other chairs, but I think my father had already fallen through one, so he opted for the bike. Outdoor chairs in the *Way Back Machine* consist of two varieties: aluminum frames with crisscrossed vinyl webbing and cinder blocks.

Everybody from this era has witnessed someone gently sitting down on a pretty, blue crisscrossed chair with a plate of food in their lap, followed by a tearing sound and then...*Bam!* Their ass lands on the ground. It made for hilarity long before *America's Funniest Videos*.

I made about twenty-five trips to the shed that day. I would take in beer, bring out a sandwich, take in beer and some coleslaw and bring out another sandwich. I didn't mind though because as long as I was doing that, it was still summertime.

In the afternoon we would gorge on watermelon and corn on the cob and listen to them shoot skeet at the Carney Rod and Gun Club. I grew up hearing gunshots every weekend. They were not inner-city gunshots that would cause someone to duck and cover, but distant shotgun blasts with a built-in echo. It was part of the soundtrack of my youth.

On a great day, they would be parachuting at Spalmers Airport, and we could lie in the grass and watch them jump out. I remember counting as the little dots in the sky fell until their chute opened; it was entertaining to watch but used to scare Tonya Chadman because she thought dead guys wearing unopened knapsacks would be littering her yard.

Right around dusk, kids would just start milling towards Mr. Hudson's truck, near the top of the park, waiting for him to end the holiday with a bang. Every year he would drive all the neighborhood kids to see the fireworks. It was a different time, so there were no seat belts. Hell, there were no seats! We would be sitting everywhere, hanging off of apparatus, like firemen. We would go to the coolest place to see fireworks in Baltimore, Luskin's.

Luskin's was an appliance store that sat high on a hill overlooking the beltway near Cromwell Bridge Road. At nine-thirty, every Fourth of July, the sky above Luskin's would light up, as they would shoot fireworks off their roof. I don't think I actually ever went in the store, but if you played word association with anybody who grew up in Carney, Parkville or Loch Raven and said "fireworks," they would respond "Luskin's" with a glint of joy in their voice.

We would park so close that we would lie on our backs looking straight up as the spent sparks rained down on us. I always enjoyed Mr. Hudson's truck rides and I don't even think he knew half the kids he took. He was one of the coolest dads in the neighborhood because he would flip you the bird, even if you were walking with your parents.

July fifth was full of leftover fun, because we would scour neighbors' backyards looking for the firecrackers that didn't go off. We would gather them up, wrap them in napkins and light them. *Boom!* Never failed. I remember one year Jimmy Flanagan had a whole box of Ohio Blue Tip matches, and we did that for twelve hours. We were on a mission. I'm ninety-five percent sure he found those matches somewhere in the neighborhood.

If we had a lot of free time, we would unroll those red caps that were meant for our cap pistols and hit each individual one with a hammer. If we really wanted to get our ears ringing, we would take entire rolls of caps and hit them with the fat end of a baseball bat on a brick. *BLAM!* The ringing in our ears was sensational and lasted for hours. I am totally sure that our forefathers did the same thing, *sans* the baseball bat, so we were celebrating properly.

Halloween was our annual sugarfest. Whoever invented the act of dressing in jaguar pajamas and wearing a plastic mask that had a slit in it to cut your tongue just to have total strangers hand you SweeTarts and Mary Janes was a veritable genius. Halloween preparation was fun and easy. As a family, we would drive to Valley View Farms in Cockeysville where it cost ten dollars for all the pumpkins one person could carry to the register. My dad once carried twelve. Total strangers applauded him, making him feel like a hero; his fame only cost him ten bucks!

The plan was to pick out all of the desired pumpkins first. After they were selected, we would place the biggest ones in our father's outstretched arms and begin quickly piling the others on top. Every year I would notice some pitiful-looking dad standing around, impatiently, with his arms sagging from the weighty pumpkins and all hunched over in excruciating pain, while his kids were still sorting through hundreds, searching for the perfect pumpkin. Rookies.

Once home, I drew several sets of eyes, some noses and mouths on a sheet of paper and cut them out. I would mix and match them until I found the proper face, and then tape them to my pumpkin. With the proper serrated steak knife, I would whack out a couple of triangles and a mouth. Easy peasy.

It was customary to carve our pumpkins on the same night that *It's the Great Pumpkin, Charlie Brown* would air. We had waited all year to see that show and would laugh heartily at Snoopy flying his Sopwith Camel, like it was the first time we had experienced it.

One year, my mother, who was an excellent seamstress, made all of our costumes. She used to sew all the time and made curtains, dresses, jumpers and slip covers for the furniture. I would accompany her to Woolworth's to select the patterns. Her Singer sewing machine was white and blue and lived in her bedroom.

As impressed as I was with her sewing skills, I didn't really want her to make my Halloween costume. I enjoyed creating and wearing something crazy. One year I wore a bathrobe, a tool belt, one army boot and a gardening glove and carried a golf club. On my back was a sign that said "To be released Tuesday," and I went as a mental patient.

I knew she would opt more for a cute costume rather than a spooky one. She assured me, though, that she'd make me a scary one, so I agreed.

She called us kids together and excitedly showed us her creations. She had made matching ghost costumes for Karen, David, and me, and we were forced to trick-or-treat together. Sewn down the front of each of our costumes was the word BOO! *Oooh, scary.* I felt like a cast member of the Peanuts gang. I'm happy to report, however, that I never received a rock.

We lived in the perfect trick-or-treating neighborhood. We would warm up by walking Uxbridge Road; all it took was one trip around the block and we were returning home with a candy-laden brown grocery bag. Keep in mind, this was before crazy people ruined the holiday, so happy parents also handed out homemade cupcakes, popcorn balls and candied apples.

You knew you were halfway around the block when you saw what we dubbed as The Great Pumpkin. He was tucked away in Mr. Tisdale's hedge, and he would talk to you when you walked by. Mr. Tisdale was hiding somewhere in the house where he could see all the costumed kids; he had a microphone and a speaker behind this great, big carved pumpkin. He did it annually, and everybody really looked forward to a visit with the talking pumpkin.

I remember one time he asked Fitz, who was dressed as a pirate, if he had any candy barrrrrrrs. I thought it was funny, but Fitz didn't get it and tried to stab the Great Pumpkin with his aluminum foil sword.

I swear there were a thousand kids walking around our block, not to mention on Alda Drive, Oakdale, and Oak Summit roads. The little guys would make the trip before dinner when it was still light outside so everyone could see them and make a big deal about how cute they looked. While they made their rounds, we were busy applying make-up and making last minute adjustments to our costumes.

It started getting dark around five-thirty, so we would leave early and be done by eight. Parents never walked with you, no one used flashlights, and I never remember a time when it rained. Once I even crossed busy Joppa Road and walked all the way over to David Thomas's house, on the other side of Carney, dressed as an old woman. I tried that recently and was arrested.

About halfway through the night, we would come home and get a fresh bag and head back out. Some ambitious ghouls would even change their costumes and hit all the great houses twice! At the end of the night, it was customary to dump our booty on the floor and sort it. Piles of lollipops, Smarties, Sugar Babies, Sugar Daddy suckers and Pixy Stix were everywhere. And let's not forget the Black Cows, Razzles and bags of candy corn.

For most kids, a certain sugar coma would come shortly thereafter. Karen and David loved lollipops, so I would always trade them. Trading up was a common practice, so I went for the Goetze's Caramel Creams. I wasn't sure what was in their center, but I absolutely loved it. Years later, I found out they were manufactured only a couple miles away from Carney, in Downtown Baltimore.

Candy bars were expensive, because the only size was gargantuan, so no house ever gave those away. If you found one in your bag it was from a next-door neighbor or godmother. My mom would go through everything first and throw out any unwrapped stuff as she checked for razor blades. She never found one, so I figured out it was simply an excuse to apprehend some of our little goodies.

The neighbors were great and enjoyed getting into the Halloween spirit too. Mr. Collins, who lived across the street from the Millers on Summit Avenue, would design his whole yard with displays and decorations. He ran a wire from high up in a tree to his front door. When you knocked on the door, a ghost came shooting down from the tree and made you wet your pants. The next year, as you looked over your shoulder expecting the same ghost, he'd jump out of a barrel on the porch and made you wet your pants. There was a lot of pant wetting on Halloween.

The night before Halloween was called "Moving Night," and we would soap windows and move stuff around. Mrs. Silk on Alda Drive used to let us autograph her door with soap so little mischief-filled children wouldn't soap her car. The idea wasn't to break anything or cause damage, but to switch all the trashcans and picnic tables and swing sets around so the next day everybody had to go and find their stuff and move it all back to their own yard. Good times.

My dad had his own plan on Halloween. While we were eating

dinner, he would fire up the hibachi on the back porch. When we headed out to partake in the miracle of candy receiving, he would carry the glowing coals down to the Chadmans' and set it up on the open tailgate of Mr. Ed's bright yellow station wagon. Together they would eat hot dogs and drink beer and protect the neighborhood. As word of this adventure spread, other men showed up and they, too, drank beer and protected the neighborhood. They became known as the "Vigilantes." As far as I know, the Vigilantes still get together every Halloween night on Uxbridge Road. My dad was the innovator and the Vigilantes are a piece of his proud legacy.

Earlier I mentioned Black Cows; these were delicious, chocolate-flavored caramel suckers on sticks. My dad liked to have them in the house, but not because he liked to consume candy. As a matter of fact, I don't ever remember him eating a piece of candy, but he did start salivating though whenever my mother baked.

He saved Black Cows for teeth extraction. I don't mean as a form of punishment, but to assist T. Fairy. Loose teeth at the Beller compound were very hard to remove. By sinking your wiggly teeth into a Black Cow, they would come out easily. The first time it happened to me came as a complete surprise. I thought Dad gave me the sucker as a treat. It didn't dawn on me that my mother had instructed him to, "Get that damned tooth out of his mouth!"

I had been complaining about it all day and had cried her a river; she grew physically and mentally done. My dad arrived home, gave me a Black Cow and, magically, the tears stopped flowing. After I had softened it up a bit, he told me to bite into it, and so I did. When I pulled the sucker out of my mouth, my molar was attached to it. Honestly, I was amazed because I had forgotten I even had a loose tooth. The only problem was that I couldn't get the tooth out of the candy, so I put the whole tooth-extracting tool under my pillow. *I hope the T. Fairy wears gloves.*

If you were paying attention, you would notice that I haven't yet mentioned Thanksgiving; that's because we didn't consider Thanksgiving a holiday. We considered it an event. It is, by far, my favorite day of the year. Whenever you can get thirty people together, have them all bring a hot dish of yumminess, hang out watching football and absorb sixty-eight hundred calories all in one day, there's no other term for it but event.

My maternal grandparents ran Thanksgiving like they invented it. I loved showing up and finding my own place to hang out while everyone arrived. It seemed that this was the day to try new things, and I looked forward to that. On the upstairs bar there was a bowl of mixed nuts still in their shells. In 1972, I had never seen, much less operated, a nutcracker, and it was real work. By nutcracker I am not referring to the toy soldier variety, but the metal one invented during the Bronze Age.

They had a special bowl with all the cracking implements, some of which resembled dentist tools and that curvy thing on the Russian flag. Displayed were long, pointy, pronged, metal things, forked things, medieval hardware and, of course, a hand-held nutcracker. The nuts came in different shapes and sizes, and the only one I could name was a walnut. I ate the others, regardless, but to this day don't know what they were called. Over the years, I have had many nightmares about strange plants taking root in my abdomen.

During one sweet day, my grandfather handed me a red cardboard canister, about a foot long, and told me to open it. The sound of air rushing in was only topped by the salty smell from the air that rushed out. Inside I found a slightly bumpy oblong-shaped wafer, which I was told was a new breed of potato chip. *Potato chip?* And underneath it were many clones.

I took out a stack and laid them on a napkin. One at a time, I picked them up and observed their similarities. I was amazed at this invention. I grabbed the canister and read the ingredients for the first time in my life. I wanted to know how such a thing was made. I clearly remember reading new words like dextrose and mono-triglycerides. Scientists had invented Pringles, and I was in love with them. Boy was I thankful. Life would be different from that day on as I rejoiced at the laboratory-fabricated, artery-clogging snacks.

My grandmother would prepare things I would have never tried on a normal day, but I tried them all on Thanksgiving. Rutabagas, turnips, four-bean salad, yams, even a dish featuring pearl onions were sampled. For hours leading up to the big meal, we would snack on dips and chips and cheese and crackers, all the while playing a card game my Uncle Richard invented called "Crap on Your Neighbor." The name says it all and basically reiterates the idea that shit rolls downhill. The dealer would deal everybody a card. The player next to the dealer had the option to pass his card to the next player if he or she thought the card was low enough. This would continue all the way back to the dealer, who could take a new card if needed. If someone had an ace, you couldn't change with them and you were stuck with what you had. There were names for all the cards, like Kingski, Queenski and Tener. My uncle was very quick to call you a loser, followed by his annoying, degrading cackle.

When the feast was ready, we filled our plates and ate like Vikings. My grandmother owned a long piece of furniture in her dining room, and it would be covered with pies and brownies and cookies and Cool Whip. Maximum density couldn't even describe the wonderful bloated feeling experienced by all. Before long, every room in the house was filled with people, naps and flatulence.

The forty-minute drive home only prolonged the wait to devour a late night turkey sandwich (on white bread with mayo), the perfect ending to the perfect day. I am thankful for Thanksgiving.

E. BUNNY AND VALUMTIMES

For Easter each kid in our house had four matching baskets ranging in size, and, if you are counting along at home, that makes sixteen straw baskets. Each basket had its own purpose with the smallest one housing the giant chocolate egg and the largest one nesting a small hard-boiled egg with a name on it.

The egg hunt was massive, and it felt like it lasted for hours and crossed the tri-state area. Left by E. Bunny himself, there appeared a handwritten note which included the official egg count, the quantity of eggs left in each room and a proudly worded list of each child's recent accomplishments. Edification was always a part of E. Bunny's note.

On the day before Easter, my mom would call us in from outside, and we would dye eggs. Everybody in the family, including our pet cats Morris and Catherine, had one with their name written on it; the rest were decorated with a menagerie of designs, colors and thumbprints. I frequently tried to create one that contained seven different colors. One of our favorite things about dying eggs was when the event was over. We would all gather around to witness the pouring of the dye into the sink. The colors always looked cool as they circled down the drain and resembled the death of a rainbow.

There were at least thirty-five eggs hidden around the house, which was exciting because we had only dyed eighteen. That meant that the magical and mysterious E. Bunny had dyed the rest. As much as we thought our eggs rocked, E. Bunny always showed us up.

In the middle of the hunt when someone would find the first egg E. Bunny had made, everyone stopped to *ooooh* and *aaaah*. They were swirled and shiny and remarkable and the most beautiful things we'd ever seen. Every egg was prettier than the last, and I never had the heart to crack one open and eat it. One year in late September, while getting dressed to go to church, I felt something in my sports coat pocket. Sure enough, it was one of E. Bunny's eggs from the Easter before. That find said something about his choice hiding places, but it also said something about the frequency in which I attended church.

We were allowed to take the baskets to our rooms. Many a night I awoke from a deep sleep to find myself digging into one, searching for a special treat. Jellybeans always worked their way to the bottom, so when I finally dug one out and popped it into my mouth, it was usually accompanied by plastic grass. I just chewed it up with the candy and went back to bed.

When done correctly, the candy would never overlap, meaning that just as the Halloween candy was running out the Christmas candy would arrive and then the same with Valentine's Day and on to Easter. As I grew older, I appreciated all the work that went into each holiday and found out the hard way that the hoopla was only meant for the young ones.

One Valentine's Day in 1978, I came home from high school to find a heart shaped box filled with candy on everybody's pillow except mine. On my pillow was a rolled up brown grocery bag. I opened it up and discovered three oranges with a note which read "Be someone else's Valumtime this year. The neighbors are starting to talk." *Nice.* There was also a record album titled *Music for Longhairs,* and yes, that was a hint.

Losing a tooth was also a special time in our home and created an anticipated visit from T. Fairy. It was well documented that T. Fairy would take our teeth to make piano keys. For that exchange you would find under your pillow a nice shiny dime and, if you were really lucky, a quarter.

I recently recalled, through an expensive court-ordered, hypnotic therapy session, where T. Fairy had forgotten to pay me a visit. It's amazing how much little things, like not finding a quarter under your pillow when you were five, will affect the way you treat strangers on the subway when you're fifty. Go get some change, people, and make the world a better place.

Obviously, E. Bunny and T. Fairy were the same person as S. Claus. That person was my dad. He loved to surprise us and rarely missed an opportunity to practice the extraordinaire. My parents made life on Uxbridge Road as special as they could, and we knew no different.

One Christmas we came home to a giant, and I mean a giant, box sitting in the corner of the dining room. It was about four feet wide and high and resembled a huge square block wrapped in red Christmas paper. It had other things protruding from it, which were also wrapped. There were a couple of different sized square boxes sticking out in places and a tube pointing straight up in the air. It kind of looked like a massive version of a Neverending Gobstopper. It was addressed to our mother with instructions not to open it before Christmas.

My mother was in shock and stared at it all night in hopes of learning its contents. She walked around it with her hands across her mouth in shock at the gargantuan gift.

I, too, stared at that thing for weeks, trying to figure out what was inside. A pony would need to be fed, so I quickly scratched that off my list. I eventually decided it was a robot driving a Big Wheel. I was certain.

Finally, on Christmas morning my mother started unwrapping all of the exterior boxes and poles to learn that they were only imposters. Smirking with delight, my dad helped her lift the box straight up. Inside it she found a new kitchen implement called a dishwasher. It was at that exact moment when I learned that Jan and I had been fired. It was the best job I ever lost.

WHAT?

I used to *half listen* to everything and everyone. The word concentration was only a part of my vocabulary because it was the title of a game show hosted by Hugh Downs. It was not that I was stupid I was just bored. I am still afflicted with some of the associated symptoms today and often feel as if I am missing something. That is the main reason I need to personally handle the remote control for the television. As soon as a commercial hits I am off to another channel. On many occasions you can find me watching two movies, a sit-com, a murder mystery and a cooking show featuring avocados, simultaneously. Thank you. It's a gift.

Another perceived flaw is being distracted while in a one on one conversation. We've all done it. You are sitting and talking with someone when someone else walking by catches your eye; instinctively your eyes follow them. You don't stop listening to the conversation, but it is judged that way because your significant other thinks we listen with our eyes. It is annoying, I know. When I was a youngster my concentration was pretty bad. I would hear things wrong, not question them and then recite them back later with masterful imperfections.

Standing in church wearing my newly purchased, personally polished brown leather shoes, I was reciting the Lord's Prayer with the rest of the congregation at Linden Heights United Methodist Church. I had finally memorized it and was loudly bellowing it out when I blurted "lead our snot into temptation." Heads whipped around, so my mother grabbed my arm and squeezed me in embarrassment. Later, when she explained it was "lead us not into temptation," I got a little confused. I mean, I knew what snot was. I usually wore it on the forearm of all my shirts.

I was hard on shirts, especially T-shirts. The collars were always stretched and completely out of elastic because I would pull on the collar to wipe my mouth. For five years I sported a Kool-Aid moustache, which always led to chapped lips. The chapped lips would expand around my mouth, causing even more pain. And when it was cold outside, my runny nose would add snot to the mix. *Was that not temptation?*

I truly thought that there was another meaning for snot. I assumed snot was a homonym and was something important like perseverance or grit. I mean, even President Kennedy stated, "Ask snot what it can do for your country." *I don't know...cure chapped lips maybe???*

When our Boy Scout troop merged with a larger Catholic troop, I was thrust into their religious rituals and, once again, had to use my special skills to adapt. When we would go camping it didn't matter how deep in the wilderness we had burrowed, we all got up early on Sunday and found a Catholic church. I remember sitting there in the pews, half asleep, when everybody stood up and started shaking hands. This was during the aerobic portion of the mass.

They were all saying something as they did this, and I heard what I heard, so I played along. I enjoyed the meeting and greeting part and as I shook fifteen strangers' hands I said, "Pleased to meet you... Pleased to meet you." Finally, some kind old lady held onto my hand with both of her hands, leaned in and *clearly* stated, "Peace be with you."

For a moment I felt silly for hearing it wrong but replied, "Oh, I'm sorry, and also with your shoe."

THE FAN

If someone walked in through our back door and took an immediate right, they would run smack dab into our stove. The only thing that separated it from the dining room was the small wall that housed the telephone. Mounted to the wall, hanging high over the stovetop, was a cabinet and immediately below that was the kitchen's exhaust fan.

Unlike today's versions of vents and fans, which are mounted above the stove, fans in the **Way Back Machine** are actually airplane propellers embedded in the wall. There's a tiny and sometimes greasy chain that hangs down from it. When you unlatch the chain, a vent quickly opens to the outside and the fan kicks on.

Its main purpose is to blow out scents and smells and grease and cauliflower. Yes, once I launched cauliflower towards the fan and it ended up in the backyard.

Another cool thing about the fan was yelling through it. It sounded like the same effect as taking your finger and jamming it up and down very fast into your jugular as you talked. I think this is how auto-tuning was created. Karen and I used to have conversations that way all the time. I would be inside, and she would stand on the porch, and we would holler back and forth through the fan. I imagine bobble heads talk that way naturally.

Every now and then, on a Friday night, my dad would surprise us and whip up a great treat. He would put Karen up on his shoulders, and we would all gather around the stove, as a family, to make Jiffy Pop. There were wonderful moments of anticipation when the blue flame on the front burner came to life. When we heard the sizzle of the oil heating up, we knew in a few minutes the inflated aluminum ball would be filled with delicious, hot white popcorn. We stood there in utter amazement as one pop turned into a drumroll of pops and caused the once flat piece of aluminum to quadruple in size.

Whenever Karen was up on my father's shoulders, family events would seem better, whether it'd be on a family walk or in the pool or especially in the kitchen. She was his favorite helper. For his birthday one year, she gave him a Muttley necklace, and he used to wear it all around the house. Muttley was Dick Dastardly's green dog and had a hilarious laugh that my dad could imitate perfectly. Karen would cackle like crazy when he would launch into it.

They had a tremendous track record of working together cohesively. I only remember one failed attempt. It took place on the Harbor Tunnel throughway on the way to our grandparents' house. The state of Maryland had recently removed the live toll-taker; in her place was installed an automatic coin machine which demanded exact change.

As we pulled in to feed the machine, my father summoned Karen to the front of the car, handed her the exact amount of coins, and told her to toss them into the change basket. I felt jealous that Karen was chosen to perform this cool task but stood up to witness it happen anyway. The sounds of the coins jingling around in the basket were replaced by the sounds of them bouncing on the toll road. Karen had missed the basket.

"Oh, for Christ's sake!"

My father had no idea how many coins had made it in and how many had missed, so he reached inside his pocket and started heaving money into the bin, one coin at a time. I turned around to check out the level of disappointment and frustration on the driver's face behind us. It was high. Finally, the bell rang, noting its acceptance. My father, now sweating bullets, anxiously put the bus into first gear and rolled up his window as we sped away from the automatic toll taker.

Karen's popcorn-popping record was stellar though. Unfortunately for us, our desire to pop every kernel would get the better of us, and soon smoke would be billowing out of the Cessna engine and into the backyard. I would've loved to say it was operator error, but my father would never have owned up to that. It had to be a packaging issue (eye roll).

After the smoke cleared, we would sit around and eat popcorn, one tasty kernel at a time, until we got to the layer of coal chunks that were welded to the bottom. Then, in a well-rehearsed ceremony, we would go outside and walk down the porch steps to the popcorn graveyard. In a patch of dead grass, we would bow our heads and solemnly dump the burnt popcorn.

One very eventful day, I was standing on the back porch when a burst of white smoke came out the exhaust fan and enveloped me. The smoke was followed by a scream, and I quickly recognized it as belonging to Karen. I had heard her scream about a thousand times, so I thought she was playing; it sounded pretty cool coming through the fan. When I heard my mother yell, I realized something abnormal must've happened, so I sprinted inside to investigate.

My mother was in the middle of baking her third Harvey Wallbanger cake of the day. The Harvey Wallbanger was a popular cocktail at the time, and she was making it for a friend from the Joppa Lounge.

The first cake accidentally fell into the cat litter box in the basement. It was sitting on the freezer, cooling off, when someone opened the freezer door, accidentally causing it to slide off. The litter pan broke its fall. The second one spent too much time in the oven and came out resembling a brick, so she was then on to number three. Karen was assisting with the electric mixer when, somehow, her long blonde hair got caught in the beaters.

When I arrived on the scene, the mixer was making this incredible humming noise and belching smoke. Karen was screaming and there was Harvey Wallbanger cake mix everywhere.

My mother finally turned off the mixer, then pushed in the red button which ejected the beaters, and Karen, who had been sucked into the mixing bowl, was finally able to stand upright.

We used to fight over who had licking rights to the beaters. However, after spying them all wrapped up in Karen's hair like a pair of sticky dangling earrings, I decided she should keep them.

I don't quite remember how long it took to surgically remove the beaters from her hair, but I do remember Karen sporting a bob haircut soon after.

Needless to say, Mom had to jaunt back to the ACME to buy more ingredients to construct a fourth cake.

REINCARNATION

When David was three years old, we switched rooms with my parents and moved our bedroom downstairs next to my sister Karen's. It was common knowledge that all parents hid treasure in their bedrooms. It was the responsibility of all children to search for said treasure whenever they had the opportunity.

In their haste to secure the treasure more efficiently upstairs, my parents left us the only window air conditioner in the house. Honestly, I really don't think they could have moved it because it weighed about nine hundred pounds and was hand-built by Thomas Edison himself.

The front was designed with dark brown panels, and when you turned it on, the compressor took three minutes to finally get up to speed. The sound resembled a B-52 when it revved its engines. It would start with a slow wobble and get faster and faster until it reached a steady speed. It was very powerful though, so in a few minutes ice would form on the windows, and occasionally it would snow in the bedroom. Karen pointed out to me recently that she used to beg us to let her sleep on our floor. We let her crash in our doorway a few times, but we didn't succumb easily, if at all, to her pleading, so she sweated all the way through her teens.

During the move from up to down and from down to up, my mother had what she thought was a moment of interior decorating genius and totally removed everybody's bed frames. She left the mattress and box spring sitting on top of each other on the floor in the middle of the room. She meant it to be artsy, but I'm pretty sure it was because she hated dust bunnies.

Everyone in the house got in better shape because we had to do deep knee bends just to get in and out of bed. Think about it. For two young and playful boys, it seemed adventurous to crawl into a bed so low to the ground. David and I could wrestle around and hardly make any noise.

Every night before bedtime, I would lie on my back and hang off the corner of the bed, facing the door with my arms in front of me. He would run down the hall and then turn the corner into our room, and I would grab his legs in mid-gallop and throw him high into the air over me and onto the bed. He never tired of it, and we set a record for getting yelled at at bedtime every night for a whole year straight.

David hardly ever talked to us, but he made great noises. One of his favorite things to do was tickle my armpits. He would make the cutest face, curl his fingers in and out and go, "e-E-e...e-E-e." He would make me laugh every time, and I couldn't get him to stop. He thought I was enjoying it because of my laughter. When Karen joined in, I was really in trouble. We were in a fit of hysterics every night before bed.

It was around this playful age of three that I was convinced that David must've been reincarnated. We shared a double bed, which accounted for his later prowess in swimming skills (see Bedwetting); I would always go to bed hours after he was asleep.

One night, while I was lying in bed, reading, David rolled over and plainly stated, "I could have found a cure for that."

He appeared sound asleep, and I thought maybe I was too, at first, but I wasn't. I stared at him in shock, waiting to find out which disease he had cured, but he said no more. I thought he was either possessed or he was a seventy-four year-old reincarnated German scientist. What made it even more astounding was that, as I had just mentioned, David rarely ever spoke a word!

My parents thought I was making it up, of course. Imagine that... me making something up? A couple of days later he announced, "The expansion bridge won't reach."

I jumped out of bed this time and got my parents. We stood in the doorway, listened, and stared at him for several minutes, willing him to say something like "I will invent the I-Pad," but he kept silent.

Very early the next day, while he was playing with his trucks, I kept my eye on him. My thought process was that while he was pretending to be Ralph the Kenilworth driver, his *vrooms* might be replaced with something astonishing. As I watched him play, his voice deepened and he uttered something that resembled a chemistry equation.

I perked up with a pad and pencil in hand and tried to jot it all down. When he finished, I sat down and wrote it out again, trying to make sense of it, but it made no sense at all. It wasn't the periodic table and it wasn't the engineering plans for a drone. It might have been the schematic for the condenser in that big-ass air conditioner, but I wasn't certain.

He never spoke like that again, however, so there was no exorcism. The "e-E-e's" persisted, and we continued to get in trouble every night at bedtime. I was tasked with putting David to bed each night at the time. I enjoyed that job so much that my punishment for enjoying that task was that from now on David had to go to bed by himself. I blame it all on the lack of bedframes.

SATURDAY

By far, my favorite day of the week was Saturday. I would wake up early and eat half a box of Cap'n Crunch cereal while watching cartoons. I mean, how could anybody sleep through the comedic antics of Bugs Bunny and the Road Runner? I laugh just thinking about that poor coyote and how he was foiled again and again by the ACME catapult. There were great cartoons when I was growing up with great characters: Ralph and Sam punching the clock while sheepherding, the Tasmanian Devil and who could forget Marvin the Martian?

Cartoons weren't just entertaining, they were educational too. I learned about our whole judicial system and the proper use of pronouns because of *Schoolhouse Rock*. I can recall the lyrics to "I'm Just a Bill" and "Conjunction Junction" at a moment's notice. I also loved "Three is a Magic Number," and "Mother Necessity" just blew my mind. I picture that big freckled kid playing hide-and-seek while teaching how to count by fives every time I hear kids yelling "Ready or not, here I come." I even wanted to name my first-born Rufus Xavier Sarsaparilla. Google him. There should be a **Way Back Machine** channel on cable; I would watch.

I also viewed *H.R. Pufnstuf, Josie and the Pussycats, Johnny Quest, The Monkees, Fat Albert and the Cosby Kids* and *ooh, The Banana Splits Adventure Hour*! There were so many good things on TV; I was begging for someone to create the VCR. They finally did in 1971, but I couldn't afford one until 1986, and by then Fat Albert had discovered NutriSystem and was known as Seemingly Pleasant Al.

In the middle of the day they would show movies made just for kids. *The CBS Children's Film Festival with Kukla, Fran and Ollie* was a favorite of mine. I remember watching *Skinny and Fatty* and crying like a little girl whose brother had just ripped the head off of her brand new Malibu Barbie doll. For the record, I had the same reaction with the movies *The Red Balloon* and *Paddle to the Sea.* Thank God I had long sleeves because I didn't like to look for the Kleenex.

Skinny and Fatty was about these two Japanese boys who became friends, and, you guessed it, one was skinny and one wasn't. The thin boy helped the heavy one and taught him to think and act on his own and was very influential until he and his family moved away. I was a chubby kid and totally related to this movie and was moved to tears when I saw it. I have never forgotten it.

Saturday afternoons meant roller-skating at Carney Elementary. By simply placing four folding chairs in the middle of the Cafetorium, a square room was transformed into a circular skating rink. Mrs. Collins, whose husband I spoke of as owning Halloween, was a skating guru and would run the event.

She had one of those old suitcase record players and would set it up on the steps of the stage, in front of the blue curtain. We were introduced to the latest music. FM wasn't available in any radio that we owned, so other than an occasional song between baseball games in the car, I heard all the popular hits while roller-skating. I considered her my modern day Casey Kasem.

To this day, when certain songs from back then are played, I'm immediately hurtled through time via the **Way Back Machine**, trying to stand up on four little wheels. "One" by Three Dog Night immediately comes to mind as an example of this, although "They're Coming To Take Me Away, Ha-Haaa!" really stands out too. After all, that song describes most of my friends as it was written about a person needing to be dragged away to an insane asylum.

Throughout the day, Mrs. Collins would stage races and contests for the kids with the winner receiving a free pass for admission the following week. It was just a little white piece of paper with a roller skate on it, but it would hang proudly in my room all week, that's to say if I would win one; I was a horrible skater. You could find me either holding onto the wall or onto the hair of the person next to me while trying to keep myself upright, but more often than not, you could find me on the floor after falling flat on my ass.

Limbo was a huge hit with the skaters but not with me. I was too circular to fit under that pole. Dr. Goshorn of Woodhaven told me that I had an anti-limbo body. That meant fat. The little girls, like Kelly Dooley and Stephanie Grayson, used to own the limbo contest; I was more of a racer or flailer.

Once during a race, I tried to cut the corner hard because I was losing to Anthony Ritchey, and I just couldn't let that happen. The chair flipped over, and we both went crashing to the floor. The thump even turned the record player off. I just lay there, embarrassed, while Anthony crawled across the finish line.

When the chair hit the floor, it sounded pretty bad, so I played the pretend-you're-unconscious card until a big crowd gathered. Everybody was staring down at me like I was dead; it was pretty cool, and I was milking it! I'm sure every kid has played that card at least once. Feigning sleep in the car so you could be carried inside the house falls within this category. I was helped up to some applause and limped over the stage. And for the rest of the day, I got to be a guest DJ by picking out which music to play.

A great Saturday would end with my dad taking me on a trip to Berg's in Perry Hall for ice cream. I mean, there were real live cows there! Berg's was a dairy store in the middle of nowhere. The store was located at the edge of a pasture. To the right and left of the front door stood wooden fences that held back the actual cows who made the ice cream. I'm not saying that they physically stood there and added sugar to the cream, churned it, and refrigerated it; they supplied the fresh milk.

I remember standing still and peering through the fence in awe at how big the cows were. They would stand there and stare at me as I stared at them. They used to chew in slow motion too. I can still hear them ripping the grass right out of the ground. My dad used to pick me up and hold me by my waist while I stood on top of the fence. He would always greet them with "Hello, ladies," his favorite line. I loved Saturdays!

MUMMIES

We didn't have a ton of snack foods in the house. When they did show up, we considered them special treats. My mom loved to bake and made the best Red Velvet cake and Lemon Meringue pie on the planet. My dad used to talk about her piecrust in his sleep. Some guy named Charles delivered potato chips to our house in a big golden can. The golden can was engraved with Charles Chips on the side and was the size of a five-gallon Spackle bucket.

When the lid was pried off, the scene inside was a vast and lovely sea of crispy, salty goodness. The can would be retrieved from the closet occasionally and only when requested at my father's command. He was in charge of the culinary can and the disbursement of the chips. If he wasn't around, the can never came out. Nobody touched it, not even accidentally.

I recall Karen sitting on the floor next to his chair when he opened the can. An invisible timer would start, and we would snack on the chips for precisely seven minutes. You would get a disapproving look if you took more than he thought you could eat in one handful, so your grasp into the can had to be quick, like a claw machine. If you drove your hand in too deep and broke up a bunch of other chips during retrieval, you would not only get "the look," but he would also stop chewing. When he froze in place while in mid-chew, it made "the look" that much more intense.

You knew snack time was over when Dad would rub the salt from his hands over the can then close the lid. During the next commercial break, he would put the Charles Chips can back inside the closet for what seemed like a month. The sound of the closet door shutting on my salty appetite still resounds in my head today. No one dared to open the can when he wasn't home either. It lived in the coat closet, right next to the vacuum cleaner. It sat in the back corner and was covered by hanging coats. It covered a small hole in the hardwood floor that only *I* had knowledge of.

I discovered the hole one day, when playing hide-and-seek. I was hiding in the closet, and it was pitch black, except for this tiny light emitting from the floor in the corner below the Charles Chips can.

I squatted down to peer into the hole and swore I had found a secret room in our house. *What could be down there and how do I get there?* There must have been a hidden passage somewhere, so I started feeling the walls and moving hangers, hoping to trigger the opening, much like the secret switch in the bust of Shakespeare that revealed the bat pole.

Nothing worked. I used to look in that floorboard hole for hours, trying to catch a glimpse of hidden treasures. I saw shiny things and wooly things and, once, I briefly saw a blurry figure walk through my field of vision. It scared the living daylights out of me! I remember hearing a story about a mummy being seen in a tomb of riches. *Was it King Tut...or maybe something pirate-related?*

My imagination was squelched one melancholy day when I dropped a bag of marbles in the hallway and one of them rolled under the closet door. When I went in to look for it, I found it wedged right inside my secret hole. It was so flush with the floor that I couldn't get it out, ever, so it just lived, forever, under the Charles Chips can.

One day, eight years later, my mother sent me down into the basement to get the winter clothes out of the barrel, which was stationed next to the furnace. The barrel was a shiny, black fifty-gallon drum with a lid that latched on tight to create a perfect seal so no bugs or varmints could get inside it.

Twice a year we would switch out our winter clothes with our summer clothes. I'm sure they went in there neatly folded, but somehow they always came out wrinkled and disheveled. Anyhow, as a game of hide-and-seek ensued, hiding inside the barrel was ideal. Because it was so tall, you could never look inside it, so it was a perfect place in which to hide. It sat upon a wooden pallet, which made it even higher, so to get inside it you had to be a gymnast or a member of the flying Wallendas. It was the perfect type of hiding place. As soon as you were found, the person who found you immediately hid there. It was that good.

I was pulling the wrinkled clothes out of the barrel, sorting them by child and laughing at all the stretched out necks of my T-shirts when, for some unknown reason, I looked upward. As I stood positioned near the staircase that led down to our basement, I had innocently scanned the compact area underneath the steps and had encountered one of my dad's secret hiding places.

He didn't intend for it to be secret, but it turned out to be that way as the area had progressively become hidden by accumulated storage. Apparently, under the set of steps was a smaller storage area, which could only be seen when looking up.

He nailed the lids of my ancient baby food jars to the bottom of the steps and then screwed the jars on. Each jar had a hand-written label and was filled with nuts and bolts and washers and those little pins that screwed onto a bicycle pump for blowing up a football. I always thought it was cool that he did that with empty jars of strained peas and pulverized pears.

As my eyes followed them up the underside of the stairs, I started noticing other things wedged in the beams of the ceiling. There were curtain rods, fishing poles, and even a telescope box. I never knew there was so much crap jammed in the ceiling. I had never really looked up in the basement, with the exception of trying to find the pull chain light switch.

At the top of the stairs, there was a wall switch that illuminated the right side of the basement by the workbench. There were other pull chains positioned above each quarter of the basement and each one would need to be turned on and off individually. As someone walked through the basement, they would turn each one on, and when they left, they had to turn them off.

Everything worked perfectly until someone pulled the chain, turning off the light over the workbench. When that happened, the next person had to walk down the stairs in the dark. I hated that! Monsters and ghosts lie and wait for kids to come down the stairs in total darkness. Good thing I could wet my pants at will because monsters hate urine.

I stared at the ceiling, trying to figure out why the toilet plunger was wedged in the joists, and then something little captured my attention. It looked clear, but reflective and totally unrecognizable from a distance. I grabbed a nearby stool and climbed on top of it to get a closer look. I moved a small spider web, and there it was in plain view, the bottom of a marble wedged in the ceiling. I looked down from the stool and realized that my shiny wooly treasure was nothing more than a black barrel of winter clothing and that the mummy I saw was, in fact, my mommy. I'd sorely wish I had never discovered that. I mourned my destroyed imagination for a minute and then stormed upstairs in anger and ate some potato chips. A rebel was born.

THE TUBE

The infamous baby Beller high chair lived in the dining room. It was wedged in the corner, in front of the transparent shelves which divided the living room. It was a standard wide model with an off white tabletop which was stained with seven year's worth of baby food. Both Karen and David fell asleep in their oatmeal three years apart. Petrified Cheerios were embedded in the seat and there were dried spaghetti noodles permanently spot-welded to the railing.

During dinner the youngsters were often seen with their legs whipping happily up and down. Karen used to make noises when she ate; she gave birth to the phrase "nom, nom, nom, nom." It was very easy to eat Karen up. She was cute as hell, with pretty green eyes and blonde hair.

As a matter of fact, we were all towheads. My hair was white until I was in the fourth grade. I'm sure it made interesting conversation when we were out in public, because my dad had black hair and my mom was a screaming redhead.

Karen always wanted to share with us whatever she was drooling over. I have many memories of her holding an orange Popsicle out for me to taste. We have home movies of her eating a Popsicle in her high chair that seem borderline pornographic. Karen loved the Ice Cream Man, too. No matter where we were or what we were doing, when those jingly Ice Cream Man bells would ring, her world would stop. We could hear him merely entering the neighborhood and knew his routine well. He would go all the way down Uxbridge Road, without stopping, and then make two or three stops on the way up. If we didn't come out, he would stop at our house anyway, taunting us. The proper etiquette of summoning the Ice Cream Man, no matter if you were at dinner, sitting on the toilet or in confession, was to yell at the top of your lungs, "WAIT A MINUTE!" Through the roar of his engine and his loud jingling bells, the Ice Cream Man could always hear a child, especially Karen. Years later our father taught her how to whistle; she could not only stop the Ice Cream Man, but an eighty-eight-car train.

Once, outside of the Travers' house, I stood patiently in line while everyone else was waited on, and then, in a flash, the Ice Cream Man, in his impeccably clean, white suit and hat, jumped back into his truck and sped up Uxbridge Road. I could see the pictures of Astro-bombs and frozen chocolate Éclairs on the back of his truck, waving good-bye, as he drove away. I felt crushed! *Where would I score an Eskimo pie now?* When Mrs. Travers realized he had forgotten me, she took me inside her kitchen and made me a vanilla ice cream cone. *Wow, a backup plan, and I made a quarter!* She then swiftly walked me across the kitchen, took my twenty-five cents and ushered me out the door. Capitalism at its finest.

When David took over the reins of the high chair, he was so quiet that we used to forget about him. Watching a baby eat is pretty hysterical; David, however, made it into a movie of the week. He used to eat like he didn't have fingers. He would pick up a handful of food and then turn his hand outward and eat from the palm, near his wrist.

One wonderful afternoon, my dad called us on the phone and told everyone to get the camera and gather in the dining room for a surprise. I put David in the high chair, and Karen and I took our places at the table. After a few minutes of anticipation, my dad walked in with a bag in his hand and turned to David. He pulled out a honey-glazed donut the size of small tire and set it in front of him. It was the biggest donut I had ever seen. It was larger than a cake! The expression on David's face was hilarious. He looked at the giant pastry and then at my dad and then back at the donut. He could hardly pick it up, but when he finally held it, he squealed with delight.

Next, while my mom was taking pictures, my dad placed a chocolate donut in front of Karen. She said something unrecognizable; I'm pretty sure it was in another language for *"Woo-hoo!"* It was even bigger than the one David was gnawing on. I asked my dad where he had gotten them, and he told me in his usual dry way, "At the giant donut shop." Then he pulled out another honey-glazed mammoth and handed it to me. I was ecstatic and dove my mouth right into it. David was licking his donut to death, and Karen was covered in chocolate. It was a great day.

My dad liked to have fun with food, and it rubbed off on the rest of us. Whenever my parents would go out, Karen and I would stay up late, watching TV and eating unhealthy, but tasty snack food. Around midnight, Karen would make me the tastiest sandwich on the planet.

MISSING PINE PARK

She had learned from the best, my mom. I would, in turn, make her a fried egg sandwich. We always ate great food in the middle of the night.

My mom worked for the Equitable Bank in the Parkville Shopping Center. Teller Beller, as we called her, always worked late on Friday nights. Around 7:30, my dad would make the announcement, "It's time to feed your mother," so we would pile into the car and drive to the bank. While we were waiting our turn in the drive thru, we were giddy with excitement.

My dad always took the outside lane; that way, we had to use the special space aged tube instead of the drawer. We would talk to our mom through the intercom while my dad packed the tube with Mom's dinner, and then with a push of the magical button, we would fire dinner at my mom through the vacuum tube system. It was the highlight of our night. Right across the street from the bank was an Arthur Treacher's Fish & Chips; on special occasions we would fill the bank tube with deep fried goodness and send it to my mom at the speed of light. *We found out the hard way to not include her drink.*

WE TRY HARDER

It has been said that next to your parents and your coaches, the most influential people in your life are your teachers. Carney Elementary had a few class acts, and together we helped one other. I know they earned their money struggling to teach me, and I'm pretty sure most of them spent that money on wine. I was the child that helped them grow.

I already discussed Mrs. Branson and her "duct taping skills," but she was obviously instrumental in teaching me something valuable. In fact, I credit her with the three R's: Relax, Release, and Repeat. Relax with your feet on the desk. Release the paper airplane. Repeat. I remember one day she took me by the shoulders and shook me so hard that my head resembled a bobble head's. I also crapped my pants, and, you guessed it, my mother had to come and pick me up.

In the second grade I had a blonde beauty named Ms. Scarborough. She seemed very friendly and smiled a lot. I'm pretty sure she was also a witch because I can't remember another thing about her. Witches have memory erasing spells, you know, especially the hot ones.

Ms. Erickson was my third grade teacher. She had long black hair and liked to wear blue dresses. She was instrumental in teaching us to how to cover our heads properly when leaning against the lockers during air raid drills. I remember she had a boyfriend who came in one day to teach us to speak German. *Decke* meant ceiling and that was the extent of my German, next to potato salad.

In the fourth grade I had Mrs. Rask. She almost always wore plaid, had very short hair and called me Mr. Beller. Once during recess, while playing Greek dodge, Rick Temple, nicknamed Footie, face planted into the concrete and broke his tooth. Mrs. Rask rushed him to the nurse while supporting his chin in her hands. When she came back, her whole skirt was covered with his blood. She wore it the rest of the day like that. Later on, she made a fortune by creating a colorful plaid pattern for Vera Bradley called Footie's DNA.

Mrs. Lotus was also a fourth grade teacher; we went to her room for English or something like "how to talk good." She taught us a way to remember lists of words through association by using our imaginations. She wrote twenty random words on the board as kids called them out to her, and, in a matter of minutes, she could repeat them all back to us and then taught us how to do it. To this day I still remember those words. Carpet, paper, bottles, bed, fishes, chairs, etc...

I tried to learn how to play the trumpet in the fourth grade but really struggled to learn how to read music. Herb Alpert and the Tijuana Brass were my inspiration. My father was their biggest fan and played their music every weekend. I eventually had all the songs memorized from "The Lonely Bull" to "Tijuana Taxi." "Lollipops and Roses" and "Spanish Flea" were very popular songs and used on the television show *The Dating Game*. I could blow all of them on my Boy Scout bugle; it was a different story, however, when it came to the trumpet.

I gave it the old college try and had Mark Slater write all the finger notes in my book. It worked out great, and I became a pretty good trumpet player... that was if Mark was around. That lasted about a month before I was busted. He was absent one day, so Mr. Webster, our music teacher, discovered I couldn't play my way out of a wet paper bag.

Mrs. Forster was my fifth grade teacher, and I loved her. She knew how to talk to kids and so, in turn, I just wanted to please and impress her. If I excelled at something, she would give me a little round sticker that said "We Try Harder." At the time, it was the popular slogan of Avis Rent-A-Car, and she wanted to empower us. It worked too; we all tried harder in her class. Curiously, she possessed a giant tumbleweed that she kept on top of her cabinets. She told us it blew across the road during a cross-country trip, so she pulled over and swiped it.

On my birthday she let me get up and get a drink of water whenever I wanted. She made me feel special.

It was common elementary school knowledge that letting children drink water when they want to was against the law. Their schedule allowed us to only drink at pre-determined times and from specific water fountains. We liked drinking from the water fountain by the office, which was plugged into the wall; its water was nice and cold. When the class left the room and ventured to other parts of the school, such as other water fountains, the Cafetorium, gym or the music wing, we were required to walk in straight lines. We literally followed a silver line on the floor.

If you stepped off the line, mad dogs or electrocution were sure to greet you. The teacher was then required to randomly pick someone who hated me personally to physically turn on the water fountain and count to five. Apparently, the FDA had determined that five seconds was the time allotted for children to re-hydrate. Heaven forbid if your lips touched the metal spigot. Sirens would go off, and you were yanked out of line before you could say I love the National Sanitation Foundation.

Mrs. Black and Mrs. Norwood were the other fifth grade teachers. All I remember about Mrs. Black was that my sister had her, and I wasn't allowed, by threat of bodily harm, to let her know we were related. You see, my oldest sister Jan had a different last name than I did, so she never had to hear "Your fat little brother is a pain in the ass, and if I could, I would bury him alive in the garden area next to the rain gauge."

Mrs. Norwood had established the "Norwoodian Museum," which had helped to enlighten all the kids of Carney Elementary about famous people and historical events. I remember a time when John

Blank dressed like a boat captain talking about the Titanic, but I thought he was Mr. Howell from *Gilligan's Island*. She loved little smiley faces and drew them on everybody's papers. I'm one hundred percent sure she invented emojis.

Mr. Kuzemchak was the gym teacher and he rocked. One rainy day, I was chatting with him and found out that we both loved the new television show, starring David Carradine, called *Kung Fu*. After every episode, I couldn't wait to relive the highlights with Mr. K. We used to act out every little detail together.

He had a Johnny Unitas crew cut and was the gatekeeper of the "Charlie ball." The Charlie ball was this ginormous canvas ball that stood about four feet tall. Someone had painted Peanuts Gang members all over it, hence the name. He would roll this thing into the middle of the floor after lining up all the kids against the wall. When he would blow his whistle we would all charge toward the ball while he sat back and watched the carnage. Kids were bouncing all over the place. My only bad memory of Mr. K was when he made me run laps around field number two for saying the word "crotch."

Mrs. Romine was the music teacher and cast me as Captain Von Trapp for the school play. I had no idea who he even was and thought it was a bit part until the class took a field trip to Westview Cinemas to see *The Sound of Music*. I was very excited about having the lead but still made my way to the bathroom at intermission to throw up due to nerves.

My sixth grade teacher was Mrs. Coker. She lived next door to David Thomas, and for the first time in my life I saw a teacher outside of school. It felt unnatural. She was a strict teacher by reputation, but one day she inexplicably put on "In-A-Gadda-Da-Vida" by Iron Butterfly and placed black lights all over the room. I thought for sure she had eaten an entire tray of hash brownies in the teachers' lounge, too. I can't remember what we were learning, but it definitely gave me the munchies. Actually, now that I think about it, we were learning about electricity; she kept asking us, "What turns you on?"

Mrs. Prescott was a popular sixth grade teacher; all the smart kids were in her class. One day we heard her scream at the top of her lungs. It wasn't a rodent or a bug that caused her alarm; it was David Simonton who, quote, whipped it out, end quote. An urban legend was born!

Mrs. McBride was the other sixth grade teacher, and I often went to her room just to gaze at her. She was a blonde-haired, blue-eyed, go-go boot and mini-skirt wearing hottie. She was the first woman I ever saw who worked the cat eye make-up look. I didn't learn a damn thing in her class. She called me over to her desk once to have a little conference, and I asked her out to dinner. She was my Mrs. Robinson, or so I had envisioned.

In the sixth grade I became President of the Story Telling Club. Imagine that, a club where stories were told. I'm still its president. We would go into the kindergarten wing and tell animated stories to the little ones. They were so cute and watched with excitement as we read or narrated to them a story. I was hooked.

My favorite book of all-time was *Drummer Hoff.* I must have checked out that book a gazillion times. At one time, my name was written in the back of the book, on the sign out card, about fifteen times. It was a great rhyming story, and I had memorized it quicker than *Green Eggs and Ham.* It had these very interesting drawings and told the story of a drummer who was actually in charge of a sergeant, a major and even a general. I bet you that in the Carney Elementary library my name can still be seen in the back of the book. I was drawn to the idea of rhyming, and poems were fun for me, so I started writing them.

The first poem I had written was called "Summer." It was short and sweet. I sat at the picnic table in my backyard and made copies for all my relatives. My second poem paid homage to my dad, who loved National Bohemian beer. He used to whistle its theme song, which they played during the television commercial, so I wrote new lyrics for it. Sing along if you remember the tune.

"National Beer, National Beer, you'll like the taste of National Beer, the first National Beer was made of deer and the icky stuff in an elephant's ear." My father liked my poem but assured me that it didn't taste like that.

As part of the sixth grade curriculum, we had to enter a contest, sponsored by the Parkville VFW, to write an essay specifically titled "What America Means to Me." I wrote a twenty-stanza poem, and the first letter of each stanza, or paragraph, spelled out what America meant to me. It took a lot of time and thought; I was very proud of it.

On the day of the award ceremony, the whole school had to march into the Cafetorium for an assembly. I was very excited until saw my mom sitting in the back. I thought she was there because I was about to be suspended. When she received the phone call from the office, *she* also thought I was about to be suspended. She had to come to school so many times to retrieve me for getting into trouble or throwing up that she really wasn't sure why she was sitting there. Imagine both our surprises when I came in third place for my essay. When we arrived home, she gave me a We Try Harder sticker.

YANKEE DOODLE DADDY

I always felt better playing at somebody else's house compared to my own. I think that is because so much was new. I learned the rules and the dos and don'ts of all of my friends' houses and would even recite them to the residents. It was my own house where I didn't read the behavior manual.

My house of choice to play in was Timmy Fitzpatrick's. His basement was semi-finished as it had a tile floor and was loaded with great places to hide. His back sidewalk and patio were a perfect place to lie out our combined Hot Wheels track. They had a small above ground swimming pool, which is where the G.I. Joe submarine was invented. Instead of buying a submarine to play with, we created our own by setting our G.I. Joe in a black, adult-sized swim fin and watched him slowly sink to the bottom of the pool. It worked like a champ.

Fitz also had a level backyard for playing catch. I remember throwing the ball back and forth, listening to the 1971 World Series on a transistor radio that was sitting on his picnic table. In the *Way Back Machine*, all the World Series games are played during the day. Night games are still years away, so we listen, dejectedly, as Roberto Clemente and the Pittsburgh Pirates defeat our beloved Baltimore Orioles.

Clemente was a superstar baseball player. Sadly, his career was cut short when he was killed in a plane crash while on his way to help earthquake victims in Nicaragua.

I owned about five miles of bright orange Hot Wheel tracks and two powerhouses. Powerhouses were these orange battery-operated buildings that the track went right through. Inside was a set of turning soft wheels that would grab the car and shoot it out the other side. If you placed them right, you could get the cars to circle the track over and over without ever stopping. We would hook our track together, grab every matchbox car we had and make the Fitzpatrick Speedway. My favorite car was lime green and called the Splittin' Image. It was the coolest car I had ever seen.

Sometimes we would place the powerhouses at the end of a ramp and jump cars from one track to another over a distance of fifteen feet. We shot cars straight up in the air, into his swimming pool and even made up a game resembling step ball where we would catch them in our baseball gloves.

Fitz's parents hung a big-ass bell on his back porch, right next to the door. When they rang it, he was required to come running or face severe punishment. It also required a response the second you heard it. I heard that bell every day of my young life. Once, Fitz and I were at the Carney Rod and Gun Club about a half a mile away, trying to find some clay pigeons. Clay pigeons were small, round fragile disks that were catapulted into the air and used as target practice for the shotgun wielding weekend warriors. The echo of shotguns in Carney was just as common as a bluebird's song.

Finding a clay pigeon that wasn't broken was a real challenge. If they weren't blown out of the sky by shotgun pellets, they would break when they hit the ground. Originally, they were white and black, but a couple of years later they made them bright orange. Now who wouldn't want one of them turned upside on your coffee table, acting as an ashtray? I had my bike and met Timmy there to search the grounds. We had to search the woods at the end of the range, which is where they would land if someone were a bad shot. They were a rare find and very valuable to a Carney kid. When we finished, I decided to give him a ride home on the back of my bike.

I loved my bike. It was orange with hand brakes, a banana seat and a little sissy bar. Banana seats were all the rage, and you could easily have someone sitting behind you *not* holding on for dear life. The sissy bar was a metal bar that arced from one side of the back of the seat to the other. Fitz had a purple bike with a very tall sissy bar. His bike was, by far, the coolest in the neighborhood because it looked just like Evel Knievel's chopper.

Currently, his bike was out of commission. While playing a game of follow the leader on our bikes, he followed me right under the monkey bars in the park. Regrettably, he failed to make it out the other side. His sissy bar was so high that it caught on the top of the monkey bars and stopped him dead in his tracks. Fitz was thrown forward and stripped all the gears off his bike with his nether region. I wish I had seen it happen, but the sound was very memorable. His older brother David was still trying to put it all back together, so we were doubled up for a while.

We were coming down the steep hill from the gun club that dumps onto Summit when off in the distance we heard that familiar bell. Fitz was sitting behind me, holding on to the little sissy bar behind him. We were going at a pretty good clip making the turn when he screamed, "I'm coming!" Unfortunately for me, he was only four inches away from my ear and he scared the hell out of me. I lost control and couldn't make the turn and drove right through someone's tulip garden. I was trying to pedal out when the bell went off again. He screamed louder this time and I briefly lost hearing. I was still trying to navigate out of the yard, carrying this dead weight behind me while suffering from a mild case of tinnitus. When I heard him scream the third time, we went right over. I was ready to kill him for screaming in my ear not once, but three times! Needless to say, he found his own way home.

Every family had a unique way of calling you in. One family simply stood on the porch and clapped; some parents screamed their kid's name at the top of their lungs; my father was unique and just whistled. When I say whistled I don't mean "Yankee Doodle Dandy," I mean a steam-engine-cover-your-ears-and-cower whistle. I have no idea how he could make a noise that loud. He didn't use his fingers or anything. He would just stick his head out the front door and let it rip. The only thing louder was the air raid siren at Parkville Junior that went off every Monday at 1PM. He was a close second.

The loud sound resembled a Whippoorwill and could be heard for miles. I swear he changed migratory routes for some species of birds. My friends were very aware of the repercussions I would be in if I didn't come, quickly, so they established a relay system. Many times, if I were out of whistle reach, which meant Canada, friends would yell to me to tell me my dad had beckoned. It was funny because I could never see the friend, but I *would* hear them yelling for me. Everybody looked out for each other that way. If someone was punished, then they couldn't play with you, and it would cramp your style. Fitz was late that day and was grounded in his yard for three days.

One day, while hanging out with Fitz, his brother David who had just killed a deer, laid out the pelt to dry in the grass. He salted it down with a whole canister of Morton salt and even cut off a small piece of meat and ate it raw. I watched him for hours, just waiting for him to throw up, but he never did. Several people I knew, including my father, were deer hunters. Mr. Chadman had his shotguns hanging in his basement, and the hangers themselves were deer hooves. I can still picture them sticking out of his paneled wall. I never once thought of taking the guns I had access to and playing with them. I also wasn't that upset that they were on a quest to wipe out Bambi and all of his relatives, just so they left Santa's team out of their crosshairs.

Fitz's mom took us crabbing once. It was my very first time. We were on the shore, a tall land pier to be specific, and dropped long strings with chicken necks attached into the water. Crabbing is a Maryland tradition and the only time I can think of where I actually worked to secure food. If you count standing in line for hours at a sporting event waiting for a sausage and a beer while close quartered next to a bunch of sweaty intoxicated people, then I guess I've done that a thousand times. With crabbing, the sweaty intoxication comes later during their consumption.

I had eaten crabs before, many times, but they were either claws or hand-me-down piles of meat, so this was the first time I saw them alive. We caught fifty-two crabs with those chicken necks, and each one was a challenge. I thought they would clamp on and I could just yank them right up and out of the water. Much to my anger, they would fall off, so I had to pull the string slowly until right before they surfaced and then scoop them up with a long, metal crab net.

We were steadily putting them into a cooler and listening to them scattering all around. The crabs I had seen were orange, but these were bright blue. When I inquired about the change, I was told that steaming turned them orange. *Strange.* That reminded me of looking at my veins and seeing blue, but when I bled it was bright red. It was kind of the same thing in my mind. *Hope I don't get steamed.*

Some man walking along stopped and asked how we were doing.

"We caught a mess!" I shouted and opened the cooler for him to see. He made a face and moved along. Unbeknownst to me, Maryland crabs had to be five inches, point to point, in order to be legal, and apparently all of our crabs were not. Fitz's mom was steaming mad at me for spouting off. When the man was out of sight, we started the mass exodus.

They had instilled the fear of God in me as we spun out of the parking lot. The crab police were hot on our tails, and I would soon be in crab jail. The fine was a dollar a crab, and my meager math skills had that total at a million dollars. The whole way back to Carney, I was looking out the back window for whatever was chasing us. The man I showed the cooler to was an undercover agent for the Chesapeake Bay and knows we were law-breakers, so I am thinking the vehicle chasing us would be stealth in nature so that I couldn't make it out. We flew around the beltway with a cooler full of contraband, and I felt like we were on an episode of *Adam-12*.

"One Adam-12, One Adam-12, a 4-17 see the woman with illegal crabs."

"One Adam-12 Roger, we're en route."

Oh shit!

Eating the evidence as quickly as possible was the only solution, so when we got back to Timmy's house, Mrs. Fitzpatrick quickly steamed all fifty-two of the illegal crustaceans. I can remember her asking if we wanted Old Bay, and when Fitz looked at me for a response, I just shook my head in some random manner. *I mean, what was Old Bay?*

When she brought the first batch out to the picnic table, they were bright orange but were all covered in mud. *Yuck. What the hell was the matter with her? She didn't even clean them off.* Fitz went and retrieved the garden hose and, in seconds, had washed them all clean. *Let the hammering begin.*

About twenty minutes later she came out with another tray of the steaming goodness, and when she went back inside, out came the hose again. This time, she looked out the window and saw what we were doing. She came running out the backdoor and into the yard, screaming at us for washing off all the Old Bay. We thought it was mud.

Little did I know, but Old Bay Seasoning was made in Baltimore and was the perfect blend of various salts, peppers and paprika. It enhances everything edible it touches, and *now* I even put Old Bay in my cereal. Love that stuff! It is hard learning a tradition sometimes.

The same thing happened to me with soft pretzels. My Uncle Bruce was visiting for my birthday one spring. At the bottom of the back steps, he handed me a soft pretzel, complete with chunks of salt and mustard. He was holding it out in his hand via a translucent piece of wax paper, but it didn't look appealing, so I told him I didn't like them. He looked disappointed until Fitz yelled, "I love soft pretzels!" Within seconds Fitz was sitting on our cinderblock wall, eating a soft pretzel, with mustard all over his face. It was killing me, so I asked him to rip off a piece, and when he did, I fell in love with the soft, salty dough. I ran in my house to tell my uncle that I *did* in fact love soft pretzels, thinking maybe he would run right out and get me another one. He was my dad's youngest brother, so he stared at me just like my father would until I slowly sulked away. My loss.

MY T FINE

Nothing on the planet was more soothing to my mouth, especially after eating fifty-two illegal crabs, than a tasty snowball.

It wasn't until I spent some years living in California when I found out that snowball stands were a regional thing. I don't mean the kind of snowballs you launch at a passing car; I mean the wonderfully cool, icy treat consumed on a hot summer day. The best snowball stand in my world was only a short walk from our home. Up the small hill, right on Summit, across Magledt and through the short patch of woods on Joppa Road, you could find heaven in a cup. "My T Fine" was written on the big sign on the pitched roof of the small hut. An old lady, who lived in the house next door, owned it. She looked like any one of the normal assortment of old ladies; however, she was truly brilliant and had launched a snowball dynasty.

I remember paying her for a treat and watching her dump the coinage into a cigar box. She offered about twenty flavors and all of them were homemade. My favorite snowball flavor was sky blue with marshmallow on top. They tasted divine.

A wax-lined paper cup was filled with shaved ice from a mechanically powered, vertically standing machine. When its lever was pulled, a distinct sound was produced while the shaved ice shot out of the bottom. The ice would be gathered by hand and molded until it towered out of the cup like a white volcano.

The flavors were housed in glass bottles with rubber spouts to keep the bees at bay. They lined the shelf and literally resembled the rainbow in syrup form. Your flavor of choice would then be poured into the mountain of ice, turning the cold, white concoction a beautiful, bright color. For an extra eight cents, a scoop of melted marshmallow would be dropped on top. I always wanted to dunk my head in that container!

There were a couple of benches to sit on; the snowball devouring ritual began with sitting down briefly while carefully eating the top of your snowball before moving on. Many a disappointed kid could be seen sobbing over the sad sight of the top of his or her snowball melting in the street. Those poor kids apparently hadn't yet learned the proper method: sit and sip.

It was a hopeless situation and only had to be experienced once before proper snowball eating etiquette was learned. Before plastic spoons and sporks were the norm, each snowball came with a flat piece of wood, sealed in paper. Ripping the paper open with your teeth allowed your mouth to get used to the taste of wet wood before you dipped it into the ice-cold yummy-ness. You were considered a true kid if, upon leaving the snowball stand, onlookers could tell which flavor you just had by the color of the mustache you were sporting.

The snowball stand was, in fact, a community hangout. During the summertime when school was out, I would run into other friends, serendipitously, and find out what was happening around Carney. If it was hot enough on the walk back, you could pop tar bubbles with your toes. Bare feet was the popular footwear of choice for most of the summer, so at the end of the day your parents would make sure you scrubbed the hell out of your feet to remove the tar. It was worth it.

We went there a hundred times a summer during the day, but it was a really special treat if your parents escorted you in the evening. The true definition of family time consisted of excited conversations and laughter heard as the family walked to the snowball stand. My T

Fine took on a whole new ambience when it was lit up at night. I would marvel at my parents as they ate their snowballs. Because they were our parents, they were allowed by law to use their wooden spoon to sample any snowball of their choice. Reciprocation was not mentioned in the snowball bill.

There was just no way to remain adult-like when wolfing down a snowball. I guess nobody really grows up. Remind me later to check their feet for tar.

SWIPES

Every kid in Missing Pine Park participated in paybacks, whether they wanted to or not. They knew that if they didn't, some day it would be *them* on the business end of a pile on. Currently, we were in full out pink belly mode. A pink belly is achieved by gang-tackling someone. While holding down his or her extremities, the group simultaneously slaps the person's belly with their flat palms about fifteen to twenty times. And there you have it: a pink belly. We used lots of terms for endearment like that in Carney.

Another favorite was to distract someone by telling them a joke while someone else got down on all fours behind them. When the cohort was in place, the joke teller would push the guy backwards, and he would fall over the guy on the ground. Hilarious! I don't remember anybody getting hurt. Well, hurt that bad, anyway. Smear the queer was another little shenanigan. And this could take place at any time and in the middle of any other game. There were no rules regarding it, and it only stopped when everyone was exhausted.

Basically, when the opportunity presented itself, someone's name was yelled out and the event began. The target would be chased, surrounded, and then a wrestling match would commence until the person was on the ground and then every single kid would pile on. This was funny if you picture it because kids of all sizes and ages would jump on top of the pile until the kids at the bottom started screaming under the weight of the pile. Ten minutes later we were all playing the original game again, only with dirty knees and tattered clothing.

Once, on my way home from school, I jumped into a pick up football game on Alda Drive in the empty lot where the road curved. I had the pocket of my dad's shirt ripped from my body by Jimmy Hobson. I shouldn't have been wearing it anyway, so I was pretty sure my father would be giving me his version of a pink belly. Unfortunately, he liked to perform that ritual on my ass.

Jimmy was a few years older than me, and since I felt he had ripped the shirt on purpose, I yelled, "Smear the queer," and wrestled him to the ground. To my shock, no one jumped on. I guess our pile on tradition didn't make it a whole half a mile away from Missing Pine Park. No harm, no foul, until I returned home, that is.

Most boys growing up in Carney were blessed with a "whiffle." A whiffle was a haircut where they basically shaved your head, leaving only one-sixteenth of an inch of hair. If the barber formed a flat area on top of your head, you would resemble the great Johnny Unitas. He was a Baltimore Colt and Hall of Fame legend, and it was an honor to resemble him in appearance. You knew you had a proper whiffle when every bump and scar could be plainly seen from New Jersey.

Imagine fifteen Charlie Browns walking down the street at night illuminated from behind by a car's headlight. Upon seeing all the profiles, I could instantly name everyone by the shape of their bald head. Also, when I get in the *Way Back Machine*, I can name the make and model of any car based on the headlights alone.

Getting a haircut was always fun, not! There was a barbershop next to Len Dees. I only remember going to his place once as a kid. There was one time when the barber came to our house, but not to cut anyone's hair. He helped my dad carry in the big, giant stereo he bought as a surprise for my mom. It is funny because I didn't even think my dad knew him that well. I imagined that he just stopped by on the way home and asked him for help. That was the kind of neighborhood we lived in.

The stereo was huge; it was a piece of furniture actually. It looked like a long dresser of sorts but had no drawers. Its solid wood composition made it very heavy. Found on its right hand side was a top that opened to reveal the record player inside. The left hand side didn't open; but that was where you housed all the albums. My dad put it in the living room and outlined it in little tiny Christmas lights. I had never witnessed anything more beautiful.

Up until that time, all Christmas lights were screw in light bulbs and were about three inches long. These were the same tiny lights that we use now. I couldn't stop looking at them. If you stared long enough and let your eyes blur, all the colors would triple in size and blend together. It was psychedelic!

This is the same trick used for perfecting illumination on a Christmas tree. We call it "the squint test." When putting the lights on a holiday tree, sometimes there are bare spots. By standing on the other side of the room and squinting at the tree, all the lights will blur and blend together. Performing the squint test will aid you in finding out where the holes are. This Beller tradition works every time and is a famously used in many, many households.

My barber worked at a place called JP and Company at Satyr Hill Shopping Center, right next to the ACME. It was run by a gaggle of hippies. I always found it interesting that all these longhaired guys ran a barbershop. Imagine getting a manicure with someone who has horrible cuticles and dirt under her nails. They liked to play games like spraying me in the face with a squirt bottle and pretending it was acid. They would yell, "Don't open your eyes. It will burn!" After a few seconds I would hear them laughing. Crazy hippies.

Sporting my Johnny Unitas whiffle, I walked out my front door and heard Fitz yell loudly from the park, "Swipes!" *Damn, they called it.* You see if I had yelled "No swipes!" first or showed them the little letters SP on my belt, which of course meant "swipe protector," I would have been okay, but I didn't. So when I walked into the park, I just decided to get it over with and took off my baseball hat.

"Swipes" is when everybody makes a fist with their strongest hand and then using their thumb nail, runs it up and down the back of your neck to the base of your skull. After four or five times the next guy would step up and do the same. When you experienced swipes at school, kids didn't use their thumbs; they used those hard-as-shit, green ink erasers. You could always tell some poor kid who had just been swiped because of the red racing stripe up the back of his neck.

As soon as everybody was done, we played a game of baseball, and before we went in for dinner, I tackled Fitz and gave him a pink belly.

LEFT IS RIGHT, RIGHT IS WRONG

If you have ever seen Dick Van Dyke play Mr. Potts in *Chitty Chitty Bang Bang,* you would recall how much he loved his kids. My father had never invented a machine that made us sausage and eggs in the morning; however, he did invent plenty of other ways to have fun.

After dinner one night, Karen, David, and I had ventured out through the front door to play "Witch." My father followed us outside and sat on the steps to watch us while my mother cleaned up. Our job was to get on her last nerve; we were really good at it too.

My dad let us run around for a while and then he called us over to teach us a new game. His game was similar to charades, but he called it "Lemonade." I have no idea why he called it that, but it has become a Beller staple at outings.

The concept is easy. Two people act out something after announcing the initials of what they will be attempting; for example, if they would be pantomiming someone "flying a kite," they would say F.A.K. before starting. The other players would call out guesses until someone guessed correctly. Then, two new partners were determined by another creative way. A category is chosen such as "cars" or "candy" or "trees." The two actors who just performed huddle together and each would pick a type of tree. They turn around to the group and one of them announces the names of both trees like "birch and maple." The person who guessed F.A.K. correctly, picks one of the trees and then gets to act with the corresponding person. If you have some very bad acting, it actually makes the game funnier.

On one particularly hilarious evening, David had announced the letters S.O.A. We prepared ourselves for his Broadway style of acting while he started staring at the sidewalk, smashing his foot down in an awkward way. We were baffled and could not, for the life of us, figure out what he was doing. He didn't change his actions and kept on repeating the same movement over and over again. David was only about five years old, so we thought maybe he didn't quite understand the game. All of a sudden, my father busted out laughing. He had obviously figured it out but was enjoying the spectacle so much he didn't say anything. Finally, through his chuckling, he announced, "Stomping on ants!" My dad was a genius.

Once during a camping trip, my mom was doing her best impression of M.A.C. or "milking a cow." Unfortunately, it looked like she was making a cake and nobody guessed it. I don't think I've ever seen my mom make a cake using milk right from the utter of a cow, but around the campfire anything goes.

In the early seventies my father had won a sales contest at work and swept my mom off to Spain for a week. We have some great home movies of them romping about a Spanish marketplace, strolling around some ancient ruins, and of a camel that had fallen in love with my dad. He kept licking my dad's face and tried to knock off his Northside cap. They returned home with chocolate and gifts and *pesetas* for my siblings. They had brought home for me the coolest thing ever. It was a Spanish poster, which was actually an ad for an upcoming bullfight. In the middle of the poster, written in bold, it listed two bullfighters. They were Manuel Benitez, whose nickname was El Cordobes, and Neil R. Beller, Jr. My parents had it made for me in Spain.

I loved it, and it was proudly displayed on my bedroom wall for years. All my friends were extremely jealous. It was quite unique and made me feel very special until I saw a similar one hanging in another house on Uxbridge Road, that is. It belonged to Herman C Bell III. My parents got the same poster for him with his name on it. He didn't even look like a bullfighter.

Sunday nights in our home were all about the television. As the weekend faded away, I can remember getting ready for school to the sounds of *The Lawrence Welk Show*, *The Ed Sullivan Show* and *The F.B.I.* Efrem Zimbalist Jr. was the star of *The F.B.I.*, and I was always excited when the announcer said that the show was "In Living Color!" Our television was a black and white set, so I couldn't wait to see that show in color. Obviously, crime would look better with hue and saturation.

There were many variety shows in the **Way Back Machine.** The Smothers Brothers, Sonny and Cher, and even Glen Campbell have their own show. I'm sorry, but I can't even think of Glen Campbell without visualizing Johnny Carson singing "Rhinestone Cowboy." The man behind the most popular variety show is Ed Sullivan.

His show was originally called *The Toast of the Town,* and I believe it was the longest running variety show in history. My father loved doing impressions taken from that show. For a short while, he walked around the house doing his best "My name José Jiménez" impression. He would draw a face on the north end of his left fist and talk to us in a very peculiar voice. He was pretty good at it.

He was a southpaw and did everything backwards. I used to ask him if it was difficult being left-handed. "Hell, yes!" he barked. He then went on to describe all the things that right-handers could do that left-handers couldn't. He couldn't use scissors or alley-owned bowling balls because they were designed for righties. Even cars in America are designed for right-handed people, so he threatened to move to England. That difficulty takes place in the **Way Back Machine** obviously, because there are many things designed for lefties presently. I was so intrigued by his plight that I researched the discrimination of left-handers and wrote about it for my senior project; I received an A for my effort.

Once when I was in Scouts at a "camporee," a lowly boy from another troop approached me and asked me if I had a left-handed smoke shifter. Being asked to search for one of these was part of an old joke in Scouts and a rite of passage for the new scouts. It was the same for the elevator passes we sold to freshman at Parkville Senior. For the record, there were no elevators at Parkville.

The greatest thing about the scout was that a few minutes later, after he had checked with another troop, he came back with one. Some genius had turned a paper plate over and traced around his four fingers. He then turned over the plate and traced around his thumb. By placing your digits in the proper place, one could stand next to a campfire and use their left hand to shift smoke away from everybody.

My father loved to surprise my mother with music. He would cue up a new forty-five record on the stereo and move the arm over halfway so the song would repeat. She would listen to Neil Diamond and Simon & Garfunkel, endlessly, until we had cemented each note to memory. I read a book called *Snow Treasure* one Saturday afternoon and for the entire time I read, "Without You" by Harry Nilsson was playing in the background. I, forever, have merged the two things together. One day, I had informed my dad that she was playing it over and over again and was driving me crazy. He simply replied, "You're right!" Sometimes being right is just wrong.

TIN CAN WILLIE

There were times we needed to organize an event for forty kids of all ages, all genders and all intellectual capabilities. The latter was the hardest because there were some real idiots roaming around. It was also very important to look out for the little guys, and since we had so many kids around, babysitting became a group sport.

Many, many, many times, as I was flying out the door with one arm in my coat sleeve, my mother would yell, "Take your sister with you!" It wasn't a big deal, I guess. Except for my lack of responsibility or the fact that I had spent a lot of time telling dirty jokes with my friends, I was a pretty good babysitter. There was usually someone for her to play with, so she wasn't really a nuisance. The hardest thing to do, however, was to get her to come home with me. Somehow, Karen had always gone out and about with me, but I had returned home solo.

Of course, I would go back out and find her, and that would require some door knocking, but eventually she would turn up. Once I found her in line for the Good Humor Man in front of the Winstons' house, and I knew she didn't have a red cent to her name. It didn't matter to her though. She just kept moving up in the line until I discovered her and grabbed her arm to walk her away.

So, with Karen in tow, I headed for the park. I could see a gathering as we approached it. I knew jocularity was moments away when I saw the Pepsi can. Tin Can Willie! If you jump into the **Way Back Machine**, you see that aluminum has yet to be a part of our everyday life. Soda cans are made out of tin. They are hard and heavy and difficult to dent. Pop tabs are not attached and can be found scattered upon the ground near any soda machine.

We used to keep an old, blue Pepsi can near the steps of the park. It looked like litter, but was actually a priceless piece of Americana. To the kids in our neighborhood, it was the only thing needed for the ultimate game of hide-and-seek. As more and more kids wandered over, a seeker was chosen. I said chosen but meant singled out, because no one ever wanted to be the seeker.

To start the game, everyone would stand in the street by the manhole cover at the top of Missing Pine Park. The can would be thrown into the park, and everybody would run for cover, within a selected area, while the seeker retrieved the can. Once he or she picked up the can, they had to place it in the middle of the manhole cover, and the hunt began.

If the seeker spotted somebody hiding, they had to sprint to the can and bang it on the manhole cover, yelling the whole time "Tin Can Willie on Fitz behind the Sullivans' hedge!" for example. From that moment on, the honor system kicked in, and Fitz would have to come out and sit on the park steps which acted as the collection box. It was a very important rule to yell where the hider was so everyone was assured you had actually found him hiding. Every good newspaper reporter knows that as attribution. Without that detail, we'd have had anarchy.

After the last person was apprehended, the first person caught would become the new seeker and the can was thrown again. In addition, if while the seeker was looking in the opposite direction, someone who hadn't been caught yet ran out and kicked the can or threw it, everyone would be freed and the "lucky seeker" would begin at square one. The only other reason the can could be moved was if a car were coming; at which point the seeker would yell "Car!" so nobody would run out and get smashed. A brave seeker would leave the can on the manhole and hope the car didn't crush it. After the car would pass, the game would resume as normal. The most excitement was had when the seeker surprised someone hiding and they both sprinted toward the can. The mad footrace usually went to the hider who would kick the can out of the seeker's hand while the seeker was in "mid-Willie." What fun!

I've always had a good arm and learned that if I filled the Pepsi can a third of the way with pebbles from the street, I could launch it way past the flagpole. This also gave the can a distinct *maraca* sound when it was banged on the street, and who doesn't love *that* sound? We would play that game for so long that occasionally some kids went home for dinner and returned without anybody even noticing they'd left. Once, a group of kids walked through the woods and went all the way to Len Dees to get some lunch and later continued playing like they'd been there with us the whole time.

We were probably in our fifth hour of Tin Can Willie when everybody was in the box, except Bobby Flanagan and Tony Miller. It was starting to get dark, and I was getting tired; I had been sitting there for a couple of hours and had heard the same exact jokes about four times.

The one downfall of playing Tin Can Willie was the more kids that played, the longer the game endured. The great part about it though was the multitude of assorted hiding places. The tunnel was always a good starting place, but the seeker could see into the tunnel when retrieving the can, so you'd be forced to be on the move until they hit the street. Quickly climbing up a tree was also advantageous, but hard to get back down fast. Diving into the bushes or blending in with the scenery were your best choices.

Waiting for the game to end, I heard the familiar yell of "Car," and when I turned around to look, the Millers' car was driving down the small hill. I had just then remembered Tony telling me earlier on that his mom needed to take him to Thom Mcan to buy new shoes. I was thinking about what I'd say to her when she'd stopped to pick him up. I stood up to address her after the car had come to a halt, and, before I knew it, the back door had popped open and Tony Miller jumped out of the car, laughing, as he lumbered towards the can.

It had been erroneously left on the manhole cover; he scooped it up and threw it into the park. Nobody on the steps even knew what had happened until they heard the can hit the ground. What a move! It was, indeed, the best Tin Can Willie game move ever. We laughed like crazy as we all ran off to hide.

From that day forward, the use of automobiles in a game of Tin Can Willie was definitely outlawed around Missing Pine Park.

TRAIN TRACKS

I never enjoyed having someone else's hands in my mouth. It wasn't an everyday occurrence, but it did happen. The bottom of a football pile, the sharing of bubble gum, and when my parents were removing bad words are all examples of the aforementioned. Due to one of nature's wicked pranks, when most kids reach the sixth grade, their teeth go into business for themselves. Overbites, mouth breathing, teeth grinding and facial imbalance are all reasons to get braces. Coincidentally, they are also side effects of getting kicked in the nuts.

My dentist suggested to my parents that I visit an orthodontist. I certainly didn't think that was a good idea and asked for a family discussion on the matter. I saw them do it all the time on The Brady Bunch, and it seemed like a good use of democracy. I quickly learned, however, that our house resided under the dark blanket of a dictatorship.

I never had a good experience at the dentist, and an orthodontist was, in my mind, a step *up* the pain chart. I think my dentist used me as a guinea pig to obtain records for Guinness. I'm positive he holds them for the number of cotton balls shoved in a kid's mouth, the longest conversation held without spitting, and owning *the* hairiest nostrils.

I was told that I had an overbite, and it would haunt me later in life. *Umm, can you say Steven Tyler?* I saw no problem there. Once, after he filled my mouth with wet cement, under the guise of obtaining a mold of my imperfections, he disappeared. I waited patiently for about fifteen minutes and filled the void by counting the ceiling tiles. There was always one that was out of line or in backwards, and it really bothered me. When he didn't return, I sat up and started playing with "Mr. Thirsty." After I had sucked up everything in the room, I started to get mad. I walked over to the door and peered out and saw no one, so I retreated to my chair. I learned everything I could from the gingivitis chart hanging on the back of the door and even perfected my squirting ability with his mini water jet. I rifled through all the drawers in the room and after I had stuffed my pockets with Q-tips, I left to search the building.

The lobby was empty and so were two other exam rooms. I even checked the room where they boil all the medieval instruments to clean off everybody's spit. *Where in the hell was everybody?* Upon hearing some laughter, I tested the last door, which turned out to be the break room. Sitting around a small table were the dentist, his two assistants and the receptionist. They all looked up at my cemented mouth and started laughing. The dentist had forgotten about me! He thought that one of his hygienists had dug the cement out of my mouth and sent me on my way. They kept giggling as they stood to attend to me, but I was done. I yanked the mold out of my mouth, pulled off my bib, set them both on the table, and walked out the door.

I could only imagine what a trip to the orthodontist would be like. I had heard stories that nighttime outer wear resembled barbed wire, and that when they applied braces to your teeth, they used rusty tire irons, sheep shears, and super glue. Much to my disapproval, my parents took out a forty-five thousand dollar loan and made me an appointment.

My orthodontist was in the basement of a bank next to Satyr Hill Shopping Center. I dreaded going for my initial visit, but my mom insisted, so we descended the stairs and entered the dungeon. Upon entering, I quickly surveyed my surroundings, looking for an alternative exit. There was none. The décor was unimpressive at best and consisted of a combination of Ocean City spin art and plastic chairs. I sat and stared at the floor while my mom checked me in and then followed an assistant back when they finally called my name.

After a thorough examination, which included prying my mouth open with a small bear trap and having me bite down on a piece of Styrofoam, I was again left alone for several minutes.

I had just reached my wit's end when the door opened and someone walked in. My mind was made up to react in an unfriendly manner until I heard a sweet voice. I looked up to see a pretty orthodontist assistant. Her smile was inviting, and she immediately caused me to change my demeanor. I tried my very best to suck in my stomach and make my teeth feel straight. She looked inside my mouth with a small mirror on a stick. She smelled very nice, and her pink shirt made her blue eyes gleam with friendliness. Her name was Amanda. *Perhaps braces aren't going to be that bad after all.* She installed these little things called spacers and sent me on my way. I couldn't wait to go back.

Right across from the bank on Joppa Road, there was a huge wooded area that was going to be developed into a shopping center. It was to be called North Plaza Mall. *A Mall? In Carney? Seriously?*

Five days later, as I was walking across the bank parking lot, I noticed that they had already started bulldozing the wooded area to prepare for the mall. It brought back memories of the beginnings of Missing Pine Park.

I was due to get out my spacers. They had become very loose, so obviously Amanda had done great work. I really enjoyed the spin art this time as I waited to be called back. I was wearing my favorite shirt and was having a great hair day, so I felt pretty good about myself. I lay in the chair, checking out their ceiling tiles. I noticed that one was out of place but didn't even care. I heard the door open and briefly saw a pink shirt out of the corner of my eye. I said, "Hello" with a step in my voice, and then she entered my field of vision. It wasn't Amanda. It was Claire and she was mean. Apparently Amanda was just the closer. I never saw my special spacer-er again.

Over the next few weeks, they cemented and screwed enough metal in my mouth to manufacture a small robot. I wore headgear that prevented me from sleeping on my stomach and bags of very small rubber bands that were designed to snap in my mouth at inopportune times. I wasn't allowed to eat anything harder than marshmallows, and every three weeks someone would use pliers to twist tiny wires so tight on my teeth that my eyes watered and my sphincter puckered. In the *Way Back Machine* orthodonture is closely related to proctology.

Following years of scars on my inner cheeks from the jagged metal, a severe hatred of spin art, and meeting a litany of orthodontist assistants, who I was sure would grow up to be roller derby stand-outs or prison guards, I finally had my braces removed. All I wanted to do was rub my tongue back and forth on my teeth because they felt so smooth. I was in the ninth grade at Pine Grove Junior High and needed to get back for an intramural softball game. Before she returned me, as a celebratory gesture, my mom took me to North Plaza Mall and bought me a pretzel. I visited the mall several more times but vowed that I would never go near the orthodontist's office again, even if Amanda was out front selling spin art, wearing nothing but a smile.

WHAT'S BLOWING?

Growing up, our house was full of laughter. It was usually at the expense of others, but laughter nonetheless. Once, while standing in the kitchen fighting over the last of the Kool-Aid, Karen hauled off and punched me square in the nuts. I, of course, went down like a stone, which made Karen laugh. My parents were standing close by and apparently witnessed the whole thing. I remember my mom saying, "Oh, get up. She didn't hit you hard," and my dad quickly chimed in, "She didn't hit him hard. She hit him low!"

Getting hit in the nuts is the worst feeling in the world for a male. You can't explain it to a woman, nor will a guy ever understand childbirth; they are completely different arguments. Before becoming pregnant most women understand the extraction methods and the accompanying pain involved. There are no filmstrips, or videos, however, on the massive sucked-in feeling associated with a solid, testicular jolt.

There is a high-pitched sound reverberating through your inner body that turns hearing off, if only because your soul doesn't want to hear the horrible, strangulated sounds that emit from your mouth, nose and other orifices. Sweat immediately stains your face, and red dye number two turns your whole body magenta. Hair follicles detach from your skin, and every nerve ending in your body rushes to your balls to join the party. Yeah, it is pretty funny. Not!

I am pretty sure Karen stored that little tidbit of knowledge away for some future girls-weekend-to-go-clubbing-stiletto-move, and that is the only reason I am glad to have been her test case. On the bright side, it was the perfect training for me becoming a baseball catcher later in life. The equipment a catcher wears is known as "the tools of ignorance." It is a well-documented fact that most major league catchers were punched in the nuts by their little sisters.

Every Saturday night at ten, *The Carol Burnett Show* would be shown on CBS. I used to sneak out of bed, into the upstairs hallway and listen to my parents laughing. Occasionally, I would catch an entire sketch of "As the Stomach Turns" and find myself chuckling to the sounds of Harvey Korman. As a kid, I totally thought he was the voice of the Great Gazoo from the *Flintstones*, and, as it turns out, he was.

The *Saturday Night Live* of the day was called *Laugh-In,* and it came on Thursday night. Boy, what a wacky show that was. I learned and used their new catch phrases like "you bet your sweet bippy" and "here comes the judge." I didn't even know what the hell they meant.

On the way to bed one night, I was walking up the stairs and did an entire impersonation of Ernestine the operator complete with "ringy dingy's" and "Is this the party to whom I'm speaking?" My mother was rolling, and I was hooked. I liked this comedy thing.

I loved to make people laugh. When Karen laughed hard, her nostrils would move in and out real fast, and on more than one occasion milk shot out of her nose. I made my father spit out his beer once, which was truly a feat, because he was hilarious himself. My father would pepper us with dry jokes sometimes referred to as "way homers" due to the extended sink-in time of his humor. My dad and Karen and I were up late at night when a commercial came on TV, featuring Mr. Clean. He was that bald guy who only wore white and sported an earring. At the end of the spot, the whole kitchen was immaculate, and it showed a bottle of the clear liquid product sitting next to a clear bucket filled with clear water. My father got up to get another beer and said, "I had a clear bucket once... but I could never find it." I woke up laughing three hours later.

Needless to say, April Fools' Day was quite an event on Uxbridge Road. When I was little, my father would wake me up with little white lies like "It snowed last night and it's blue." Running to the window and hearing "April Fools" only had to happen once, and then *I* was on the offensive. I couldn't wait to pull practical jokes; I was never without one up my sleeve from then on.

For one of my jokes, I utilized the telephone. Its earpiece was cupped which meant that shaving cream could hide in there perfectly. When someone would put the hand piece to his or her ear to listen for the dial tone, they would literally get an earful.

Saran Wrap on the toilet bowl was a gem, especially under the seat. My all-time favorite prank was switching the salt with the sugar. We always had a sugar bowl on the table because Frosted Flakes just didn't contain enough sucrose. We also made Kool-Aid by the fifty-gallon drum and each packet required a cup of sugar, so our mother bought it by the skid. Seriously, one time we ran out of Kool-Aid, and to prevent a David meltdown, I made a gallon of sugar water and added red food coloring. I might have thrown in a cherry cough drop too. He was sold.

The great thing about the salt and sugar prank was that I used it two years in a row. The first year I sat there and watched Karen and then David spoon what they thought was sugar all over their cereal. The faces they made were epic. Karen literally looked like she had swallowed a sea urchin. David just spat out everything back into his bowl. I walked away, laughing, until I found out about dad's coffee. I didn't sit for a week ... okay, two weeks!

The next year was even better because I didn't physically do anything yet earned a payoff anyway. You see, my brother had overheard me saying that I was going to switch them, so he had planned on outsmarting me. Right in front of our father, he made a bowl of cereal and then poured salt right out of the salt shaker into his bowl, thinking it was sugar all the while. For two years in a row, he made the same face and spit everything out. The best thing though was my father's reaction. "What the hell's the matter with you?"

I also remember developing this fun little game to pass the time, and it took off like a shot. In response to whatever my mother would say, I decided I would say something that rhymed with it.

"Where are you going?" was followed by "What's blowing?" which was followed by "I said, where are you going!" I could see a long future with this little scheme, and I played it well.

"Did you finish your work?"

"Who's a jerk?"

"Go and get Karen"

"The music's not blaring."

"Did you hear what I said?"

"Who did you say was dead?" About halfway through the year, my mom started to get a nervous tick. The rest of the family saw how much fun I was having and decided to join in. Slowly, they all ended up playing along.

"Where are you going?"

"Where is what growing?"

"Did you say it was snowing?"

"God is all-knowing."

"GOING, GOING, WHERE ARE YOU GOING?"

I knew we had her when my dad joined in as well. He had laughed until his eyes had watered.

I think we pushed her over the edge, however, because one day when I came home from school, my mother had put posters all over the dining room ceiling. They were packed in there like a patchwork quilt. If you looked up, you would see James Dean, Sonny and Cher, John Wayne, a psychedelic cat, Raquel Welch and many other popular sixties things. She took flowered contact paper, cut the flowers out and put them on the kitchen cabinets; there was a yellow, blue, and green mood lamp on the stereo. We had driven Mom mod!

It wasn't long before that same flowered contact paper made it to our 1960 blue Chevrolet Impala to cover the rust spots. It was evident that mom got us all back for repeating her. I insisted she drop me off five blocks from my friends' houses, and I spent most of the ride on the back seat floor to avoid being seen. Sure, she was cool and hip and right out of *Laugh-in*, but it was completely embarrassing. She had the last laugh, indeed.

THE TABLE

Suppertime at our house was the absolute best part of the day. There was joyous laughter, life's lessons were talked about openly and the day's events were discussed among our happy family. Wait a minute... That was from an episode of *Leave it to Beaver*; dinner at our house was like a prison experiment. You sat and ate what was dished out and you weren't allowed to speak. If you didn't eat everything on your plate, you sat there until it petrified, and then you were forced to eat it later.

Our dining room table was oval-shaped with a removable center leaf. My father, as you might've guessed, sat at its head, and I sat to his immediate right, which unfortunately for me was within striking distance. Jan was placed at his left, and then came my mom; Karen was at the other head, while David sat next to me.

I have already established that my dad worked in retail. His days off were Friday and Sunday; on Saturday he worked his longest day. We usually ate dinner around five-thirty, mere moments after he returned home from work. He would walk through the door, kiss my mother with a loud resounding smack, take out his pocket protector full of pens, glasses and paperwork and sit down at the table. We would then make our way to the table, find our seats and sit down in silence. Sometimes our meals involved his participation. For example, if my mom were serving her awesome chili, he would butter and stack up the saltine crackers and distribute them like poker chips. Nobody else at the table was allowed to butter the crackers; I don't know why, but I never asked. Even if he had a cold and was pulling out his hanky every ten minutes to blow his nose, he still buttered the crackers.

Our mother was a great cook. I loved her cooking and it showed. We didn't have an abundance of food in the house, it was just the way we ate it. Buttering a piece of bread and then dumping sugar on it was considered a normal snack. In the refrigerator there was always a jar of bacon grease to use when cooking green beans or other things that didn't have enough fat in them. There was a Fry Daddy on the counter, and sometimes my father would make French fry sandwiches using it.

He had learned how to make French fry sandwiches growing up in Allentown, Pennsylvania where they also dined on Lebanon bologna, lard and cream soda. While the fries were bubbling away, he would carefully smear butter onto two pieces of white bread. After the fries were cool enough to touch, he would line them up on the bread with the precision of a brick mason. There wasn't one out of place. He would salt and pepper the concoction and then put the other buttered piece on top. Oh, my god, they were delicious.

Another favorite in the Beller household was ring bologna. Its name says it all as the processed beefy perfection came in ring form. A little bigger in circumference than a silver dollar, this food seemed invincible too. You could slice it and eat it with mustard, boil it, fry it, or grill it. It didn't matter what you did to it; it was still yummy as all get out. Years later my brother coined the name "cheese gigs" for our favorite way to eat ring bologna. Cheese gigs were assembled in this order: Ritz cracker, brown mustard, ring bologna, Monterey Jack cheese, Old Bay seasoning. Make a plate of them and nuke them in the microwave for one minute and you are in bad-food-for-you heaven. I'm not even kidding!

Karen was always the last one to leave the table because in fifteen years she had never finished a meal. Scratch that. Once, for a babysitter, she ate an entire family-sized box of macaroni and cheese with a spoon, right out of the pot. She loved that and green beans. Everything else on her plate somehow ended up in my stomach. I couldn't bear to see her still sitting at the dining room table when it was dark outside.

As I was clearing the table, she would look at me with extremely sad, puppy dog eyes and ask me to eat the leftover food on her plate. She made a game of it and would often get on the floor with her hands clasped together and beg me. Every time I would come back to remove more dishes from the table, I would also pick up something off of her plate. She would even make neat, little piles so it was easier for me to scoop up. We had a good system. Additionally, there were times when I would purposely put less on my plate because I knew that in thirty minutes I would be eating from hers.

David never played along when it came to food threats. When my father commanded him to eat his dinner or go to bed, David would respond with "Goodnight." He would often be in bed by 5:45. I couldn't believe it. He chose to miss out on the tumbling; after dinner all the sofa cushions would be on the floor for the post meal Olympic try-outs.

One hilarious night non-talkative David decided to break the kids-keep-quiet commandment and talk during dinner. He decided to tell us the new word he had learned that day from Jimmy, the youngest Flanagan. Out of nowhere he chimes in with, "When Karen gets mad… she's pissed." I froze in mid-bite, in a total state of shock, as the breeze from my father's right arm made the top of my hair move. In a millisecond David hit the back wall and was on the floor. Needless to say, he never went there again.

If ever there was something serious to talk about, it happened at the table. Report cards were the scariest of topics because of my keen ability to constantly underachieve. PTA meetings usually consisted of teachers telling my parents that I would rather entertain the class than learn. Well, that was a no-brainer. If I could get out of doing math by making the class laugh, I was all in. The dinner table was also where we learned about Jan's cheerleading woes.

Jan wanted to be a cheerleader at Parkville Senior High in the worst way. She spent the majority of her time jumping around the living room, trying to do a split, spelling out words and placing her closed fists on her hips. I think they use magnets to keep them there. I spent the majority of my time catching all the lamps that she had knocked over. She was very loud and could make the whole house shake to the sounds of D-E-F-E-N-S-E. Karen used to shadow her and also learned every cheer and was equally as loud; however, her spelling was better.

Every year like clockwork the names of the new cheerleaders would be posted, and Jan's name would be on page naught. She held in her emotions all day at school, but as soon as she hit the dinner table, she would burst into Niagara Falls tears. Jan was a professional *zub-zubber* too. Her whole body would shake, she'd go through a box of Kleenex, and the crying would last for days.

Once she cried through seven straight episodes of *M*A*S*H*, which I consider the funniest TV show ever. Okay, it's a toss-up between that and *The Dick Van Dyke Show,* but seriously, how could anyone cry through *M*A*S*H*? In her senior year she didn't make the squad either, but she was asked to be the mascot and spent the whole year wearing knight's armor around the house. She was ecstatic, and by default, so were we. Gimme' an A-B-O-U-T-T-I-M-E!

Other than the television, the dining room table served as the focal point of the house as people would congregate there. We favored card games and would sit at the table to play rummy for hours. Besides using it for games, anyone using the telephone sat there to get some privacy. Jan pretty much monopolized the phone. I think I used it eight times between the Nixon administration and 1975, when she graduated high school.

All of our homework was done at the table too, as well as my Peter Brady volcano science experiment. Our pre-Halloween ritual took place at it as we had made an assembly line, filling bags of candy. We all had a specific job of putting something inside the bags. The last person would staple them together with these cool staplers, which resembled vegetables that my dad brought home from work.

Our stereo was in the dining room as well, so we listened to lots of records while sitting at the table. Records could be made to play over and over again if you placed the arm of the record player in a certain position. Ray Stevens, who had the smash hit "The Streak" also had a record called "Gitarzan," and it was Karen's favorite. There were three singing parts to the song: Tarzan's, a Monkey's and Jane's.

Karen and David and I were each singing a character's part, and our harmony sounded top-notch. The music was loud, which caused us to sing louder, so it was hard to notice that my mother had just walked in from the grocery store. Karen had her back to her, so as my mother called to her, she didn't hear it; Mom called her again. At that exact moment Karen's solo came up in the song, and she blasted out,

"Shut up baby, I'm trying to sing!" I burst out laughing at the perfect timing of her line, however, my mom didn't exactly find the humor in it and poor Karen had to pay the price for her virtuoso efficiency.

The only time the table became a serious place was when my father was balancing the checkbook. It was the only time I saw him wear his glasses, so I knew he must have been doing something important. I wasn't sure what balancing the checkbook even meant, but I did know it drove him crazy when my mother would rip a blank check out of the book and head for the store. She could never remember what she had bought when it came time to record it in the book.

At North Plaza Mall there was a store called The Copper Rivet. It was a cool store where everybody in Parkville bought his or her Levi's jeans. While laughing, my dad took his glasses off and said, "Come here and see what your silly mother did." In his hand he had a cancelled check for The Copper Rivet and in the checkbook my mother had written The Silver Stud.

M-80'S, MAILBOXES AND ACORNS

I will never forget the day I discovered what an M-80 was. One of the Flanagans was discussing them; I thought they were talking about the newest Yamaha motorcycle. When they handed one to me, I wasn't very impressed until someone mentioned they contained a third of a stick of dynamite. *Holy pyrotechnic flash powder, Batman!* Actually, it wasn't that powerful, but it could sure do damage to a rural United States parcel receptacle, also known as a mailbox.

A bunch of us were hanging out in the Flanagans' backyard on their brand spanking new basketball court. It was the only court in the neighborhood, and the more I think about it, it was the only basketball hoop in the neighborhood. The Flanagans lived on Appleton, and their house backed right up against the woods.

A gate opened up to the woods from a beautifully blacktopped basketball court in their backyard. The court was such a cool place to hang out that even the grown-ups would come there to play. I can vividly remember sitting on the railroad tie wall that lined the north side of the court, watching my father and the other dads play basketball on a Sunday afternoon. I didn't even know my father knew how to play basketball. What a treat it was to see him perform his fifteen-foot jumper. Notice how I didn't say it went in.

"H.O.R.S.E." was the basketball game of choice for most kids. H.O.R.S.E. is when one person tries a crazy basketball shot, like standing on one foot with your back to the basket. If by some chance it goes in, the next person has to make the exact same shot or they would get the letter "H." This would repeat with "O" and so on until someone had H.O.R.S.E. On a good day, when we had more time, we would play "B.I.G. A.S.S. B.R.O.W.N. H.O.R.S.E."

The Flanagans were so gracious because they allowed anybody to play at any time. Karen and I used to walk up there to play while they were all inside eating dinner. They made it easy to intrude. By the way, Karen had a wicked layup.

The Flanagans were a cool family for many reasons. I mentioned previously that they had about twenty-seven kids, so surprises were few and far between. I can't imagine a secret being kept in that house, and, as a matter of fact, I can't imagine their family eating dinner all at once in that house. They were like two and a half times the Waltons! "Goodnight, Bobby. Goodnight, Linda"...this went on for eight hours until it was time to wake up.

Once, the gang was hanging around in their backyard, near their swimming pool. "Hanging" was what we called it when there was nothing substantial to do. The Flanagans had the biggest above ground pool I had ever seen. It was long and oval-shaped and had banners crossing it. It resembled a circus tent. I never swam in it but peered over the side once and noticed it was full of fish. Live fish! They were swimming around in it like it was a virtual salmon stream. I don't remember the story behind it, but I'm assuming it was what had remained after a fishing expedition, or an act of God. I think He hung out there too, and had an awesome hook shot.

On another day, Fitz, Buddy, Tony and I were standing at the bottom of their back staircase when Michael came out of the house complaining about his chores. I guess with an entire workforce living under the same roof, chores needed to be assigned hourly. Upon first glance, I was pretty sure it was Michael, but I would get confused sometimes. I recognized the Flanagan girls much easier than the boys.

Rosie, who was older, looked like an angel to me, and Paula helped get me through puberty. Well, she and Dorothy Hamill did, but that's another story. (Dorothy actually made me quiver.)

About an hour later we were entrenched in a game of "redline". And an hour after that, I saw my first mailbox explode, courtesy of an M-80. It flew about ten feet in the air and made an amazing, resounding *boom*! The funny thing was how fast everyone had scattered after detonation. We were all just casually walking down the street one second and running through briar patches the next. I wasn't much into blowing up things, but I sure felt fulfilled to have witnessed such an eventful blast.

Usually our amusement was built around anonymously knocking on doors and running away like hell, fleeing the scene of the crime. Most outside doors were metal on the bottom half, so a couple of raps on one would make any unsuspecting inhabitant jump right out of their living room chair. Anybody in the neighborhood was on the menu too, as I remember our door being banged on before hearing kids scatter. I can guarantee you that my father wasn't home when that occurred. All the kids were scared of him, and rightfully so.

Some weeks later, I was taking our trashcans out to the street; it seemed like a normal Friday evening. They picked up the trash on Wednesdays and Saturdays, so I always knew I had a Friday night date with our heavy ass tin cans.

I had just reached the street, around nine-thirty, when I heard a shocking *KABOOM* from the bottom of Uxbridge Road. I immediately scanned to my right and spotted Buddy and Michael hiding behind the front of the Gables' parked car on the left side of the street. Two houses away at the home of the Orlas, I saw a faint mushroom cloud rising into the nighttime sky. *Oh my God, they just blew up the Orlas' mailbox.* There were no hard feelings against the Orlas, I'm certain. They were a nice enough family. Their youngest son, Joey, was about five years younger than me and Jeanne was a few years older. She once came with us to our grandparents' house as a friend of Jan's. I remember her wearing a black bikini, a nice memory. I am really not sure why their mailbox was selected for demolition that day.

The car that Buddy and Michael were pinned against was facing me, and I could see them looking under the car trying, in vain, to see what was happening, but they couldn't. The whole, suspenseful scene had developed right before my eyes. Mr. Orla had bolted out of his house and stood in the dark at the top of his sidewalk. The light in his living room window barely silhouetted him, so they couldn't detect him. As he surveyed the road turning towards me, I noticed the streetlight's reflection in his Mel Cooley glasses. That type of glasses was worn later by Drew Carey and by one of the elves on the original *Rudolph the Red-Nosed Reindeer*.

I stood there, motionless, for a couple of minutes, observing how frozen-in-time everything seemed. Above the tree line in the Orlas' backyard, I could see the remnants of smoke slowly dissipating. Crickets were gossiping to each other in the park. I could also hear the faint sound of *The Rockford Files*, which meant the commercial break was over, as I remained out there, my eyes glued to the dramatic scene unfolding.

All at once Buddy and Michael simply stood up and started to nonchalantly amble up the street. *What the hell are they doing?* Mr. Orla must've been thinking the same thing and soon took off on a dead sprint towards them. He was gaining ground quickly before Buddy looked over his shoulder and noticed him, and then the race began. They both took off, running up the street. The boys were neck and neck with each other, and Mr. Orla was about twenty feet behind them. I couldn't believe how fast he was moving. It was so dark out that as they ran up the street, they kept disappearing. In fact, I only saw them when they ran under the streetlights. Each time they did, he was gaining on them. And they were all heading straight towards me.

As they rapidly approached, I took one step toward the street and realized I was still holding our trashcan. The two frontrunners saw me, changed their course and then ran through my yard towards Buddy's house. As they ran by Buddy said, "Hey, Neil," like I was passing him in the hallway at school or something. Nothing piqued in his voice and neither of them seemed out of breath or scared. I, however, felt afraid for them.

Seconds later, Mr. Orla blew past me, but he wasn't laughing, nor did he say hello. I heard the sound of a chain-linked fence being scaled, twice. Consequently, I heard the Millers' German Shepard barking like crazy, and then I heard the yelling.

Mr. Orla jumped the fence, but the dog chased him back. Mr. Miller had come out. He and Mr. Orla got into a screaming match. *Perhaps it was time for me to go back inside the house.* Nobody could punish kids better than Mr. Miller. He would never let any other parent give him grief about his children and would always defend them. However, as soon as the opposing parent left, he would take his kids to task. I learned that from experience the previous year.

Here's how it happened. Buddy and Tony and I were in their front yard playing "witch." Witch is a game where one person, the witch, has to stay on the sidewalk and everybody else has to jump across the sidewalk without being touched by the witch. If the witch touched you, or you touched the sidewalk, you'd then become the witch. It was dark, and we were slipping on all the acorns that had fallen in the yard, so we picked them up and, because we were boys, started throwing them at each other. FYI, acorns hurt more than being pink-bellied! They were obviously invented by a member of D-CUP.

Buddy ran out into the street to hide on the other side of the hedge. The Millers' entire front yard was outlined by a hedgerow, which made for many perfect-hiding places. There was only one way out of the yard without diving through the hedgerow, and that was the sidewalk. I also know, from a failed Evel Knievel experience, that it was impenetrable to bicycles as well.

So, Buddy was on the other side of the hedgerow, and Tony and I were in the yard, firing acorns back and forth at him, but we couldn't seem to locate him because it was so dark. Buddy lifted his arm up to fire from his hiding place and became illuminated by the headlights of a passing car. Thankful for the outlining, I fired a handful at his silhouette, and about five acorns found the side of the passing car. The pissed off motorist slammed on his breaks and skidded to a halt. Tony and I shared a quick glance and then scattered. Buddy ruined my theory on the impenetrable hedgerow and ran right through it.

The car peeled out in reverse and stopped right in front of the sidewalk. Tony ran around in circles for a few seconds and then followed Buddy around the side of the house and into the backyard. My immediate reaction was to dive into the closest bush and burrow under as far as I could, like a gopher. I was wearing my black pea coat, so I blended in pretty well, but it didn't matter because the driver ran right past me. I could hear the ruckus Buddy and Tony were making in the backyard because they were climbing a tree to get away. I could hear branches snapping and breaking as they were shushing each other. I knew they'd been caught, so I took the opportunity to skedaddle out of the yard, past the car, and I kept on running for about two hundred yards up the street.

I could hear a man yelling at them to come down, out of the tree. It was kind of funny that they climbed the tree anyway. It was obviously Buddy's idea, and I'm sure he didn't count on Tony following him. As I calmly walked by a few minutes later, they were both only about ten feet off the ground, hugging the same branch. The man had had enough by now and walked to the front door and banged on it. His car was still running with the door wide open and the headlights shining up the road towards the Graysons' house.

Mr. Miller answered the door, and I could hear him tell the man that his kids were in their rooms and had been there all night. The man screamed back that he was lying and to check the tree in his backyard. Mr. Miller explained that lots of kids climb trees and slammed the door. I had goose bumps of fear as I walked past the house. The pissed off man walked back to his car and burned rubber out of there. It looked the same as when Steve McQueen peeled out in *Bullitt*, but I never witnessed that in person, so I stopped to watch the tire smoke in awe. I was interrupted by Mr. Miller yelling out the back door, "Get your asses out of the tree and in the house right this minute!"

I could hear the punishment being doled out all the way from my house. Acorns and tree bark weren't the only reasons for their bruises. The next day, kids came from all over the neighborhood to visit their house because of the awesome-looking tire marks left in the street. I could've sold tickets.

CATHERINE

On one Easter morning my father held out to us a basket, which held three slips of paper. Each had a color written on it: white, black or brown. Karen picked first, followed by me, and lastly, went Jan. We soon learned that each color corresponded to an adorable baby bunny. Rabbits! Our first pets were rabbits. My dad had spent all his recent free time making a giant cage for them in our backyard.

Each bunny had its own sleeping area, dining room and jellybean collection system. My father had thought of everything, except the fact that we wanted a dog. The only time we ever visited "Hasenpfeffer Alley", as we called it, was when he threatened to send them back to the farm. *What can you really do with a bunny?* Occasionally, I would convince one to hop over so I could pick it up, but that was about it. Oh, sure I had visions of thwarting the likes of Elmer Fudd and company, but the only Tasmanian devil around was David's stuffed one, named Spike.

David loved Spike and took him everywhere he went, except for school. Since I shared a double bed with David, it meant I also shared a double bed with Spike. I loved to tease David by hiding Spike or putting him in precarious situations. I turned over a shovel of sod next to the sidewalk and placed a sign in the ground that read "Here Lies Spike." David dug up half the yard before he realized I was joking. I hung him from a noose once with a suicide note. David cut him down to crazy laughter, but my favorite prank took place during dinner one evening.

We were all sitting at the table eating when my mom got up and went to the freezer, to get some ice for her water. As the fog drifted out of the freezer David looked up and saw Spike's frozen, stuffed body staring back. I knew his reaction would be priceless, but I had no idea he'd climb right over the table and through the meatloaf to retrieve to him. He adored that stuffed animal and still does.

After the rabbits were mysteriously led back to the farm, exotic cage and all, we felt horrible about not visiting them more often. We went pet-less for a couple of years, that is, if you don't count David's friend Greg Bon. He was a little guy by nature, but huge in the brain department. Once while a huge wrestling match broke out in the living room, he uninvolved himself and merely shimmied back until he was sitting, comfortably and upright, under an end table. Through the melee he simply sat there watching *The Partridge Family*.

One evening my father walked through the front door, wearing his brown winter coat. Sticking out of his white fur-lined pocket was a little kitten. She looked so lovable. She was white with black and brown patches. In our creative void we named her "Cat." This went on for several weeks until one day someone added a "thrine." She became known as Cat-thrine or Catherine.

It was quickly determined that the Bellers were cat people. I'm not talking about Nastassja Kinski either; I'm talking about cute and cuddly Kodak moments all over the house. Catherine was an outside cat and would always leave us presents on the front porch. We would have been very pleased if the presents weren't all dead.

Catherine was smart, too. She knew right where the litter box in the basement was, she came when we called and she even let David shove her in his Lincoln Log container without putting up a fuss. We were having such a good time with her, we wondered if lighting could strike twice by us getting another cat.

All that changed while I was attending a Webelos meeting. Webelos was one step above Cub Scouts and one step below Boy Scouts. I have absolutely no idea why we were called Webelos, although many unorthodox nicknames and theories had been discussed.

Our den mother, Mrs. France, informed us that her cat had just delivered kittens. I always loved the term delivered. I imagined a pizza delivery-type guy rapping on your door and handing you a box with a warm kitten inside.

Being a recent cat aficionado, I quickly picked out my favorite kitty and begged my mother to let me bring him home. Unfortunately for me, I had broken a major house rule.

House Rule Number One: Never ask Mom or Dad about something in front of the people the answer could affect.

By putting my parents on the spot, they would sometimes agree to things that they'd never allow if they were asked about in private. This rule was put into effect when I had asked a friend to stay for lunch when my mom clearly wanted to go shopping, or maybe it was when I volunteered her, in front of my teacher, to make thirteen dozen cupcakes for class the next day.

Either way, I was in violation for breaking our version of "Don't ask, don't tell" and the bad karma had started to escalate. Much to my excitement, we brought home the orange tabby I had picked out and named him Morris. He looked just like the lazy finicky pitch cat that was a superstar on television. His looks proved to be deceiving as our Morris was slightly mentally challenged.

It was well known in our house that Dad took naps on the couch every Sunday afternoon. No matter what you were doing, you had to do it in complete silence. This included everything from watching television to involuntary body functions, such as breathing. As usual, David didn't get the memo.

Our father was sound asleep on the couch. He rested on his back with his right arm touching the floor. He lay there in a deep slumber, wearing his signature white T-shirt. Two-year-old David was playing with Morris in the hallway and a chase began. Morris ran up the hallway, turned left through the kitchen, and pounced into the dining room and continued around towards the living room with David clomping close behind.

The frantic feline sprinted into the living room looking for an escape. Morris climbed my father's arm like an off ramp. In an instant my father sat straight up. Morris ended up stuck to my dad's shirt, as all four paws embedded in his chest. My dad looked down in shock as Morris looked up in horror. David entered the room, laughing, until he met up with dad.

My father pried Morris off his chest and put both of them in time-out for about two hours. It was very funny to witness, but I waited until the next day to laugh.

Morris was also an outside cat and would often be seen roaming the park, looking for little furry things to leave on the porch. Catherine, however, had already found them all, so he would only leave weeds and small shrubs. He had a habit of running up the screen door, climbing it swiftly until he reached the roof.

The only problem was that he couldn't get back down; he would sit up there and meow for hours until we would get him down. In the middle of a pouring rainstorm, we heard a noise outside and opened the door. There was Keith Hudson, our next-door neighbor, positioning a thirty-foot ladder to get Morris off of our roof. He was sitting in the rainspout and had literally created a dam. Water was pouring over the side of the house, all around him, but he just sat there meowing. Stupid cat.

The last time I saw him climb the screen was also the one and only time I saw my father get scared. My dad was standing at the front door looking out into the darkness and breathing in the warm summer air. He was very close to the screen when Morris surprised him by running up the porch, leaping onto the door, and finally making his way to the roof. My father jumped about five feet backwards, yelling obscenities as he fell against the steps. Ten minutes later, he removed the screen and put in the storm window.

GIMP

When school let out for the summer, it always seemed like a solid year before we were forced to go back. I made the most out of every day; in three months I played enough to fill twelve. School never ended before Labor Day, which was the official end of summer to us. When you heard the story on the Sunday night news about all the Bay Bridge traffic, you knew school started the following Tuesday.

In my world the summer wouldn't end until we attended the Chadmans' Labor Day cookout. It also meant that earlier in the week, my mom and I would visit the husky department at Sears for some Wrangler jeans. I hated shopping in that department; it was easily my least favorite day of the year.

One year I really screwed up and paid the price in a big way. Tonya Chadman had asked me to go swimming, so I ran home to get my swimsuit but couldn't find it. I noticed that some people had been swimming in cut-offs, so I grabbed a pair of jeans to make my own. I struck out again, as I looked everywhere but couldn't find the scissors. Wanting to persevere, I found myself in the kitchen. I laid my jeans on a cutting board. Using a serrated kitchen knife, I sawed and hacked my way into a pair of cutoffs.

Twenty minutes later, however, my swimming adventure came to a screeching halt, as my mother stood on the back porch and screamed for me to come home. When I walked inside through the back door, she stood there, holding two empty pant legs, demanding to know what the hell was wrong with me. I had no answer.

Unbeknownst to me, those jeans were my new back-to-school jeans, which she had just purchased the day before. After I changed, she angrily drove me to North Plaza Mall and forced me to buy another pair at The Copper Rivet with my own money. I almost fell out of my shoes when the clerk said, "$13.13." Highway robbery!

To this day, I still hate back-to-school shopping. As a matter of fact, I continue to get queasy when I see back-to-school signage. I have also put forth legislation to have the word husky removed from the English language.

At the beginning of the summer, Missing Pine Park was the scene of a summer camp put on by Baltimore County Parks and Recreation. I'm pretty sure there was no interference by the evil members of D-CUP as there were no tragedies to recall. I did rip the crotch out of my pants on a tree branch once, but it missed all the dangly parts. However, I'm pretty sure D-CUP planted the tree there.

For this camp, a counselor would show up with crafts and games and kind of act as a community babysitter. I remember her name to be Babs; she was the only Babs I had ever met. She had red hair, was a whiz at checkers, taught me how to make potholders and introduced us to "gimp." I don't remember Jan ever going to camp, but she did make a fifty-four foot chain out of gum wrappers. She would sit there for hours. Oh, the talent!

Gimp was a plastic lacing used to make bracelets, necklaces, key chains and all kinds of other fun stuff. It came in a gazillion colors, and there were special patterns you had to follow in order to make such items. I mastered the box stitch, but only because the spiral stitches used to kick my ass. We would sit for hours, making all kinds of things we would never use again. I am pretty sure one year I gave gimp gifts to every member of my family for Christmas.

In general moms love to receive handmade things from kids, and my mom was no exception. On any given day you could open up the kitchen's junk drawer and find thirty to forty lanyards made out of gimp and seventeen potholders.

I used to make all my gifts, as money was non-existent. Once I spent a week gluing the little metal edge pieces of a Natty Boh twist off cap onto a cardboard toilet paper holder. In the morning the ashtrays were full of them, twist off caps, not toilet paper holders. I haven't seen an ashtray in years, but growing up we had several in every single room of the house. I covered the whole cardboard tube in the little gold pieces and, in its middle, spelled out the word Mom with white pieces. Without question, she showed it to all her friends.

I'm not sure if our parents signed us up for summer camp; we just went. It was cool to see something other than a softball game being organized in the park. The grass was freshly mowed, and the county dropped off a nicely painted green picnic table for us to use. Kids were riding their bikes in from everywhere.

Due to the amount of kids in the park, the county kept the weeds along the stream neatly trimmed as well. We had lost Jimmy Grayson for about six hours one day, so the next day a crew of grass cutters and small debris movers showed up to rid the park of them.

Another reason for clearing them out was that someone had seen a snake. I don't do snakes, and if I had seen one, I would've quickly headed the other way. And I literally mean a Bugs Bunny-running-in-mid-air-before-shooting-off-in-the-opposite-direction kind of departure. It's strange how phobias stick with you; I've never met a snake I didn't want to flee from. Years later, I could completely relate to Indiana Jones and his hatred of snakes when a friend of mine from college brought his big-ass twelve foot boa constrictor to school in a pillow case; I was a nervous wreck.

Toting his snake to a baseball game that evening, he emptied the entire dugout of the opposing team, right out onto the field in the middle of a pitch, when he stuck four feet of that guy through an air vent in the back of the dugout. I'm sure there were fifty bats around, but no one thought of swinging one at the snake. They must've shared the same phobia. Eventually, the umpire made the snake leave, so my friend put the snake in the locker room's shower and returned to watch the game. About a week later the snake died of athlete's foot poisoning. A fitting end, for sure.

When the Missing Pine Park camp ended, Karen, David and I were sent to Camp Koda at the Northeast YMCA in Fullerton. This camp was where we encountered social diversity, as kids came from neighboring counties and Baltimore City as well.

The bus driver that picked us up early in the morning really grossed me out. He was always snorting like he was about to hock a loogie. We would get picked up at 8AM and spend all day there. They had a giant pool, lots of woods to play hide-and-seek in and a couple of baseball fields. I hadn't known anyone there, so I was forced to broaden my proverbial horizons.

I met this black kid named Poochie who wore a giant afro. He cracked me up. Once while playing capture-the-flag, he got his hair stuck in a tree limb, and I had to help him yank it out. He called me "his white friend, Fred." I have no idea why.

They taught us a camp song that we had to sing every morning or we couldn't play. I still remember the words: "You take the pep from a Pepsi Cola, you take the luck from a Lucky Strike, you take the zip from a Talon Zipper, you take the gleam from a lectric light-a lectric light, and then you put them all together, with the aid of string and glue and you've got the gang from Camp Koda, the gang that's all true blue." The only thing missing were the *Solid Gold* dancers.

Later in the summer, Carney Elementary held a camp that enabled you to move beyond gimp and play sports with the bigger kids. I wasn't a bigger kid, but they used to tolerate me because I would make them laugh. I was never at a loss for a joke, a crazy voice, an impression or a witty comeback.

I had memorized *MAD* magazine's "Snappy Answers to Stupid Questions" and could spit them out faster than you could say "I slit a sheet a sheet, a sheet I slit, upon this slitted sheet I sit."

My favorite comeback took place while on the phone. When someone walked up and asked "Are you on the phone?" I'd respond with "No, I am digging wax out of my ear with this lovely plastic scoop." I needed the practice as I had wanted to work for National Lampoon's *MAD* magazine one day.

We divided up into teams and played baseball on field number one practically all day. I loved playing baseball and never went anywhere without my glove. Field number one was along Fuller Avenue and had a gigantic, red radio tower surrounded by a tall fence in deep left field. It was a Carney icon and could be seen from everywhere. I used to look up at it all the time and think about the brave souls who built it. During air raid drills, when we would all run into the hallway and put our heads on the floor at the base of the lockers and wonder what vodka and fish eggs would taste like, I was sure that tower would be shooting missiles at the Russians.

Playing baseball with the bigger kids was a blast. I could hold my own, and they made me feel like a real team member. I was only intimidated once when, while playing first base, our third baseman, Ricky Marshall, threw a bullet at me that arrived in a nanosecond. The sound of it hitting my glove hurt my ears.

Ricky was a baseball god to me, and I mean that in every sense of the word because he even looked like Jesus Christ. I can see him now from the back, walking down Joppa road from Alda Drive at sunset in full uniform. His bat was placed over his shoulder and his long hair was blowing in the breeze as he walked. Man crush? No, because he was the Lord. Ten years later, he bought me a case of Malt Duck so I could impress my date Lisa, at the Bel Air High School Ring Dance. It pays to be friends with the Lord.

Carney Camp had a counselor whose first impression scared the hell out of me. He went by the name Mr. Mike. I couldn't pronounce his last name but heard it contained the entire alphabet so everyone just called him Mr. Mike. He was rather large, in a professional wrestler sort of way, and hairy. He wore black-framed glasses and could sweat just by thinking about it.

During a game he mashed a baseball that hit the fence at the foot of the red Russian missile tower, which was about two miles away from home plate. He was almost thrown out at first base. On occasion he could shoot you a disappointing look that made you apologize for things you didn't even do. I tried very hard to pass that look onto other kids, almost like I was passing on his disappointment. It worked. I never wanted to experience his wrath. My thought was to make friends with the leader so his subordinates or allies would have to succumb and let me into the group. That is the way all younger kids looked at older kids. It is also the foundation of American foreign policy.

After one hot baseball game, a few of the bigger kids were talking about something cold to drink, so Mr. Mike pulled out a five dollar bill and handed it to me. He told me to go to 7-11 and get three grape Slurpees. I had finally proven my worth and gained his trust because a grown man wouldn't just hand money to any nine-year-old kid and send him across two lanes of dangerous traffic for cold liquid refreshments. I was almost a member of his gang. There was no asking me to go either; it was an order, an initiation of sorts.

I was easily seven to eight years younger than all the big kids, so this was the fee I needed to pay for the right to hang out with them. I was sure we would be drinking beer and playing poker before the day was out.

Mr. Mike wanted a Slurpee for himself, one for Corky Cramblitt, and one for this other big kid who was nameless. Corky seemed to me to be about eight foot tall and was the older brother of Suzette, who was my age. If I climbed halfway up the fence around the basketball court, I could almost look Corky in the throat. Anybody named Corky had to be cool, so off I went to 7-11 with some friends without saying a word. 7-11 was on the other side of Harford Road, which was close to Pennsylvania, so you had to be very careful traversing it.

I was collecting pro sports Slurpee cups at the time and needed a Bruce Laird. I had seven cents to my name, and a regular Slurpee cost forty-nine cents, so if there was any change left over from Mr. Mike's bounty, I could get myself one. It was very hot outside, and the air conditioning in the store was extremely welcoming.

I loved our 7-11 and was sad and confused, years later, when they built a new one sixty yards away and turned the old one into a flower shop. Even more years later, after getting happy during happy hour, I pulled in to get a microwaveable burrito and left with a dozen carnations.

I slurped out a grape one for me and, a grape for the giant man named Mr. Mike, one for Corky and one for the big nameless guy. I was holding all four of them and sampling one as we reached the curb of Harford Road. Normally, everybody sprinted across the street between passing cars, but since I was holding a gallon of frozen wonderfulness, I had to step back. While trying to get back onto the curb, I tripped and started to fall in slow motion.

Whenever something terrible is about to happen, life seems to move in slow motion, doesn't it? Slo-mo had just occurred last week when David, trying to see what was on the sewing table in my parent's room, stood on the pedal to get a better look. In super slow motion the machine kicked on and stitched a perfect seam on his index finger. Yee -ouch!

I was no longer concerned about my own wellbeing as the sound of a grape Slurpee splattering all over the sidewalk filled the air. *Oh, shit!*

It was a miracle that I only dropped one. Sadly, by the time I jumped up, the hot sidewalk had grape DNA running in all directions. My friends ran back over to see what had happened. I knew my life would be over when Mr. Mike found out; I would never be in his gang. I planned to tell everyone that I dropped it, but that's not exactly what came out of my mouth.

"What? You were just hit by a car?"

"Yes, it came up on the curb and knocked a grape Slurpee right out of my hand." It was a miracle that I was still alive. They all touched me to experience divine intervention, and then we walked through the stifling heat back to Carney Elementary and, potentially, to the end of my life.

Mr. Mike was sitting on a bench near the playground with Corky and the nameless guy as we walked up. Along the way, I thought through the whole story of the car hitting me, right down to the color of the shirt the driver was wearing and his beady little eyes. As we approached, I could see they were waiting desperately for their Slurpees and were conversing about why I was drinking from one and only carrying two.

They sat there, stunned, open-mouthed and straight-faced, as I told them that a car had nicked me. I started handing out the frozen delight as I filled them in on the near-death incident. I handed Mr. Mike his so I could still be in his group. I could see in his eyes that he was relieved that a lawsuit had just been thwarted. I handed one to the big, nameless guy so he wouldn't crush me and then, as Corky held out his hand, I took a sip out of the third one. "Hey, where is mine?" Corky questioned. I matter-of-factly broke it to him that it was his that hit the ground.

"How did you know it was mine?" he asked.

"Well, it certainly wasn't Mr. Mike's."

Mr. Mike noted how amazing it was that my Slurpee had survived the terrible accident and that my arm wasn't broken after being hit by a 1967 light green Chevrolet Caprice driven by someone resembling the lead singer from Herman's Hermits. He didn't seem concerned at all by Corky's loss. We all turned and walked away, leaving Corky standing there, in shock. As we departed, I asked where the poker game would be held.

Eight years later, I was waiting for my friend Greg Hoffman outside the yearbook room at Parkville Senior High when I was called inside it. Greg was helping to lay out the yearbook with the class advisor, Mr. P, and wanted to show me the varsity baseball page, which featured a picture of me up to bat at home plate. As I was looking proudly at the page, the advisor said that when he was younger, he could really sting a baseball.

I turned to smile at him when it all came flooding back like a warm river of horrible memories. Mr. P was Mr. Mike! I had never made the connection before, but Mr. P was Mr. Poletynski, the coolest teacher at

Parkville. I immediately drove to 7-11 and bought him a grape Slurpee. I still feel badly about Corky. I'm sticking with the divine intervention story, but maybe I should make him a gimp lanyard.

ARM WRESTLING

We had a pool in our backyard, and in the summer I used to live in it. One day in particular Tonya Chadman and I hopped from one neighborhood pool to another for at least nine hours. Looking back, I could have totally robbed a bank that evening because there was no way that anybody in the law enforcement community could have pulled a set of fingerprints from my white, pruney fingers. Each one resembled a tiny Shar Pei dog.

Sometimes kids would come to our yard just to hang out outside the pool. If they didn't have their parent's permission to swim, they would fetch beach balls, Frisbees and other items that made it out of the water. They would also help move the picnic table to the side of the pool, which served as a diving board. Everybody knows that picnic tables can act as diving boards during picnicking downtime.

My dad enforced the "Don't pee in the pool!" rule with the threat of banishment. My friends understood this and would simply get out of the pool and pee in the yard. Thus, the grass was always greener around the pool.

We kids maintained certain pool rituals as well. Marco Polo was a staple in any pool, and if you didn't make a couple of whirlpools and then try to walk the opposite way, you were lame. I remember the filter hoses going almost parallel and the middle of the pool sinking a good two feet as we created a massive whirlpool one evening. Water was flying out of the pool in giant waves, and I think a couple of kids got heaved over the side too. Everything was awesome until Jimmy Grayson threw up. *I mean, who throws up in a pool?* We all learned a lesson that day: barf floats.

I even remained in the pool when it rained. If there wasn't thundering and lightning, I would get in the pool and try to keep my face as close to the water as possible. The rain was always colder than the pool water; it was a very weird sensation to have the cold water hitting me in the head while the rest of my body was nice and warm.

In one particular downpour the rain was freezing cold. Just for fun, I leaned over the side and grabbed the bucket that we used to rinse our feet off in and dumped its contents out. I turned it over on top of my head to repel the rain. It was like being inside a kettledrum during a timpani roll. The constant pitter-patter of rain soothed me; I sank down deeper into the water, listening to it. At that moment I learned that I could breathe under water.

I pulled the bucket down under the water, creating an air pocket in which to breathe. I'm sure I sat there for at least twenty minutes. It was so peaceful, and my brain ran wild. I figured I had created my own personal think tank. I believe that was when I invented the Flux Capacitor.

When my mom wanted to get in the pool, everyone else had to get out. My mother and I are only twenty years apart, so naturally she was a very young-looking mom. With her beautiful red hair, she always drew attention when she was on the scene. Once while I was playing football in the park, she came home from work in one of her short skirts, and as she started walking up the sidewalk, some of the boys started whistling at her. *Um, hello, that's my mother and eww!*

When inside the pool, she was all about laying on a raft in a calm state, and that was impossible with kids around.

I, of course, had learned that the hard way when I miscalculated the distance it took to successfully swim under her. My dad was pretty ticked at me, but discipline in the pool could be dangerous; he decided to take the suction hose and stick it to the middle of my back. I certainly couldn't reach it as it was practically sucking the spine right out of my body, so I had to go under water and push off from the side of the pool to escape its grip. When I finally came up, my dad was laughing his ass off.

He had his own way of entering our pool, to boot. I don't think I ever saw him use the ladder. He would stand with a straight-armed grip on the side of the pool for ten or fifteen minutes, waiting for the right time to enter. I think he was just waiting for the neighbors to come outside so he could show off. In one swift motion he would jump up and do a flip right into the pool. My dad was very strong and very much in shape. Previously, I had witnessed him do thirty-five pull-ups on the swing set without even breaking a sweat.

As I grew up he continuously challenged me to become stronger. As a parent you have to find out what motivates your children, right?

For us, of course, it was fear. As I got older, my motivations were food and then money. Whenever I asked him for something or questioned him on a fact, he would simply lie down on the living room floor and challenge me to an arm wrestling match.

"Dad, can I have two bucks?"

"Arm wrestle for it."

"Dad, can I go over Buddy's house?"

"Arm wrestle for it."

"Dad, can I see what is behind that brown wrapper?" "Watch it, mister!"

This went on for years and years. There were times when, even before asking, I would just walk into the living room and hit the floor. Not one time did I ever win.

Years later, on the night of my senior prom, my father had asked me to follow him into my room. I had felt anxious all day long. I knew my date, Carole Flynn, would look gorgeous, so I primped and played with my hair for hours. The feathered back look was all the rage, but my hair was a curly mess. After some more blow-drying, I finally felt like I was presentable. Her parents were awesome and would have accepted me even if I was sporting a mullet, but that was still years down the road.

Dressed in a full white tux with a baby blue ruffled shirt, I sat on the edge of my bed as he paced back and forth. He was obviously struggling with what he was planning to say because he started and stopped about five times. Oh my god, I realized he was about to give me "the speech!"

Nervous as hell, I watched and waited patiently as he stopped and addressed me like only a father could to his teenage son. He looked at me for a few seconds and then said, "I'll let you know when I want to be a grandfather; now get out of here." It was the single most touching conversation we had ever had. Minutes later I was lying on the living room floor, arm wrestling for the car. This time, I won, and we never arm wrestled again.

HITCHHIKERS AND ALIENS

One day, I did a down and out, caught a football thrown by Paul Flanagan, and was immediately tackled by twenty-six people. Missing

Pine Park offered the best football field in the state. Everybody played, and I mean everybody, at the exact same time. Nobody sat out unless they were "odd man out." If a game was going on and a kid showed up, he couldn't play unless another kid showed up to make it even. The rule was that there couldn't be an odd number on any team at any time.

It was considered normal and appropriate to go and knock on a friend's door and beg him to come out just so you could play football. If someone went home for dinner from one team, then somebody on the other team had to sit out. This was just how it had to be; the only other thing discussed was where the two end zones would be located.

Even the way teams were picked was a process. There was the standard everybody-line-up-and-have-two-team-captains-pick-players -one-at-a-time method. Seniority and favoritism played a big role in this non-democratic election. And most of the time descriptions were used instead of names. There was "the tall guy," "her," and "the third grader." I went by "the fat kid in the pea coat." If the crowd was smaller, the ol' standby was "one potato, two potato..." and who could forget "my mother and your mother were hanging up clothes and my mother punched your mother right in the nose." It always intrigued me imagining that while hanging laundry, mothers would just drop their clothespins and start a cage match. Awesome! Of course, all we cared about was the color of the blood.

When the ball was snapped, thirty kids wearing nothing similar took off in every direction, hoping the quarterback would throw them the ball. Screaming attention grabbers like "Here, throw it here" as they ran in circles was a basic play. The quarterback had to watch sixty kids doing this, figure out which ones were on his team, and find the open one, while a couple of other kids were counting by Mississippis in front of an imaginary line, before chasing him around the backfield. What a joy unorganized football was!

When the ball was eventually thrown, everybody in the near vicinity would tackle the receiver to the ground, tearing his clothes in the process. We called it the "Missing Pine Park pile on." In some towns this may have been considered a misdemeanor; in Carney, however, it was simply known as tackle football.

We all played hard no matter what game it was. The natural formation of the park formed our field and boundaries, and, most of the time, manmade objects, like the monkey bars and the flagpole, were deemed "in play."

One particular game of football sticks out in my mind. I was running a slant position and ran right over a patch of dirt that I had never seen before. It was right in the middle of our field. I stopped and looked at it in a puzzling fashion. When a small breeze blew by, it was then that I noticed the absence of a particular sound. The metal clanking of clips hitting a metal flagpole was lacking.

Wait a minute... Where was the flagpole? It was gone. Our thirty-foot, white, metal flagpole that hindered every sporting event in the park had been removed. *Was this a county thing, or maybe the members of D-CUP were planning on replacing it with something more sinister?*

Six months later, when I was fishing for minnows, I discovered it at the stream. *Eureka!* The stream was an interesting place, and I usually caught something that fascinated me but never a thirty-foot flagpole.

I didn't always have the best of luck with transferring a catch from the stream to my house either. My mom wasn't crazy about me playing in the stream, or in the woods for that matter, so I was forced to discreetly cover my tracks. I spent an hour a day cleaning my tennis shoes so she would never know I'd been there. She always figured it out though, and it took me years to find out how she'd caught on to me. Other than smelling the wilderness in my hair or finding acorns in my pockets, she had another way of uncovering proof ... GPS was still decades away, so she used hitchhikers.

Hitchhikers were what we called those miniscule, green, diamond -shaped, pain-in-the-ass plant things that would magically adhere themselves to socks, T-shirts, shoelaces and underwear. It would take the patience and precision of a gifted surgeon to remove all of them but would only take the existence of one to get grounded. Hated them.

"No, Mom, I wasn't in the woods; I wasn't anywhere near them. I don't think I've even seen a weed all day; why do you ask?"

Enter exhibit A: the sock with a bazillion hitchhikers on it. *Damn. Grounded again.*

As I was enjoying about fifty sips of water via the hilarious paper Dixie Riddle Cups, which made it to our bathroom wall dispenser in 1973, Buddy Miller knocked on my front door. I made Buddy wait while I pondered, "What has no beginning, end or middle?" "Give up?" A donut. *Oh, the jocularity of those Dixie Riddle Cups.*

Jan was babysitting us at the time, which meant she was on the phone, so I knew I had a couple of hours before she'd notice I was gone. Buddy had discovered something cool about two miles away from my house, so we hopped on our bikes and headed up the small hill, right on Summit and down Magledt Road to a tiny roadside marsh. About thirty yards off the road, fifteen cattails stood proudly and waited to be picked. Cattails made perfect torches, and we undoubtedly needed some. The bike ride to and fro was pretty seamless; we were back in forty minutes. It was about seven forty-five by now, so it was dark enough for the use of a torch.

I walked inside the house, unseen, and commandeered some Ohio Blue Tip Matches. (We were out of Indiana Red Tip Matches at the time.) I snuck back outside, and we both tried in earnest to light a cattail, but no dice. The thought that we needed an accelerant entered my mind, so I ran around back, and went in the basement to find the can of kerosene we used for our Coleman stove. As Buddy held the cattail, I poured a little kerosene on it and we tried again. On TV they made torches in mere seconds and they burned for an entire episode of *Hawaii 5-0*, but in our front yard they only seemed to burn for a few seconds. *What's up with that?* I decided that we must've had bad oxygen in Carney. I returned the kerosene and went back inside to put the matches away. Jan waved to me as I went by. She was an excellent baby sitter.

I marched outside and disappointedly looked at our bounty of cattails. Buddy wanted the matches again and told me to go back inside and get them. He assured me one would light this time because he had figured out what the problem was. I reluctantly agreed and trudged back inside, past the alert babysitter, and grabbed the matches. Obviously not being enforced today was Babysitter Rule Number One: Don't let the kids play with matches. The cattail was lying on the ground this time; Buddy lit a match and dropped it on top. The flash of white and orange fire that knocked me on my ass measured at least twelve feet high and singed the leaves on two nearby trees.

You see, while I was inside the house, Buddy had retrieved the kerosene and drenched the cattail as it lay upon on the ground. By the time I had returned, it had spread out into a four-foot radius, which was now burning ferociously across my front yard. All I could think about was how my dad would be breathing at me soon and plotting a clever way to use my body to repair the yard.

Buddy got up and started jumping up and down on the fire to extinguish it, but he was actually spreading it around. I ran back inside the house and yelled for Jan, who was finally off the phone and preparing spaghetti.

With the horror of someone being chased by Michael Myers from *Halloween,* she screamed at the top of her lungs, "WHAT ARE YOU DOING?"

The stentorian sound she emitted caused a nearby jet to veer off course. She ran back into the house and retrieved the pot of water that she had just put on the stove. Buddy was making some headway on the yard, however; his shoes were now on fire too. From my point of view, the whole front of the house had been lit up. I'm positive you could've seen our yard from miles away.

Jan threw the pot of spaghetti water on the ground, and the fire went out straightaway. A collective sigh went up as I stared down at the charred pile of cattails and black grass.

"Why did you do that?" was all that Jan could muster.

Buddy faced Jan and declared, "It seemed like the right thing to do at the time." Bewildered, she snatched up the pot and ambled back to the house. The burnt yard resembled the landing site of a UFO. For a brief moment I had desperately wondered if my father would believe that possibility.

For about a week I waited for my father to ask about it, but, curiously, he never mentioned it. The grass was easy to cover up by pulling up other grass and spreading it around on the burnt area, but I couldn't do anything for the singed trees. Damn aliens.

The next spring, one of the trees died, but the other one was filling in normally. On one summer day I noticed a gigantic beehive hanging from it, about fifteen feet up. It was huge and resembled a mummified basketball. Obviously, it had to go, and I was the right kid to take care of it, so I made a plan. I reached into our front bushes and pulled out the garden hose. I briefly wondered why Jan opted for the spaghetti pot months earlier when the hose was this close. I guess it seemed the right thing to do at the time. I set the trashcan under the tree to catch the fallen hive and took my position.

MISSING PINE PARK

Standing to the side, I put the hose's nozzle on stream and shot it at the beehive. The surrounding leaves protected the hive, but I succeeded in pissing off a few bees; my attack had to come in waves as I was often running for my life. No bee wants to live in a wet mummy; they would rather sting a fat kid. We'd put toothpaste on bee stings, so after several Crest applications, it dawned on me that I needed more distance in my attack.

With little success, I tried the pool skimmer and a broom handle nailed to a two-by-four. I needed something smaller but tough enough to do the job. I could never toss David that high, so I chose my favorite object in the entire free world, a baseball.

My father had taught me well as I was extremely accurate with a baseball. I went to the other side of the yard, wound up and threw my best fastball at the hive. I was sure I was going to throw a strike, but without a catcher, I hadn't planned on the ball's trajectory. The thumping sound was alarming as my pitch slammed into the side of the Bells' house. Oops! I not only missed the hive, but the ball flew thirty yards beyond it and dented their brand new white aluminum siding.

I retrieved my ball from their bushes in a stealth manner and pitched it again from the Bells' yard. I guess I wasn't as accurate as I thought I was as the ball cleared my yard and the Hudsons' yard then started rolling up Uxbridge Road towards the tunnel. Eventually, after a four-inning game, I finally struck the beehive. Through a mess of buzzing and queen bee-sized chaos, the beehive fell straight down and landed in the trashcan. *Bulls-eye!*

I waited about an hour until the party had died down and placed the lid back on. In my eyes, I should've definitely been raised to hero status; I couldn't wait to tell my family. Unfortunately, they found out before I could brag to them. While I was out playing, my mother decided to take out the trash. Needless to say, we needed more Crest.

MAN SLAUGHTER

I'm sure by now you realize that if you were to jump into the *Way Back Machine,* you will see and experience some pretty cool things even though we have no electronic devices nor do we have money to buy news toys, and high definition television doesn't exist yet. In fact, we have only four channels. Unless you wrap extra aluminum foil on the TV's rabbit ears and balance in a certain position, you might be able to get in a fifth, Washington, DC's WTTG. On most days we use creative means and our imaginations for amusement.

The toys that we did play with have probably been outlawed today, which is a shame because I think every kid should have the pleasure of playing with lawn darts, don't you? What a concept this game had. It resembled horseshoes, but, instead of a post, rings were placed upon the ground and instead of tossing shoes, you threw big-ass, heavy darts. I mean, they had actually measured two feet long and were heavy enough to penetrate a human skull, and they were a children's game! We used to throw those suckers forty feet into the air just to see how deep they would penetrate the ground. Oops, hit the water main, sorry. Now that was entertainment!

One day while sitting under the Millers' weeping willow tree, waiting for Buddy to come outside, Tony, Fitz and I were trying to think of all the dirty phrases we could make out of the initials STP. STP stood for a company that made fuel and additives; it was made popular by the racecar industry. There were red, white and blue STP stickers on just about every speed limit sign in Carney.

When that got old, we started discussing the need for inventing a new game. At any given time of the day, a game of baseball, football or basketball could be launched into action, so sport paraphernalia was always strewn about in the Millers' yard.

The normal routine just wasn't on the menu that day, as we desired to play something different. When Tony went up to see what was keeping Buddy, Buddy suddenly emerged. He was obviously mad about something. At the bottom of the stairs, he picked up a baseball bat and starting swinging wildly as he walked. He had successfully knocked everything out of his path when he happened upon a soccer ball. When he hit it with the bat, it shot off like a rocket and hit Tony right in the back of his head. His brother literally did an entire flip as he walked and landed on his face. I just about peed myself laughing.

Within fifteen minutes, we were all sitting together at their picnic table with pencil and paper in hand, writing the rules for our newly invented game, which we simply called "bat soccer." We had aspirations of contacting a bigwig at Mattel, who would, of course, jump at the opportunity we were offering and make us millionaires. Until we found that person, bat soccer became the game of the day to play. Similar to the game of tag, the players were divided into teams; dissimilar to the game of tag, everybody held a Louisville Slugger. You couldn't touch the ball with your body, and if it hit you, well, of course you were out...or dead. They should incorporate some of those rules into the World Cup. The scores would definitely go up and so would the casualties, I guess.

Years later, I came up with an even cooler game which only contained one special implement, a Hoppity Hop. You should Google them to see the giant-sized, red bouncy ball, complete with a handle to hold onto while you sit upon it. Take my word for it; these were extremely hilarious toys. They were designed as a vehicle on which you would hop around. My parents had bought one for Karen, who used to hop all over the place with it. My dad and I would play catch in the backyard as she happily hopped all around us. However, our purpose with it was to use it as a weapon.

We'd start the game by standing in a circle while somebody launched the Hoppity Hop as high as they could, straight up into the air. The person who apprehended the ball tried to tag the others as they ran for their lives. The real fun was in the tagging. There was pure hilarity involved with watching someone, who was running at a full gallop, get hit with a big rubber ball that could support up to three hundred pounds.

I was a sure shot and could hit some kid in the back of the knees, sending them flying through the air while having the ball bounce directly back to me. Once when Tony was running from me, I hit him so hard he catapulted off the singed tree in my front yard, leaving a perfect mouth ring of drool where his sharp teeth penetrated the bark. The name of this game was "man slaughter," and we used to play it in my yard after school before dinner.

Every day I would successfully "kill" about twenty-five neighborhood kids. The game was short-lived though because Brucie Green tried to fend off the giant red ball once by jamming a bucket from our sandbox onto his head. Unfortunately for him, the bucket got stuck there, and he had to wear it home. His explanation brought the local CSI detectives right to the wet ring on our singed, and now dented, tree. The ball was promptly deflated.

184.5

I loved spending time in the great outdoors. There were many times when I would just lie upon our picnic table and stare up at the sky, breathing in the moment. I would gaze at the moving clouds, the changing leaves and the glittery stars for hours. As a result, I became keenly aware of nature's signs. I acutely observed and learned to read what was happening in my surroundings. Clouds at higher levels move slower like trucks on the highway, while clouds closer to the ground speed by like sports cars. I learned that night blindness is when you have to look to the right or left of an object to actually be able to see it in the sky; if looking directly at it, it disappears. Making these kinds of observations is one of the reasons I also loved to go camping, the perfect time to enjoy the wondrous night sky.

We would pitch a tent in the backyard and sleep out there for days at a time. I used to imagine I was a yeoman farmer and wondered what I would do if, by chance, I was forced to become solely responsible for making everything, from the house I lived in to the food I ate and to the soap I cleaned my clothes with. I was infatuated with American history and wondered what people before me thought when they looked up at the stars. I wasn't sure if I believed in reincarnation, but I was drawn to the period of the late 1800s, not like *Little House on the Prairie,* more like *Ponderosa* or *Open Range.*

When a jet airplane slowly divided the sky, I looked at its fading trail and thought about the people on board and where they were going. It helped to strengthen my imagination and to build my yearning to find out why things happened.

I joined Boy Scouts to fulfill my need for knowledge, but learned how to tie knots instead. The first troop I was in was Troop 442 out of Christus Victor on Harford Road. We met for two hours every Friday night. The troop was small, but we had fun and went camping a lot. The SPL or Senior Patrol Leader was George Westfall who lived right next door to the Adolphsons on Joppa Road. The troop also included Doug and Will Stapleton, John Gerdeman, Wayne Mahaffey and Brian and Kevin Harper, with whom I became great friends.

Wayne was hilarious and stood out in my memory from the time when he and John Lathroum debated on stage at Carney Elementary. They were running for student government president, and Wayne had the crowd laughing during John's speech. On Election Day I voted for the comedian. He lost.

We used to camp on the Westfalls' family property which was down Harford Road, beyond the Gunpowder River. There was a haunted barn nearby which always had me wetting the bed, if that was even a problem for me. By the way, wetting the bed and wetting the sleeping bag are two completely different animals. Since there were others in the tent when I woke up, I had to fake a canteen spill to cover my nocturnal enuresis.

In Scouts we were training for survival camp by learning cool things like how to make fire with a Brillo Pad and a nine-volt battery. It works. The scout leaders were planning to drop us off on a Friday; we didn't have a scheduled meal until Sunday afternoon. *What?* They themselves had all kinds of events planned, but all we could do was forage for food. We dug up sassafras roots to make tea, we set up traps for catching big game and we attempted to fish. I had never been so hungry in my life!

Will Stapleton had disappeared for half the day on Saturday. We started to get worried until he was spotted in a mulberry bush. He had eaten half of it by the time we found him. John Gerdeman caught about ten crayfish and decided to boil them. Unfortunately, John was lacking in kitchen experience. He placed the crustaceans in a pot of cold water from the stream and put it on the fire; it never occurred to him to heat the water first. As the water heated up, it sounded like popcorn.

To celebrate his catch, John regaled us with a late night romp through the campsite. Streaking was all the rage, so he decided to give it a whirl. Fortunately for us, the Girl Scout troop on the adjacent hill was already in for the night and didn't witness the spectacle. Unfortunately, we had to borrow matches from them the next morning because ours were all left out in the rain. I distinctly remember the Girl Scout leader saying to us, "Never let it be said that the Girl Scouts let you down." Can you say humiliating?

I was very fortunate to have Sunil Ansari in my patrol. He and his little brother Arun had some innate knowledge of the earth that other cultures yawned at. I think they were Irish.

187

He pointed out to me a type of grass, which wasn't as green as the others, and called it sour grass. I had run over that stuff with my lawnmower for years and never thought twice about eating it. By placing several pieces between your cheek and gum and sucking on it like tobacco, it quenched your thirst by emitting a lemony taste. I was amazed, still thirsty, but amazed.

On Sunday afternoon Sunil's parents showed up to pick us up. As a patrol leader, I was responsible for organizing transportation, so I had asked them to drive. I was a little miffed when they pulled in, however, because their car was packed with their entire family. *How would we all get home?*

Sunil's father just smiled and opened up the trunk to reveal a bona fide smorgasbord. The whole trunk was filled with food! Fried chicken, potato salad, a tray of *gobhi aloo*, and, on top of that, an entire chocolate cake! I didn't care if we had to strap kids to the roof; it was a great moment, and the feast made it to my list as one of the best meals I've ever eaten out of the trunk of a car. Yes, there've been others.

On another camping trip the leaders issued each camper two eggs and two pieces of raw bacon. We had to line up and wait our turn at the troop's frying pan and cook our food one at a time. For some reason, Doug and Will Stapleton began a heated discussion about line placement, and a bout of fisticuffs ensued.

They were rolling around in the mud beating each other up, the whole time protecting their eggs and bacon. It was hilarious. We just stood in amazement and watched until it was over. I still remember Will standing there with a ripped shirt and two pieces of bacon, all stretched out and covered with grass, waiting for his turn to cook them. Sadly, there was no merit badge for participation in a pre-breakfast brouhaha.

My favorite camping trips were when we went to Antietam and Gettysburg. We would take ten-mile compass courses through the battlefields to earn patches. The compass courses were the best because we had no adults with us, and if we took a wrong turn, we could end up in Albuquerque. (Bugs Bunny reference.)

The courses were designed to teach us not only about the battles, but, more importantly, about the brave men who fought in them. We would have to follow coordinates for several hundred yards, take another reading and move on again. When you reached a predetermined destination, you needed to retrieve specific data from a monument and fill out a provided questionnaire. The questions could only be answered if you followed the course perfectly. Today it could all be done through GPS, but in the *Way Back Machine* you really need to master the use of a compass to learn about the *Way, Way Back Machine*. The *Way, Way Back Machine* takes you to a time before you were born.

Once while sharing a tent, Kevin and I sang, "Billy, Don't Be a Hero" by Paper Lace all night long. The song was about a soldier that didn't listen to his girl and died a hero in the Civil War. I used to think about that soldier all the time. He was from the same era I thought I should've been from. Learning about those soldiers struck a serious chord with me, and to this day I visit those places annually. I still haven't found out who married Billy's girlfriend.

Eventually our troop folded, and we were swallowed up by another troop who met at a Catholic church on Belair Road. Troop 746 was a huge troop with tons of kids and about forty volunteer dads. For one wonderful week we biked the entire C&O Canal. They drove us, and our bikes, to Cumberland, Maryland, and we rode 184.5 miles all the way to Georgetown.

The dads would drive ahead of us, about forty miles or so, and set up all the tents, so all we had to do was ride. The C&O Canal is beautiful and has all kinds of historical significance. The canal was started the exact same day as the B&O railroad as a race to the Ohio River. FYI, the train beat the barges by thirty years. Thousands upon thousands of immigrants dug it by hand; they also built locks, aqueducts and lock keepers' houses. It is known in historical references as the Grand Old Ditch.

I mentioned a few times that I was a heavy kid. When fat kids ride their bikes for that long, their thighs rub together in such a way that it creates a fire. I became so raw and chapped that I could hardly walk. In order to get around, I had to tread extremely wide-legged so my thighs wouldn't touch each other. My friends immediately jumped on my plight and coined my interesting stride as the "Beller Boogie." At the same time a popular song was called the "Bertha Butt Boogie," so they changed the words and sang it whenever I staggered by. By the end of the week, the whole troop was walking around, bow-legged, singing the "Beller Butt Boogie." Good times.

To make matters worse, when the trip was over and we got back to the church, my mom forgot to pick me up, so I had to ride my bike home. It took me a week before I could walk normally. I think I made it into a medical journal, somewhere under the heading "crotch rot."

I made another friend in Scouts named John Donaldson. He lived on Joppa Road, closer to Perry Hall, and his house backed up to "the flats." The flats was a mystical no man's land, located between Joppa and Belair roads. I had heard about this uncharted territory my whole life, but never ventured there. I was under the impression it was a desert and hid elements of the underworld and Area 51 all rolled into one. We decided to brave the legions of hidden land mines and security forces and camp out in the flats.

I wrote a secret letter to my family and hid it in my room, just in case I didn't return. In it I gave away my baseball cards, my glove and my chores. My family had just received a quarter of a side of beef, which was individually wrapped in hundreds of white butcher-papered frozen pieces in our basement freezer. I grabbed one that was stamped "sirloin," shoved it in my backpack and headed for John's house. We left civilization at 3PM and headed towards our demise. Foliage was sporadic, and grass was at a premium as we walked deeper into the barren wasteland. We found a place suitable for camping and rolled out our sleeping bags. We simply lay down a ground cloth in case we had to leave in a hurry. We found some rocks big enough to surround a fire, and, as evening fell, we decided to make dinner.

I pulled the soggy, thawed sirloin out of my pack to surprise John. He squealed with excitement. Moments later, though, we were both depressed because we had no frying pan. Apparently, in our haste to leave civilization, we had forgotten to bring cooking implements. In fact, we had never even discussed it, thinking the other guy would be bringing everything the other one had forgotten. I was pissed and starving, so I headed out to look for a large stick or a pipe or something to hold a three-pound steak over a fire. What I came back with has revolutionized outdoor cooking.

Partially buried in the sand and dirt of the flats was a stop sign, pole and all. I dragged it back, and to John's amazement, laid it paint-side down across the fire. It fit perfectly. After a few minutes it was sterile and glowing orange, so I threw the steak on.

Emeril Lagasse would have been jealous at this stop sign steak as it vibrated up and down on our outdoor range. It cooked quickly and perfectly, and I swear it would've held up to anything on the menu at Ruth's Chris Steak House. To this day, it was the best steak I have ever eaten. We survived the meal and the night in the flats and never had to run for our lives once.

A couple of weeks later, Kevin Harper and I were camping in my backyard when I tried to repeat the stop sign steak with a real frying pan. It didn't work and the smell of burnt meat wafted through the neighborhood. At 5AM I was awakened by a sniffing noise. I unzipped the tent and went outside, thinking it was someone playing with me.

As I turned the corner, staring right back at me was a bear. I only thought it was a bear, but it was really Bear, the Slaters' dog. He had gotten out of his yard on Alda Drive and decided to follow the steak's smell. I called Kevin to come outside while he was still half asleep. When he approached and saw the dog, he gasped loudly. Bear reacted by barking once in a heavy growling Cujo-sort-of-way. Kevin elevated his body straight up, made a ninety-degree turn in mid-air and ended up in my pool ten feet away. I burst out laughing which made Kevin angry, and a war of words ensued.

We were both tired and grouchy and scared of the bear. All I remember next was that in one giant swoop, Kevin had grabbed all the clothes my mother had hanging on the line and threw them into the pool. That was the last time I camped in the backyard.

DOO-TA-DOO!

Just around the corner from Parkville Junior High was Double Rock Park, which is where I played organized, recreational sports. I say organized because we had coaches and umpires. Double Rock had five baseball fields in the spring, and in the fall, one-football field. Field number one was the first location where I played baseball under the lights.

I always think about that diamond whenever I watch *Field of Dreams*. I remember it feeling magical when playing at night. Even the moths seemed to enjoy it.

MISSING PINE PARK

In the **Way Back Machine** our team meets at Parkville Shopping Center for the baseball parades. During the parade you find colorful floats and hear loud music; all the sports teams are dressed in full uniform. We walk in a big procession to Double Rock Park to officially start the season. The shopkeepers and townspeople line the streets and wave to us. It is a big deal and makes me feel very special.

I remember passing The First National Grape, which was a clothing store, The Colony Theatre, George's Market and my favorite sub shop in Parkville, Palmisano's.

During the summer I spent two to three evenings a week at Double Rock playing baseball. Next to field number one stood a snowball stand, and after every game we won, we would sprint to it for a congratulatory snowball. I always remember the coaches telling us we ran harder to get a snowball than we did during the game. In today's economy it would cost the coach forty bucks a game in snowballs. That's why they invented sunflower seeds.

Saying that baseball was important to me was a major understatement. I carried my glove with me everywhere I went and even slept with it under my mattress to soften the leather.

My dad wore his baseball hat with both sides of the brim bent down, almost like side blinders, so, naturally, I did the same. By the way, a proper baseball hat is a fitted one and has a size in it like five and a quarter and doesn't have Velcro or an adjustable back. Those are fishing hats and should be worn by old men in rowboats.

I followed the Orioles religiously and could even spell the catcher's name, Andy Etchebarren. Statistics flew out of my mouth with perfection and enthusiasm, and I bled orange and black. Heaven visited me in an interesting way one summer when I found out that Mr. Chandler, who lived in the second to last house on Uxbridge Road, was an usher at Memorial Stadium. Holy cow! He actually worked at the corner of 33rd and Ellerslie!

He very kindly offered me admission to any home game I'd like to go to as long as I was standing by my mailbox at five o'clock. I went to every single game I could. If I wasn't playing baseball myself, I was attending an Orioles game. He worked section thirty-five, which was right alongside of the visitors' dugout. In the **Way Back Machine** the Orioles' dugout is located on the third base side.

The games were never sold out, so he would plop me down, and if someone showed up with a ticket for that particular seat, he would move me to another. We would get there during batting practice when baseballs were being fouled off everywhere, so I usually went home with one or two balls. Hot dogs cost forty cents, a soda was twenty-five cents and so was popcorn. I would bring a dollar with me and come home with change. Imagine that! Popcorn was served in a triangular paper cone that doubled as a "doo-ta-doo" when you were finished eating from it. By placing the small end to your mouth and yelling "Doo-ta-doo!" the sound would be amplified. Empty wrapping paper tubes can perform the same task with perfection.

The first time I heard the blare of excited trumpets signaling the cavalry, I jumped up out of my seat to look for the horses. When the whole stadium yelled, "CHARGE!" in unison afterwards, I laughed out loud. From that second on I yelled, "CHARGE!" through many a spent popcorn holder.

One summer I attended at least thirty-five games. When a game was over, we would hop the fence and leave through the visitors' dugout. It was magical for me, and I loved going to the games. Looking back, my parents never even batted an eye. I would just yell to my mom, "I'm going to the game," leave the house with my glove and climb into a stranger's car to head downtown. Who does that anymore?

Going to the games with Mr. Chandler was fun, however, nothing beats my first time at the stadium. I remember holding my dad's hand and walking up the ramp, observing the bright green grass for the first time. The field was pristine, and, once inside, I stood there open-mouthed and took in all the giant features of Memorial Stadium. He would talk to me throughout the whole game, explaining and teaching me everything about the glorious game of baseball.

Mr. Chandler was nice, but he was working, so I sat alone. During one game all the midshipmen from Annapolis filled the entire mezzanine level, and before the game, players starting lobbing balls up to them. It was so neat to see all the white uniforms and how happy they were to be there.

Before it became a crime, the men from D-CUP worked for the Stadium Authority and invented Bat Day. Some genius in marketing came up with the idea to give each fan a thirty-inch wooden baseball bat. The usher of your section gave you a coupon, and you went to a pre-selected area and exchanged it for an authentic, wooden baseball bat.

Thousands and thousands of bats at a time would be banging into the concrete of Memorial Stadium in unison to cheer on our team. It would have been an awesome experience if I hadn't been robbed. Mr. Chandler gave me five coupons, and I came back with nothing. Three kids mugged me on the concourse and took them right out of my hands. I stood there motionless, experiencing what real life felt like, and it sucked. I can't even imagine the crime scene that Bat Day would create today. They would certainly have to change the name to Weapon Day.

When my own season started, I used to get excited around four-thirty in the afternoon because it was time to get ready for the game. Once while I was putting on my uniform with the big Rittenhouse Fuel patch on the back, my mother walked in and informed me that I wouldn't be playing baseball that night; she was without a car. *What? No car? How the hell did that happen?* I pitched a fit. I mean the team needed me.

My poor mother was becoming sick of baseball. Earlier in the year, in an unprecedented event, the umpire cleared the bleachers and made all the mothers leave the field. They were really on him that time and dropped all kinds of funny expressions such as:

"Shake your head; your eyeballs are stuck."

"Hey, ump, you are missing a great game."

"If you had one more eye, you'd be a cyclops."

He had heard enough, so he called time out and threw them all out of the game!

It was totally embarrassing for us as we watched the group of mouthy mothers exit the field. To make matters worse, they sat in their parked cars on the street continuing to yell at him. I'm sure she was mortified at her forced removal from Double Rock Park and never wanted to go back, but I needed to be there.

As I sat in my room sulking, she came up with a plan. My mom was very resourceful, and about ten minutes later I heard a car beeping its horn. She found me a ride! I scurried through the house to meet her at the front door to see who was driving me. In front of our home, I saw a light blue car with Jimmy's Cab painted on the side. I had never been inside a taxicab before and had no idea who Jimmy even was. My mother handed me two dollars and watched as I walked down the sidewalk in my uniform and cleats and climbed into the backseat of the cab.

On our way to Double Rock Park, we stopped and picked up three other people. Nobody spoke a word. I had no idea who they were or where they were going. Clearly, I was the most important person in the car and made it known that I should be dropped off first. They ignored me as I was dropped off last. I sprinted from the parking lot, down the big stairs, across the stream and up the big stairs to field number two only to find out that the other team had forfeited the game due to not having enough players. I never told my mother.

One year, I decided to take a stab at playing football. I played for Doug Griffith Chrysler Plymouth's Road Runners. We had black helmets with a Warner Bros. Road Runner on each side. We menaced the league. There were older kids on the team and some of them were pretty big. I was pretty big too, but in a chubby manner, so I was taught to be an offensive tackle. My role was to block other kids and generally just get in their way with my body to slow them down. My mother was totally against me playing football because she was afraid I would break something. The only thing I broke was the scale.

During practice one evening, we were playing "bull in the china shop." That's a drill where you all stand in a large, fierce circle, facing inwards. They give one kid the ball, and he tries to break out of the circle. I had never seen that drill before, and when they gave the ball to Shawn Sherman, he ran around inside the circle twice and proceeded to bury his helmet right in my belly. I flipped over backwards as he ran right over me and out of the circle. *Oh, that's the way you play?* I literally survived for three minutes without breathing. Mom was right. I enjoyed football, but one year was enough for me.

Three weeks later I went to what was called Fun Center. Every Friday night at Carney Elementary, kids would get together to play and do whatever they wanted. The gym and Cafetorium were set up with crafts and games; it was a perfect place for me to show off. I loved playing hockey in the café and would laugh like an idiot. We played Greek dodge and basketball and even created a haunted house one Halloween.

During the political election season of 1972, the gym was crowded with voting machines. They were huge, ghastly things, and we were told by the counselor to stay away from them because they were fragile. For effect, he added the direction for us not to touch them "under penalty of death." Not being afraid of death, I didn't listen.

David Schauer and I shimmied behind one and were hanging out there when our ears exploded after hearing a huge bang. Someone tattled on us, so the counselor slammed a basketball into the front of the machine and scared the hell out of us. That was very un-fragile-like of him. We were promptly escorted out.

While waiting for Fitz's Mom to pick us up, I was tumbling down the front hill of Carney Elementary with a bunch of other kids. I was dared to do a backwards somersault which looked like a rather simple feat until I attempted one. As I was blindly falling backwards, I changed my mind, at the last second, and put my hands out to brace my fall. Upon impact, I instantly felt a rubber band snap in my arm and stood up to realize I had broken my left wrist. I wore a cast for six weeks and missed the rest of football season. I think my mom felt very glad that I had to stop playing football. That way, she wouldn't have to see me get hurt.

Having a broken arm made life interesting. Every day things, like putting on a shirt, became arduous. I felt sorry for myself until my father told me a story about the time he had broken both of his arms. He explained that while riding a horse and galloping to a crossroad, he had wanted to go left, but the horse had his own GPS and turned right. He started to slide off the horse and noticed a huge signpost in the way, so my father crossed his arms to brace for its impact.

I couldn't imagine having two broken arms. After thinking about it for a minute I asked, "How did you go to the bathroom?" Without missing a beat he replied, "You find out who your friends are."

I also remember that my broken arm used to itch like hell. I tried sticking long, pointy things under the cast to scratch it, and some never came back. When the doctor finally removed the cast he discovered three pens, two pencils, a ruler, a hanger and a doo-ta-doo.

THE BROWN WRAPPER

On each side of the opening between our living room and our dining room, we had white decorative shelving that reached to the ceiling. Covering a distance of two to three feet, there was also a faux brick wall made from painted Styrofoam from the floor to the shelves.

Over the years, I had just about ripped all of the fake bricks off with my shoes by climbing up the shelves. They were completely see-through, unless filled with stuff, which was rare.

One day, while dusting, I accidentally dislodged some pieces of mail, which were, strangely, placed on the top shelf. They had all fallen to the floor. I didn't see the mail clearly, however, because it was lying in the curved fold of a brown paper wrapped magazine. I carefully unfolded the bundle. Curiosity had me peeking under the wrapper, and what I saw had changed my life forever. It was a magazine with a pretty girl on the front and at the top was the word *Playboy*.

The timing was perfect, because the day before that I found myself watching a *National Geographic* special on the tribes of Zimbabwe. It was an interesting portrayal about the delicate balance between the heritage of the ... *Who am I kidding?* I have no idea what it was about. There were topless women on the TV!

It was shown on WBFF-TV channel 45, home to *Captain Chesapeake*, who was obviously off that day. I'd be lying if I didn't check the *TV Guide* every week after that. I circled anything that even remotely sounded like there might be naked women in it. The green chick on *Star Trek* was also high on my favorite female list, and how about that Audra Barkley from *The Big Valley*?

There was another show that played on channel twenty-six called *Hugh Hefner's Playboy after Dark*, but we couldn't get that channel in at all. I know this to be true because I became intimate with the TV antenna and went through a whole roll of aluminum foil to find out.

It was bad enough that I was thirteen and already having sexy dreams about neighborhood friend Paula Flanagan. Now there were naked pictures of women in my own house. I kept my findings secret for about a whole minute before telling my friends. Immediately, my house had become a stopping point after school. You'd be surprised at how many of the boys had memorized our mailman's schedule.

We wore white gloves and handled the magazine like a priceless historical document while uttering things like "Wow" and "Oh my god, look at that." I never knew that a naked woman could look so good on a haystack. My father would only let the brown wrapped goodie sit for twenty-four hours before it disappeared, so I had to be quick and stealth in my viewing.

His memory was as good as mine. He knew exactly how he had

left it, how many inches it was sticking out of the shelf and how manicured the upper-right corners of the pages were. When I walked into the room and spied it sitting upon the top shelf, all was right in my world.

One Saturday afternoon, while in the heat of an important battle, I was interrupted by a loud call from outside. You see, in our living room, I used to painstakingly set up all my army men in squads, against the wall next to the TV set. Then, from across the room, I would lie down with every rubber band I could find. After making a rubber band gun with my index finger and thumb, I'd have the perfect weapon to lie there and shoot them all down. I was in the midst of battle when I heard the familiar cry of "Gas Man!"

In the *Way Back Machine* gas meters are inside basements, and a meter reader walks from house to house to read your meter. He yells "Gas Man" so you know that a stranger is intentionally prowling around to find and enter your basement.

I had heard that they even had keys to some people's basements. On one particular day, after barely hearing the Gas Man's warning, I heard him shout a second time, so I left my men and proceeded to the back door to check it out; the basement door was locked.

I ambled downstairs and let him in. I made small talk with him, but he was all business as he walked to the meter and wrote down some numbers on his pad. He thanked me and said, "Goodbye." (Nobody says, "Have a nice day!" in the *Way Back Machine*) As I returned to the steps, something instantly caught my eye. On a metal shelf in the corner of the basement, stacked very neatly, were about twenty brown paper wrapped magazines. Thank you, Jesus; I had found the mother lode!

Nobody else was home, so, for the first time in my existence, I spent about five hours in the basement. What a great day! It was amazing how many times I *needed* to go to the basement from that day on. I walked through it on my way to the mailbox. I looked for stuff that wasn't missing. I even decided to paint the workbench one day, which somehow required several coats. Consequently, my parents became interested in my recent motivation to paint.

On a different day, I had asked Buddy, Tony and Fitz to help me search for ghosts when the bottom fell out! Against my wishes, Buddy was eyeing Miss October and her pumpkins when we heard my mother descend the staircase. I immediately freaked out, of course. There was absolutely no time to return the girly magazine back to its brown wrapper, and so, thinking quickly, he threw it under the big pile of laundry that was on the floor. *Phew, that was close!*

To throw my mother off a non-existent trail, we grabbed some sports equipment and headed out the basement door. The idea was to return in a few minutes to put Miss October back with all her friends. It was the only recourse, so I felt satisfied with our plan.

Fifteen minutes later, we reappeared inside the basement, and to my horror, the laundry had disappeared. The washing machine was chugging, the dryer was humming and I was shaking. I desperately looked over to the shelf and noticed the vacancy of all brown wrapped items. They were gone. I immediately slapped Buddy across the chest and mouthed, "Thank you," in a very sarcastic manner.

We decided to go over to the park and hang out on the monkey bars. I was scared to death for the rest of the day. I imagined all the horrific things that my father was going to do to me, and I dreaded going back home.

Then, the strangest thing happened. Nothing. Nobody said a word to me. Nobody lectured me on the evils of looking at naked women and nobody made me get rid of the haystack I had set up in the backyard. I must have been growing up.

Going through puberty was quite an adventure for me. I knew that when girls turn into women their bodies changed and parts shifted and curves formed. When boys turn into men, however; it's a whole different ballgame, pun intended. Our voices change, and, for absolutely no reason, we get boners. Some days I couldn't even ride on the school bus. The school bus scenery had so much bouncing and jiggling around that every day when I arrived to school I sported a boner. Thank God for my loose leaf.

In high school we nicknamed the phenomenon "half a three quarters semi." When you see young boys walking around, sweating, while holding their books in front of themselves, they're sporting half a three quarters semi. It would literally happen when the wind would blow. You couldn't do anything either. You couldn't walk, you couldn't sit; other than hammering in nails, you were immobilized.

The New York garment industry then decided to add to my pubertal hell by inventing tube tops. *I mean, what the hell? Did they really need to do that?* Yes, yes, they did, and now I applaud their designer.

I am pretty certain that my father knew what I was going through because he went through the same thing when he was my age. To celebrate all the crazy hormonal signals that were being sent from my brain to my gonads, my father hung a Farrah Fawcett poster on the back of the bathroom door. *Are you kidding me?* It was the one where she was wearing a skin-tight, red bathing suit, with her head tilted back in front of a horizontal striped blanket. Not that I had it memorized.

My dad must have told his brother about my situation as well because my Uncle Wayne sent us another poster, and my father placed it right above Farrah. It was a picture of the Dallas Cowboys cheerleaders. I never went to the bathroom so much in my life and, strangely enough, totally lost interest in Zimbabwe.

NEIL IN THE MIDDLE

In the **Way Back Machine** it is called junior high, but now it is known as middle school. After leaving the innocence of Carney Elementary, I was ushered off to Parkville Junior High School and became a squire. The high school's mascot was a knight and a squire was a knight in training. The biggest and scariest memory from Parkville Junior was of the vice principal. His name was Mr. Crockett, and he scared the living crap out of me. He looked like a combination of the Agent K from *Men in Black* and the principal from *The Breakfast Club*. "Don't mess with the bull, young man; you'll get the horns." Unfortunately, I was a bull messer-wither.

During the lunchtime speed walk to the cafeteria, I was pulled over and made to stand against the wall until everyone else passed by. To make matters worse I was the designated speed walker that day and was carrying milk money for David Thomas and Harry Dillon. They shot me a disapproving look when they walked past me five minutes later and noticed me standing against the wall with "Agent C." Our lunch plan usually worked, and we would rotate turns. From that moment on I was kicked out of the rotation and had to get my own milk. I tried to explain my important role to Agent C, but he wasn't having any. He informed me that I would have to choke down my lunch on spit alone. Our paths would cross many times in junior high; the best was yet to come.

We had an art teacher whose punishment for misbehaving in class was to draw shoes. You would sit there through the whole class and draw shoes. Some teachers made us copy procedures and another teacher, named Mr. Bricken, would assign five hundred word essays. He once made me write an essay on mocking the teacher. I didn't even know what mocking meant. It sounded pornographic to me, so I used my imagination and turned in quite an interesting essay. I'm not sure if it was a good thing that I knew what every teacher's punishment was.

My favorite teacher at Parkville Junior was Mr. King. He was the very talented choral music teacher, and together with the instrumental music teacher, they wrote the school's big end of the year musical. Unlike today when a school puts on *Beauty and the Beast*, these guys wrote them from scratch. My favorite musical was called *Tomorrow*, and my sister Jan sang in its chorus. The shows were professionally recorded, and she bought the album. We sat at the dining room table and listened to it close to a hundred times.

Before teaching at Parkville, Mr. King used to be part of a professional barbershop quartet called the Oriole Four. They toured the country, won many awards, put out albums and played for thousands. When not in school teaching us, he was placed in charge of the Chorus of the Chesapeake, a barbershop chorus of one hundred sixty men. My friend, John Logan, and I received a special invite to rehearse with them one evening, and I have never forgotten it. The harmony of all those men singing is like nothing you have ever heard. I loved being there.

Mr. King was also a comic genius. He had false teeth and would slowly push them out of his mouth while he was talking. He had about a million stories and made being in chorus, somewhat cool. He was the one who told me that Edwards and Anthony's, a local store on Harford Road, sold different colored smoke bombs. *How spectacular was that?*

One very cool thing about Parkville Junior High was its fundraiser. They had something called the balloon ascension. The other students and I ran around our neighborhoods selling twenty-five cent raffle tickets for it. Then, on a specified day, the other end of each sold ticket was individually attached to a single balloon. Lastly, they were all released into the clear sky at the same time. The sky was filled with thousands of colored dots as they all soared upward. Unfortunately, many ended up in trees and antennae and the back seats of some cars. In about a week some farmer in Nova Scotia would find a balloon in his field and write in. When the farthest distance that a balloon had traveled was calculated, the finder and the ticket buyer won a prize. It was a very neat event, which continued for many years. It was stopped when it was discovered to be harmful to Atlantic Ocean seals that hurt themselves trying to make balloon animals.

I tried to cheat the system by sending a ticket to a friend in California and was sure that no other balloon would have traveled farther. I had no idea of the jet stream at that time, so, in order for my balloon to have landed in California, it would have to travel all the way around the world and 21,906 miles. *Ooops.*

I only attended Parkville for one year because the next year they were opening the very first modular school built in Maryland. It was called Pine Grove Junior High, and it was very strange. It was carpeted, air-conditioned and the only window in the whole joint was on the front door. All the lockers were in one area, and there were no internal doors except for in the science wing. The classrooms were all open format, so you could see and hear what was going on in the class next to you. You could literally write on the walls, which were orange and acted as chalkboards. All the offices were located upstairs, which meant if you broke your leg, you had to drag your ass up the stairs to the nurse. I was elated to learn that Mr. King was making the transfer, but devastated to learn that so was Agent C.

Halfway through the summer, we learned that Pine Grove wasn't going to be finished in time for the official start of school. They were running three weeks behind schedule, and nobody was sure what to do. They couldn't send us to Parkville for three weeks so they just extended our summer. *Woo hoo!* When most students' first day of school came, everybody went to school except us Pine Grovers.

The playgrounds were empty, and I almost felt guilty sleeping in. My sister Jan was hooked on a soap opera called *The Young and the Restless* and asked me if I could watch it to let her know what was happening. This backfired because then I totally became hooked.

Snapper became a part of my vocabulary, and I was interested in the Brooks and the Fosters. *Damn, what a waste of a good half hour.*

When school finally started, I was voted as class rep for the student government where we had the opportunity to decide everything: school colors, our mascot and the school song. All that stuff landed on our plates. It didn't feel like we were starting a new country, but it was very exciting. I met brand new teachers, made brand new friends and got into brand new trouble.

In choir, of all places, I was sitting next to Trish Lathroum and Diane Sadowski, who were old friends from Carney Elementary. They had never been in trouble a day in their whole lives, until they sat next to me that is. Trish had a hole-punch with her, and I asked to borrow it. For about fifteen minutes I punched random holes in paper until I had a whole hand of confetti. I then threw the confetti on Trish and Diane, and we exploded into laughter. For the rest of the period we made confetti bombs and launched them on unsuspecting recipients.

The next day, the three of us were called out of class to go to the empty cafeteria. We weren't sure why we were there until we were each called away, individually. When I was called, I had to walk down a long, dark hallway. Standing under the only recessed light at the other end was Agent C. When he breathed his disappointment at me, my immediate thought was that he had totally stolen that from my father. He asked me why I was there, and I really had no idea until he brought up something about littering. *Littering?* I guess he thought throwing thousands of fun little pieces of paper on the floor was littering. My thought was right; he did.

Agent C informed me that I had detention for a week. I tried to blame it on my mother because she had started smoking again, but regressive therapy was not his thing. He gave the custodial staff the week off, and every day the three of us had to go through the whole school picking up little pieces of paper. It didn't take too long and was somewhat humiliating, but I really felt bad that Trish and Diane were there. It was my first experience seeing guilt by association, firsthand. A few years later when I worked at English's Chicken and Steak House, I used to swing by the 7-11 where Diane's mother worked on occasion and drop off a free bucket of chicken for her. To this day she has no idea why.

My best friend at Pine Grove was Tim Crawford. We used to play a game in his basement where we would literally throw darts at each other. I'm not sure why we did it or what it was called back then, but today, in all likelihood, it would've been considered attempted murder. He was a good friend, and together we laughed a lot. We painted my entire living room, dining room, and hallway for my mom one Sunday while we watched the Baltimore Colts and Bert Jones lose a play-off game to the Steelers. Boo!

He was the very first person I called when I heard that Reggie Jackson had been traded to the Orioles from Oakland. Reggie was at the height of his career, and I couldn't contain my excitement. Tim couldn't care less and told me he would be gone after one year. He was right.

Tim taught me how to write personal letters to athletes to ask for autographs. I would include a self-addressed stamped envelope and three index cards along with a thoughtful letter. The first autograph I had ever received back was from Hall of Famer Joltin' Joe DiMaggio.

On January 3rd 1976, I proudly walked through the doors of Pine Grove Junior High wearing a brand new leisure suit. I had received it for Christmas and couldn't wait to wear it. What the hell was I thinking? I looked pretty ridiculous, as did every other boy wearing his new leisure suit. My father had a brown one and looked like Mr. GQ when he wore it. I resembled a circus freak.

Girls were developing and bursting out of their sweaters with perfect pubertal precision, and here we were, sporting enough disgusting multi-colored material to make Omar the tent maker a fine commission. I have not seen one good picture from the seventies. Not one. And I do mean not from any family, in any state of the union, not one. Maureen McCormick, who played Marcia Brady, might have had a couple, but I've never seen them.

In the ninth grade, while at Pine Grove Junior High, I was asked by a teacher to pick four people who I respected in four different areas of the career I wanted to pursue and write a report on them. Having an interest in film and television, I chose an actor, a composer, a writer and a producer.

Vince Guaraldi's memorable music graced every Charlie Brown episode I had ever seen; I always smile when I hear his iconic sounds. Agatha Christie's *And Then There Were None* was my favorite novel; in fact, it scared the hell out of me and made me fall in love with suspense. Lee J. Cobb was in something like a thousand movies, and I marveled at his acting. He was in everything from *Twelve Angry Men* to *The Exorcist*. I had been reading about billionaire Howard Hughes and his airline when I learned that he spent his early years as a movie producer, eventually owning RKO, which was an American film and distribution company. When I researched him, I learned that he produced *Hell's Angels*, *Scarface* and *The Outlaw*, all big budget movies that set a precedent in Hollywood.

After uncovering a lot of interesting things about each person and completing my report, the strangest thing had occurred. Within three months of finishing my paper, all four of the professionals I had reported on died. I still think about that. (Cue opening theme song of *Twilight Zone* "Do, do, do, do, do, do, do, do ...")

Junior high was awkward and unnerving, but I cherish all the memories from the Spanish lab with Miss Kennedy to class with Mrs. Lassiter. One day, fruit flies got loose from the science wing and terrorized the school. There were no windows so they couldn't escape. They were everywhere and found their way into everything. A huge investigation was launched in order to find the person or persons who released the pesky little bugs.

In my yearbook my science teacher, Ms. Putnam, wrote a little poem:

There once was a boy named Neil Beller.
He was a smart and funny feller.
His dimples he'd show
To let me know
At his bad behavior, I shouldn't yell-er.

I suppose she knew.

TIPPING

Every now and again, a unique thing would happen where my circles of life would interconnect. It's like when the guy you always see working at the deli starts dating your sister. When you see him at your house, he just seems out of place, unless he's carrying around a pound of paper-thin sliced American cheese.

For example, it always felt strange when someone from a different neighborhood would ride our school bus home. Everyone would stare at them because they were out of place and had the potential to upset the neighborhood chi.

My cousin Randy was a few weeks older than me, having been born on St. Patrick's Day. He would occasionally stay a few days with my family, and his ultimate goal, I believed, was to upset the neighborhood chi. He was from my mom's side of the family and was my closest cousin. All of my mom's side of the family lived in Maryland.

My mom's parents moved to Maryland from New York and initially settled in Dundalk. "Forget about it, hon!" My grandfather worked at Bethlehem Steel for thirty-eight years. His nickname for me was "Lump." Eventually they moved to Pasadena and still reside there. Whenever they visited us, they'd first stop at the Carney Bakery and bring us a dozen donuts or honey buns. Right now, I can picture the white box, tied with red and white twine. Yum!

When I would spend the weekend with Randy at their small farm on the outskirts of Annapolis, his dad, Uncle Dave, would take us target shooting and hand out all kinds of fun chores, like vacuuming the barn or scrubbing the horses. One time after cleaning up for him, he informed us that if he found any dirt on the floor afterwards, he would wake us up in the middle of the night to clean it again. I stayed awake all night, in a panic, waiting for him to bust in the room and shake us awake. He obviously learned the art of disciplining through fear from my dad.

One Thanksgiving at my grandparents' house, I was in the bathroom at the end of the hall which, incidentally, was in full view from the dining room table. I was standing sideways, and in mid-stream, when I noticed that all the people at the grown-ups' table were laughing. Uncle Dave yelled for me to shut the door, saying I was ruining his meal, but I couldn't reach the door and pee at the same time. He always seemed to bring up that story.

One very sad Saturday night in 1972, while my dad and I were watching *Arnie* on CBS, waiting for *The Carol Burnett Show*, my grandmother called to tell us that Uncle Dave had died in a plane crash. He was only twenty-eight years old. It was the very first time I had ever experienced the concept of death. My parents wouldn't let me attend the funeral, so I had my own ceremony in the backyard under a tree. When they returned home, they brought some pictures that Randy drew for me. I remember that his pictures were very funny and had some figure pointing with an outstretched arm with the caption "He went thataway." Losing his dad must have been horrible. I couldn't imagine what he was going through emotionally.

Randy and I always shared tons of laughter when spending time with each other. We would play rummy for hours and hours and together we had the biggest collection of Wacky Packages in the state. In the **Way Back Machine,** Wacky Packages are sarcastic trading cards that make parody fun of every day products like: Skimpy Peanut Butter, Quacker Oats and Ajerx. Those cards still make me laugh.

Both of my mom's sisters were very cool aunts and great cooks. I spent New Year's Eve with Aunt June once, and she made spaghetti with shrimp in the sauce. It was one of the best meals I have ever devoured. Randy's mom was another great cook and, to this day, spoils us to no end. Before going out one night, she baked a huge, three-tiered chocolate cake for the weekend. Randy and I were watching The Brady Bunch in his room when he decided to go and get us each a piece of cake. He returned with two forks and two pieces of cake; he literally split the cake right down the middle for us to share. I think we stayed up for thirty-nine hours straight after all that caffeine and sugar. Her face was priceless as she kept asking us what had happened to the cake. Randy and I just stood there in a chocolate coma, trying to appear innocent.

We used to go to the movies whenever I visited. In 1973 she took us to see the movie *Jesus Christ Superstar*. We were late getting there and missed the first ten minutes of the movie. If you have seen the movie, you will remember that it starts with all the actors driving up in a modern day bus and getting into their costumes. Having missed all that, we were shocked to see Caesar's guard wearing purple tank tops and carrying machine guns in the temple market.

When the movie ended, they all got in a bus and drove away. *What the heck just happened?* We sat in our seats until the next showing started so we could see the beginning, and then the movie made sense. In the **Way Back Machine** people are allowed to do that sort of thing.

She also took us to see *The Getaway* with Steve McQueen and Ali McGraw. It was directed by Sam Peckinpah, and is solely responsible for my career choice in television production. I still watch it once a year.

In 1974, my aunt drove us to Walt Disney World in Florida and planned to spend a relaxing week there. We were the biggest thirteen year olds you ever saw and took full advantage of our age. We stayed at the Howard Johnson's where, nightly, they ran an all-you-can-eat special for kids aged thirteen and under.

Every single night they offered a different meal and every single night we ate until they ran out of food. On the first night, after twelve plates of spaghetti, the manager came over to see what was going on. The same thing happened the next night with the chicken and then with the fish sticks and then finally with the hot dogs. I think Aunt Ginny traveled with copies of our birth certificates after that excursion. We had a great time, or so I thought, but Aunt Ginny was done and drove sixteen straight hours to get back home. We left at four in the morning and reached her house at eight that night. It took five days for me to come down off of my food high and get used to the sudden lack of calories.

The next year, we all traveled to California. The plan was that Randy and Aunt Ginny would drive out; her best friend Nancy and I would fly out. Together we would tour the country and experience America. I was very nervous, having never flown before, but excitedly geared up for the red eye flight. I sat in the first row's middle seat, having been denied the window seat by a real live cowboy. He was wearing the whole cowboy get-up; the only thing this guy didn't have was a horse. I was pretty disappointed.

When we took off, my stomach became a little upset, so, after we leveled off, the stewardess brought me some hot chocolate to calm my nerves. In the *Way Back Machine* they are called stewardesses, but, with the aid of political correctness, today they are known as flight attendants.

Ten minutes after downing the hot chocolate, my stomach was gurgling pretty well, when I realized I should have listened to the pre-flight dialogue because I was about to ralph and had no idea where to spew. I glanced to my right to see if Nancy had read my mind and found a barf bag, but she hadn't, so I glanced to my left. At that moment, the launch sequence hit blast off, and I threw up all over the cowboy. I achieved full body contact. I even hit his Stetson. I think that's why they call it Tex Mex. The good news was that I immediately felt better and I finally got the window seat.

I enjoyed California and saw everything between San Diego and San Francisco. The coolest thing was seeing Alcatraz from the lookout on the Golden Gate Bridge and knowing that Al Capone and Machine Gun Kelly served time there. I always loved to read about gangsters, especially if there were no books about Bigfoot available. When we hit the redwoods, Randy and I slid down a grassy ravine to check out this cute little stream that Nancy had pointed out. On the way back up the hill, we noticed that we had slid through poison ivy. By the time we hit Salt Lake, we were both covered with oozing blisters and red patches of the lovely, painful rash. The next four days in the back of the Volvo wagon were a nightmare.

My miserable status had only lessened when Randy and I began to find money. It started, innocently enough, after a stop for lunch. We went to the bathroom while Aunt Ginny and Nancy paid the bill and went back to the car. When we returned to our table to finish our drinks, we found a couple of quarters and thought they were left there by accident. We hit the jackpot and scored again after dinner. It wasn't until three days later, while in the Kansas City beef district, after we returned with goodies from hitting the vending machines, when they had finally asked where all our money had come from.

Needless to say, they were livid after hearing our answer. That was the day when I learned what tipping was. When they explained it to me, I felt sick to my stomach for stealing all those tips. The curious thing was that when I looked around, still feeling ill of course, I noticed that there were cowboys all over the place. Clearly, there's a direct correlation between cowboys and my weak stomach.

Before Allentown, Pennsylvania became infamous for bringing stinkbugs to America, it was known as the birthplace of my dad's family. We only saw those relatives about once a year, and the whole visit was centered on my grandmother. She was the female version of the Godfather. Not that she had people whacked at the drop of a hat, but I swear I heard her once say that her neighbor Mrs. Giovanni was going to be swimming with the fishes. She was widowed right after I was born but ran the family like the staff sergeant from *Full Metal Jacket*. She wasn't mean by any stretch of the imagination, just forceful.

She was my first girlfriend, next to my mom. She used to tell the other grandkids that I was her favorite, and that made me feel so special. She gave birth to all four of her sons in the upstairs bedroom and grew up next-door where her mother still lived. Her house was so ancient that I was afraid to walk up to the third floor for fear of falling through the ceiling. She had a dirt floor basement and an outdoor water closet. She gave every one of her grandchildren a bath in the kitchen sink and lived in that home for over fifty years. Once, I opened the drawer of her china cabinet and found more than eighty-two BIC lighters. When I asked her why she had so many she said, "They were on sale."

When I was five, I was scheduled to spend a month with her during the summer. I was treated like a king. Every day, we would open the bedroom window and yell down to the milkman which color of milk I wanted: pink, brown or white. There was a squirrel that I named Stinky who would eat peanuts right out of my hand in the backyard. My grandmother bought me a little salmonella- laden painted turtle that ran away from his bowl and hid behind a floor mirror. When I found him, he was admiring himself. I was loving life, being the man of the house; however, after ten days, my mother missed me terribly and sent my father to retrieve me.

Allentown, which was also known for Billy Joel's 1982 hit, had one of the best amusement parks on the planet, Dorney Park. There was a wooden roller coaster there that they should have named The Chiropractor because it completely adjusted your spine. The first time I ever tried vinegar on French fries was at Dorney Park, and it was also the first time I rode The Whip with my father. My mother told me, years later, that he was sporting a hangover that day, so that made the memory even better.

One crazy night, Randy visited me during spring break of our senior year in high school. I took him to a party off of Taylor Avenue. Most of the gang was there, and for some reason Mark Slater showed up wearing a World War I army helmet. Mark was always about five steps behind the garment industry and paid absolutely no attention to fashion.

One night at The Barn, Mark was wearing a pair of velour shorts. Most men wouldn't leave the house in velour, whereas Mark could care less. He was standing and talking to a group of women, who were sitting in a booth, when Doug Wann, known as Two-Buck Doug because of how much money he would throw in for a hundred dollar check, yanked Mark's shorts down to the ground. Mark was in mid-monologue and didn't bat an eye. Without skipping a beat or ceasing his talk, he just reached down and pulled them back up. Classic.

At the spring break party, Mark was in rare form, and Randy was doing his best to catch up. We walked to Loch Raven Shopping Center on a beer run, and the two of them were joined at the hip. When we got back to the party, we made plans to meet up later with Mark, and everybody took off for Burger King. There was some talk at the party to drive out to Carroll Manor and partake in some cow tipping. It was rumored that cows fall asleep standing up, and if you stood next to one and pushed her over, she couldn't get back up. They would lie on their sides and moo until the farmer would show up with a tractor and pick them back up. We decided to pass on that adventure.

At any time, day or night, on the weekend, somebody you knew could be found at the Burger King at the corner of Perring Parkway and Joppa Road. Once while standing at the counter at one in the morning and pleasantly waiting for a counter person to appear, a yellow Volkswagen Beetle pulled up, and two guys jumped out of the trunk, right next to the front door. Before I knew what happened, they ran inside and rolled up the twelve-foot Burger King rug that was on the floor in front of the registers, shoved it in the trunk and sped off. I grabbed the microphone and informed everyone that their rug had just been stolen.

Randy and I hung out for a while; however, Mark never showed up. We decided to check for him at home, but he wasn't there either. Actually, nobody was home, so we waited on his front porch. It was long after midnight, and we were already loud, but Randy was getting louder. He arched his head back and yelled, "SLATER!" at the top of his lungs. I guess he thought he would magically appear if he kept yelling.

After fifteen minutes of yelling, a car pulled in across the street, and Mr. Watson got out. He was the father of my friend Tim and was very involved in American Legion Football. He could tell you the name of every kid who ever played for him. He also threw the mother of all Halloween parties. He saw us on the porch and ran over to inquire who we were. He had just come from some function and mirrored us in inebriation.

"Who are you and what are you doing here?" he barked. We told him our story, and five minutes later, *he* was sitting on the porch, between us, yelling "SLATER!" at the top of his lungs.

BICENTENNIAL PICKLES

In 1976, the whole country celebrated its two-hundredth birthday or, rather, the United States Bicentennial. Overnight all the fire hydrants were painted red, white, and blue, and every product, on every shelf, in every store, had offered a commemorative, "patriotic" package. Specifically, I remember bicentennial syrup bottles, bicentennial cereal boxes and bicentennial clothing.

My grandmother had a red, white, and blue crocheted toilet paper holder perched majestically on the back of her toilet. If that doesn't scream patriotism, then nothing does. Entire trains, sides of abandoned buildings and cement mixers, to name a few, were all painted with patriotic colors. Using six thousand gallons of paint, NASA had even painted an enormous flag across a whole building to celebrate the occasion.

Everybody had jumped on the bicentennial bandwagon, including the United States Mint. I still have seventy dollars' worth of bicentennial quarters, and it warms my heart to know that after almost forty years they are still worth seventy dollars. Not to be outdone, McDonald's served red, white, and blue milkshakes. I think their company's cow genealogy was traced all the way back to Ben Franklin's bovine family tree.

Two years earlier, on July fourth 1974, CBS started airing what they titled "The Bicentennial Minute." This was a segment, sponsored by Shell, which came on every night at 7:59. For sixty whole seconds some famous person would explain what had happened in the U.S. exactly two hundred years ago to the day. The Revolutionary War had lots of interesting, historical tidbits of information and we, as Americans, most certainly needed Fred Sanford to share them with us.

It was a good concept, and I looked forward to watching them every day. I used to run inside the house at 7:55 and turn on the television so it could warm up. Televisions have to do that in the *Way*

Back Machine. This little dot appears in the center of the screen and slowly grows until it covers the whole screen. The sound screams static and settles in to a palatable level.

Moments later, I was learning from Jim Nabors about John Hancock's speech impediment. Other networks tried to join in on the minute windfall to teach us disco, yoga and teeth maintenance. They all failed, thank God.

Vice President Nelson Rockefeller had spoken on July third, followed by First Lady Betty Ford on the fourth. The fireworks were absolutely amazing that year, and New York Harbor was visited by a shitload of tall ships. There was a feeling of solidarity around the country... I think... I mean, how would *I* know? In my little world of Carney, Aunt Jemima syrup was now sold in a brown bottle covered with stars and the official bicentennial logo. It didn't make the syrup taste better; it just made you think the company that made it was extremely patriotic. Bull! It was a marketing ploy, and people ate it up.

There was even this guy in Philadelphia who was selling bicentennial "air." Seriously! It was in a soda-type can. You could pop that baby and smell the likes of Thomas Jefferson or something revolutionary. At any rate, it was an interesting event, and I still smile whenever I find a bicentennial quarter and pocket it. I can't wait until its value increases to twenty-six cents.

Mr. King, our chorus teacher, had written another wonderful musical, which showcased many historical events of our great nation. I was cast in his barbershop quartet that serenaded the crowd with a humorous song about having a picnic on Bunker Hill. At one point in the song I leaned out and soloed, "I'll bring the mustard." I still sing that in the shower.

For me, the most horrific part of the whole bicentennial commemoration took place in Chicago. Bill Veeck, the owner of the White Sox and master of the gimmick that I'm about to explain, decided to change his team's uniforms for the occasion. On July fourth, in a little fashion show for the home crowd, professional baseball players marched across the field behind a fife and drum corps, wearing un-tucked shirts and Bermuda shorts. *What?!?* A sacrilege, that's what!

My mother had missed a golden opportunity by not selling her bicentennial pickles. She made the world's best bread and butter pickles and could have totally made a huge profit by shoving them in red, white and blue jars. She used to slice cucumbers for days and then cook them in a gargantuan galvanized bucket that sat on all four of the stove's burners. She used a gigantic wooden spoon to stir them and looked like a pioneer over a kettle. Had I the gift for marketing back in the ninth grade, some kids in the future would be learning about patriotic pickles during CBS's "Tri-centennial Minute."

BELLE

Later that same year, we had vacationed in Ocean City, Maryland. I woke up on a Monday morning, feeling excited about the promising week ahead. My nipples were already raw from wave riding on a canvas raft the day before. However, after eating my weight in Fischer's popcorn and Thrasher's French fries, I didn't care.

We had stayed up late the night before learning how to play pinochle from my father. My cousin Randy and I played cards all the time, from rummy to crap on your neighbor, but had never played pinochle. My sister Jan and her boyfriend John were also playing which made the learning experience quite comical. We all picked up the game pretty quickly, but Jan was struggling and needed a tutor.

My dad had played cards all his life and was pretty good at any game. He even had two decks of cards with "Make Checks Payable to Neil Beller" printed on them. He had his own card lingo too, and referred to an ace as a "bullet." While helping Jan, he leaned in as she picked up a card and whispered, "What d'ya get?"

"A bullet!" she barked out. I guess she forgot that sound traveled. Randy and I just laughed. John was in hysterics. My father looked at him and said, "There's still time."

Jan was a great one to tease. She had no reservations towards people, so she never saw a joke coming. When she was in nursing school, I decided to make her a cake for her birthday. I drove down to her school and presented her with the cake. I made a big deal about how it was the first cake I had ever baked. Her friends were there, and we all sang to her. She felt quite melancholy at the event.

I handed out paper plates and gave Jan a big knife to cut her cake.

She was talking to her roommate, Diane, as she plunged the knife through the thick, vanilla icing. When she hit the cake part, she heard a little noise and stopped. Embarrassed, I explained that I might have overcooked it a bit, so she smiled and tried again. The knife wouldn't move, however. The look on her face was priceless. She thought I had burned the cake and was worried about hurting my feelings.

Unbeknownst to her, I had bought several cans of icing and had decorated two bricks. Her friends were all in on it and went into hysterics. Eventually, I brought out the real cake, but the joke worked perfectly.

Jan had some great nursing school stories. Once while on a rotation at Springfield Hospital Center, Jan tried to get one of the patients to attend an in-house function. The patient declined so Jan moved on. Another nurse made the same unwilling patient go, inadvertently placing the blame on Jan. When the obstinate patient saw Jan at the event, she approached her and punched her in the mouth. Who knew nursing was so dangerous?

A few months later, Jan gave me a tape recorder for my birthday but was absent at the gift's unveiling. My father had left a *Mission Impossible* type of message on it for her.

"Good morning, Mr. Beller. Your mission, should you decide to accept it, is to have a happy day... each and every day for the rest of your life. If you, or any of your friends, should be discovered by the enemy, you will be subjected to fifty lashes with a wet noodle. This message was brought to your sister, the nurse, who at this very minute is being punched out..." Before he could finish, my father went into hysterics, and it was all recorded. When he finally caught his breath, he continued, "...by some patient at Springfield." His laughter still echoes in my mind.

It was raining very hard in Ocean City on that Monday, so, of course, Karen Carpenter came to my mind. I agree; rainy days and Mondays suck. You can't be depressed on vacation, right, so we played inside the unit we had rented and searched all the closets, looking for hidden treasure. Around three in the afternoon, my father had discovered a "crasplunshphwift" and was excited to show it to us.

There was a canvas-covered awning out front, over the porch. Every fifteen minutes or so, it would completely fill up with rain; the weight of the water would cause one side to tilt and dump out about twenty gallons at a time onto the patio. The sound of the water hitting the concrete and the wind whipping through the now empty awning sounded exactly like *crasplunshphwift*. I hope I spelled that right. Anyway, this went on all day. Finally, after hours of asking when it would stop raining, my father informed us that we were smack dab in the middle of a hurricane.

Her name was Belle and she was quite awesome. Waves were actually crashing into the middle of the street about one hundred fifty yards from where my nipples became raw the day before. Strangers were running around, wearing trash bags, and signage was bending at will. Occasionally, something would blow by that I couldn't recognize because of its speed. It went on all day and night and then slowly tapered off as we went to bed.

Very early the next morning, my father tapped me on the toe and told me to get dressed. The sun was just as awake as I was, so we squinted at each other. As my dad and I walked to the beach, I noticed that sand was everywhere. We were staying on 78th Street at The Captain's Bridge. The road ended at a bulkhead, which you could step over to get to the beach. When we arrived, we had to climb down a twelve-foot incline. The beach was gone! Stairs, which normally led up to beachfront condos were hanging in mid-air, six feet from the ground. I tried to imagine how the renters would get up and down now.

As we walked out towards the ocean, I noticed that there wasn't one single footprint in the sand, not one. The sand was smooth, like a piece of glass. There were no bumps, no divots and no ripples. Not a single sign existed that anyone had ever been there before. I started looking for the top of the Statue of Liberty. Author's note: Rent *Planet of the Apes*.

The ocean itself had turned into a calm lake. There were no waves, no mist, and no noise. My father told me that when a hurricane comes through, it takes away all the weather imperfections and literally wipes everything clean.

For over an hour we walked the beach, talking and marveling at the power of Mother Nature. We finally found civilization when we came upon a couple of other survivors who had just been writing something in the sand. After they had passed us, we noticed that in huge letters they had written "Welcome Hurricane Belle." Before we walked away, I added the letter "r" to the end.

THE FOOTLOCKER

Before we had wall-to-wall carpeting, our home had area rugs, which covered some of the hardwood flooring. By starting on a dead run from the dining room, you could take ten quick steps and do a sock slide all the way to the front door. Although she doesn't remember this, I used to sit Karen on the floor and pull her by her feet all over the house, using her Barbie pajamas as a sled. If I got a good enough run, I would whip her past me, and she would spin elegantly across the floor before slamming into the wall, just missing the television. Pure fun.

Right above the kitchen stove was our "lone cabinet." Our mom would keep all the breakfast cereal and cookies in there as the only way it could be reached by the vertically challenged was by using a dining room chair, or so I thought...

One day, when I blew in through the back door on the way to retrieve a roll of red bang caps and my baseball bat, I caught an obscure glimpse of something through my right peripheral. It appeared to be a tiny pair of knees at eye level. I took a couple more steps before the current computation had reached my brain; then I stopped and turned back around. Standing on top of the stove was my little brother David.

The cabinet was open, and he was standing there, between burners, with his arm shoved inside of a box of cookies. He LOVED cookies. "Somebody said I could have these," he sheepishly declared. I chuckled internally and reached up to grab him down. While I yanked his arm out of the box, his hand had clutched onto about a dozen cookies, and he immediately took off on a dead run around the dining room table. I was stunned.

I took chase for no reason other than he was running from me. He had a giggle that was infectious. As he ran he seemed to have just missed slamming into the furniture because he was watching me chase him. He knew I would eventually catch him, so he tried to take a bite out of each and every cookie during his attempted, on-the-run cookie heist. Brilliant! I never would have thought of that. When I did catch him, he held out twelve cookies, each missing a bite so we couldn't put them back. Genius really.

Six months later, I was sitting in the living room with my friend Jerry Diem, showing him one of my many card tricks. He had come over earlier in the day, and we were in the park, throwing rocks into the stream. Jerry was a southpaw, and whatever he threw possessed a natural screwball effect. David was following me, as usual, and for some reason, Jerry and I moved our rock throwing attempts from the stream to my little brother.

It became a game of skill after a while, and Jerry, unfortunately, won when he hit David in the back. His throw started out way left, but then just hooked right in and...*Whack!* Instantly, we were overcome with guilt. *I mean, what the hell were we thinking? Who throws rocks at their little brother?*

I can still picture him in his green snorkel coat, with fur lining the hood, as he swerved from left to right, trying to avoid our barrage. I was crying as I followed him home, partly for hurting my brother and partly for not looking after him like my father had asked me to.

It worked out well, though, for David. Later in life, every time he would run into Jerry at a bar, the reminiscing would begin, and Jerry, through teary eyes, would buy him drinks all night long, trying to rid his rock-throwing guilt.

We had followed poor little David home to apologize. He was crying in our room, so we sat in the living room, waiting until he came out. It was an absolute necessity for us to reach him before he informed our parents. I'm sure I would've been grounded for an eternity and would've had a sore ass to boot. While we waited, I taught Jerry how to toss playing cards. I owned an old World War II army helmet that was filled with nineteen decks of playing cards. I used to dump them all out on the floor and pitch them one at a time into the helmet and keep score of my progress. Yeah, I know. How boring was my life?

I got pretty good at it and was showing my system to Jerry when David came running into the living room, carrying his G.I. Joe footlocker. He knew I was playing with my army helmet so, naturally, he wanted to play along with his own G.I. Joe helmet. I smiled when I saw him.

David adored his G.I. Joe. For a time, he never went anywhere without him. One windy day, he was throwing him off the back porch to watch the official G.I. Joe parachute deploy. It looked like fun, so I asked if he wanted me to throw it higher. We played for a while; I would hurl it as high as I could, and then David would try to catch it before it hit the ground. There were some trees around back, so we went to the front yard to launch it from there.

Unfortunately, the wind picked up and steered his Kung Fu Grip Joe right onto the telephone lines that ran above our front yard. When I saw his beloved toy hanging there, I felt terrible; when I looked at David, however, I was sick to my stomach. David constantly wore a smile, but at that moment, he was wearing the saddest face I had ever seen. I quickly apologized and hugged him and promised him I would get it down.

David sat on the front steps and watched as I tried, unsuccessfully, over and over again, to shake G.I. Joe loose. I needed to extend my arms another twenty feet, so I became creative. I taped two brooms together, using duct tape, and started swatting at the line, but I still couldn't reach it. I retreated to the backyard and grabbed the pool skimmer.

You might be thinking that smacking a low power voltage line with a metal pole would be troublesome. You would be correct! Fortunately for me, I switched them around and hit the line with the broom. G.I. Joe had remained there, motionless. I tried everything I could think of. I even threw everything I could think of. Finally, I called the fire department, but changed my mind when they answered the phone. The last person in the world I wanted to make sad was David. I felt worse than horrible.

That night, I lay in bed and prayed. I didn't pray often because I didn't want to bother anyone who might be busy helping others who really needed it, but I prayed hard that night for G.I. Joe. The next morning when I awoke, I quickly went to the living room and peered out of the picture window. He was gone! I ran outside, still dressed in my pajamas and slippers, and there, in the middle of the yard, was David's Kung Fu Grip Joe, parachute and all. *Thank you, God!* David was elated and put him back in his footlocker.

Several months had gone by since that had happened, and my hope was that he had forgotten all about it, but maybe not. When he opened his footlocker, Jerry and I nearly fell over. Stored inside it were about seven-dozen Christmas cookies! David's eyes bugged out; he quickly garnered his holy-shit face and said, "I forgot these were in here!" Upon closer examination, I could see and smell chocolate chip, sugar, peanut butter, and oatmeal cookies. Our mother had never set them out for public consumption, so this covert cookie monster did all his thieving on the sly.

He must have stored them away one or two at a time, like a crazed squirrel and his nuts. He swiftly grabbed one and took a bite. Jerry and I followed suit. They were yummy. We sat there with my little brother for about an hour, laughing and eating Christmas cookies in March. In my opinion, cookie tins now had taken a back seat to G.I. Joe's footlocker. I didn't know if it was the army-issued camo smell or the Kung Fu Grip, but they were the best cookies I had tasted in a long time.

NOTES

Every home has a communication center, and ours was the refrigerator. Its front was covered with magnets; therefore, notes of all kinds could be found there. Certain magnets represented long-term notes, some attached short-term notes and others were simply used for reminders. It was the perfect place for communication, because the second anyone entered the house, the first place they stopped was the refrigerator.

Friday was my dad's day off, and he always did the grocery shopping, so Friday afternoon was a great time to survey the refrigerator. Over the years, after gaining lots of experience in fridge surveillance, Karen had become a specialist in using the proper "recon" stance and had developed a code for the purpose of passing on the icebox info to us kids. She then barked out what she saw like a star quarterback, "Hunts, two, left, chalk." This, of course, meant: the Hunt's Snack Pack pudding could be found on the left side of the second shelf, and it's chocolate. She missed her calling as a brigadier general.

Depending on who had left the note dictated how long it stayed, what it was written on and where on the appliance it was placed. "I'm going over Bernadette's" could be written on a napkin with a crayon and haphazardly attached on the lower left side. "I need a loose-leaf for biology" was scribed in pencil on a torn sheet of notebook paper and placed in the upper right corner, while "Nobody goes into our room to look for the treasure" was penned in indelible ink on the back of an envelope, right smack-dab in the middle of it all. My father had left that particular one for us once when he and my mom had gone out. I'm not sure what the treasure was, but we made a valiant effort to find it. Recently, my mother brought out from the attic a giant box with a bunch of our saved notes inside it. To my surprise, they weren't all from the refrigerator. Her favorite one was from the Carney Elementary School's nurse that simply stated "Neil got himself caught in his zipper REAL BAD!" *Good lord, I thought I had burned that one.*

There were many notes that easily conjured up laughter and trips into the **Way Back Machine**. Some, however, definitely required further explanation. For example, David, who didn't utter a recognizable word until he was five, once wrote "Eh-ah tinkled me." Right away you would think it was a bed wetting reference, but in fact, he pronounced my name Eh-ah and was telling everybody that I had tickled him. David wasn't allowed to leave many notes, though, because one time he didn't use paper but scribbled right onto the refrigerator itself.

There was a time when we were asked to make our own chore list. That list ended up making top billing on the freezer door. It was amazing how everyday tasks were now, in our minds, transformed into money earning chores. Waking up, brushing my teeth, and combing my hair had all made my personal chore list. My father instantly replaced my choices with trimming the lawn and changing the transmission on the Chevy. Report cards also made the refrigerator, much to my chagrin. I think that in all my years of schooling, the most popular letter on my report cards was "N" which stood for "needs improvement." My teachers used to include notes as well, saying things like "Neil would rather entertain the class than put forth an effort towards learning." Nice.

Perhaps the most memorable note of all time was left by my father, which was attached to the front door and is currently framed in my office. It was a Friday afternoon; I had just gotten off the school bus and was walking down Appleton while talking to Michele

Lamantia. Apparently, my dad was trying to enjoy a nap after grocery shopping. He was hoping for some peace and quiet, which were totally rare commodities at our house.

As I approached the top of the park and cleared the Sullivans' hedges, I could see the collection paperboy parking his bike on our sidewalk. At the time, Baltimore had two newspapers, *The Baltimore Sun* and *The News American*; they would come three times a day. One boy would deliver the paper and a different boy would come around at the end of the month to collect a check. *What a horrible job.* Anyway, when I saw him walking up the stairs to our front door, I knew he was about to experience the wrath of Dad and that I would reap the repercussions. I picked up my pace, but I got there too late.

Since I had certainly seen my dad slam the door in many a solicitor's face, I was sure this kid had probably caught wind of his lack of openness, too. Still, he proceeded, right into the impending death trap. He had opened the storm door and reached his hand to knock on the front door, and ... wait for it ... stopped abruptly. He momentarily leaned in, shut the storm door carefully and hustled right back down the stairs. I tried to say something to him as he flew past me, but he was nothing but a blur. I walked up the steps, chuckling to myself, and opened the storm door to reveal a note written in all caps: WHOSOEVER MAKETH A NOISE SHALL HAVE A TERRIBLE MISFORTUNE BEFALL HIM. It was signed: GOD. I turned and walked away, too.

MORSE CODE

Living in a bedroom next to Karen enlightened me to new levels of humor. She possessed numerous, creative, hidden talents and attributes which have undeniably aided her later in life; however, in the *Way Back Machine*, I am positive she will end up in prison.

Learning how to copy your parent's signature was vital in the life of a kid. Think of all the notes, permission slips and tests that your parents were required to sign that you didn't necessarily want them to see and you'll know where I am coming from.

Our mother had a very unique way of writing her name. There

was a hitch, a loop, a swirl, a thingamabob and some other forms of calligraphy around it that I clearly couldn't figure out how to replicate. Karen had mastered it though. She could not only sign *Carol M. Beller* to perfection, but she could also add a note, using the proper verb tenses and folding the paper in such a way that would baffle forensic investigators. Had she known what it was, I'm sure she could have figured out how to duplicate DNA. I held nothing but disdain and jealousy for this trait, that is, until I needed a failed test signed; I walked into her room with my head down, ready to make a deal.

It was pretty easy to find something to trade with her, as I always seemed to have some dirt on Karen. For some unexplained reason, I would walk around the corner at the exact moment she was doing something stupid. Once, I trotted around the side of the house just in time to see her striking a match and starting a small fire underneath our wooden back porch. The fire spread rapidly, and as I sprinted down the basement steps to put it out, I noticed that she had picked the perfect, pyromaniacal location, right next to the lawnmower's gas can. *Hello! Can you say huge explosion?*

I came to learn that these random acts of insanity were only a ruse. She was very sly and would do such things to throw off my scent towards her true genius. Plus, she had even performed magic. Her bedroom was at the end of the hall. Our room was on the left and the bathroom was on the right.

While heading towards the bathroom early one morning to have a private moment, I was abruptly interrupted. Karen's door swung open; she stood there in the middle of her room. It opened without her even touching it. Her hair was teased up, and I swear ground fog surrounded her feet. She looked just like Ted Nugent. I was paralyzed. As I remember it, she levitated right into the bathroom and the door shut. She was not a morning person, so the sight of her scared me. I don't mean scared in the same way that those little monkeys from the *Wizard of Oz* scared me, (OMG!) but scared, as in, she might turn me into a frog.

Having one bathroom in a house of six people made modesty non-existent. Many times, someone would be on the toilet while somebody else was in the shower and still another was brushing his or her teeth. I don't ever remember closing the door. On many occasions, we took turns when given the task of answering our father's call, while he was prisoner to the toilet, to retrieve him another roll of toilet paper. It was kept in the hallway closet, not in the bathroom. Everybody else in the house had to do the swift-penguin-walk-of-shame, but not Dad. T.P. delivery was a scary moment too. Not only did you have to hand it to him when he was vulnerable, but you had to explain why the other roll was empty.

So, with my failed math test in hand, I knocked on her door, went inside and explained my dilemma. She acted kind and caring and wrote out my mother's name with extreme professionalism. She even added a little quote, stating that I would be trying harder in the future. I was quite impressed. I was even more impressed when random kids started showing up early in the morning; she was signing notes for them too. *Holy cow!* She had a whole forged-note operation going on. Karen was a one-person syndicate. She could replicate every parent's signature in the neighborhood. A pure innovator she proved to be, but this was far from her best masterful moment. One night while I was babysitting David and her, I witnessed another act of brilliance on Karen's part.

David had been asleep for hours, and Karen and I were watching TV. The three of us had been laughing all evening because we had chili for dinner and that, no doubt, meant hours of fun with bodily noises.

I still can't contain my laughter when I go into the **Way Back Machine** to a time when re-creating the campfire scene from *Blazing Saddles* is an everyday occurrence. It was commonplace in our house, upon hearing such a foul noise emitted, to yell out the name of a pie. That's right; you read correctly, a pie. I'm uncertain of the beginning of that tradition; maybe other families shouted out types of pasta, but in our home it was pie.

The last person to yell something like "lemon meringue" was the loser, of course, and for no particular reason. That evening, I was in rare form and about fifteen minutes after David went to bed, I personally lit up the room. Amid laughter I yelled, "Peach!" and Karen quickly followed with "Pumpkin!" To our surprise, we then heard a faint, muffled voice from a darkened bedroom calling out, "Blueberry!" It was that kind of night.

At about ten o'clock, I sent Karen to bed and I settled down to finish watching television. She had been in her room for twenty minutes when I could've sworn I noticed a light turn on down the hallway. When I looked at her door, however, everything was completely dark, but then I saw it again. I stood in the hallway for five minutes and finally spied a light at the bottom of her closed door switch on and off about forty times. My apprehension to investigate was enormous, as I could've sworn she was experimenting with lightning or something related to nuclear fusion.

When I opened the door, it surprised her, so she swiftly jumped on the bed. "What are you doing?" I demanded, but she just giggled, not offering to explain. I turned off her bedroom light and continued to chastise her about going to bed right away when she asked me to flick on and off the light three times, very fast. I didn't have the energy to fight her, so I did it and turned to leave when another strange thing caught my eye.

Out the window and across adjoining backyards lived the Graysons. Like the Flanagans, they had about thirty-two kids, but they were all girls, except for one boy named Jimmy. The third youngest was a skinny girl named Bernadette and she was one of Karen's best friends. The Graysons' house was dark, except for one window on the first floor, which had been randomly illuminated by a light blinking on and off. As I looked out the window in disbelief, Karen jumped up and started flicking her light in response; Bernadette, did the same. *They were texting!*

I couldn't believe what I was seeing, but felt intrigued at the same time. They had had an entire conversation with their light switches, right in front of me. Karen started translating, out loud, what their conversation was about; she was filling in Bern on our evening. After a brief display from Bernadette, she fell onto her bed, laughing hysterically. "What is so funny?" I really wanted to know.

"What did she spell?" It took her a moment to gain her composure, and then she responded "Apple!" *Oh, good God!*

MOMENTS

Every life experience starts with a moment. Whether its outcome is good or bad, the instant you learn about, say, something shocking or something beautiful, is the moment that you remember most. I picture my moments as snapshots in time. That is why I love baseball so much. There are times during each game where everything seems to come to a complete stop. The pitcher stands on the mound, about to make his delivery. He comes to a set and glances at the runner leading off of first base. The whole game pauses as they stare each other down. The batter positions himself in his power pose, waiting for the pitcher. Everybody watches with anticipation until the pitch is released. What a great moment.

In August of 1974, I spent time with my grandparents at a campground called Tuckahoe Acres on the Indian River in Delaware. They owned a small trailer; as they were both retired, they would take various grandchildren down there for long weekends.

It was a great place for clamming, and if they were running, it was all we ate. I loved clamming. The only tool we used was a clam rake, which was similar to a metal garden rake with a small cage on the end. My grandfather and I would wade out into the three-foot inlet with a small rope tied around our waists. The other end of my rope was tied to an inner tube with a bushel basket nestled inside, which is where we put the clams after catching them. My grandfather was tied to a little dinghy that held my grandmother. For hours, we would tread slowly and carefully, raking in the mud for delicious mollusks. The water was dark, so I wore old tennis shoes, which, thankfully, prevented me from stepping on anything creepy.

Halfway through the day, a horseshoe crab swam through my legs, causing me to freak the heck out. I jumped straight up out of the water and landed on my grandmother's lap. I scared the hell out of her too! We both screamed simultaneously. Horseshoe crabs look like giant water spiders and are one of the nastiest arachnid-type animals in the ocean. They have been around for four hundred fifty million years and are considered living fossils. They are wrong on many levels and even smell bad. To put it bluntly, they are pre-historic, leggy sea farts.

That evening, we were outside, sitting around the fire after dinner. It was a peaceful evening, and we had our fill of clam fritters, fried clams and clam chowder. Around the campground you could hear people laughing, the hum of Coleman lanterns and an occasional squeak of a camper's door opening or closing.

I enjoyed the fire time as the night settled in. On this particular day we were listening to the radio. I noticed I was hearing everything in stereo, and it was coming from all over Tuckahoe Acres. We were all listening to the same station. My grandparents just stared at the fire, listening, as their faces reflected the reds and oranges of the flickering flame.

For the moment, all other banter in the area had died. It was dead quiet, except for the radios. We sat there, illuminated by the glow of the fire, and listened to President Richard Nixon resign. Sadness filled the air and not because of Watergate, but because during that moment, I was ashamed of my country.

Four years later, I was sitting in Mr. Decrispino's history class at Parkville Senior High. He was an interesting teacher and known for his cleverness. He once separated Jodi Laser and the person she was talking to in class by putting his pen down on his desk and having it roll slightly to one side of the room. He then stated that the room was off-center and started moving people all around to level it out. During this antic he separated Jodi and her friend, along with a couple of others, and when he put the pen down again, it didn't move. The room was now level, and he started teaching again. She was none the wiser, and I was very impressed.

To thwart students from leaving his class to use the bathroom, his hall pass was a replica World War II land mine. It was a fake, of course, but if you had to pee, you had to carry a bomb with you to do it. On this particular day no one was leaving. When we walked in, he handed out *Time* magazines to everyone in the class. They were all the same issue, and it was titled "The Cult of Death: The Jonestown Massacre."

I was glued to it and read that magazine from cover to cover. That was the moment I realized how sad people could become. To be so desperate and lonely and follow someone so blindly that it leads to your own death is a sadness I never want to realize. When I saw all those kids lying face down in the jungle, it depressed me. It was surely a moment I'd never forget and it was painful to read about. I don't like those moments.

While sitting in the left-turn lane of the light at Loch Raven Boulevard and Joppa Road, I witnessed a very funny moment. I was waiting for the light to change, so I was killing time by watching people put gas in their cars nearby. In the *Way Back Machine* you can't spend downtime at a red light by texting or searching the web for cheeseburger sales; you actually have to observe life.

This woman pulled in, and I could clearly see that her gas tank was on the passenger side of the car, which was facing me. She got out of her car, went to the pump, lifted the hose and started looking for the gas tank on the driver's side. I started laughing immediately because she had no idea where it was.

She hung the hose back up and walked around the car and had a big "A-ha" moment when she eyed it, at last. The hose wouldn't reach, so she got back into her car to turn it around. The only problem was that she drove all the way around to the other side of the pump, so the tank was still on the opposite side of the car. She got out and picked up the hose and started looking for it on the driver's side again. My light changed, and as I went around the corner onto Loch Raven, she was still looking for the tank on the driver's side. I almost wet myself laughing. I could have invented YouTube and *America's Funniest Home Videos* right at that moment.

My Uncle Bruce was getting ready to leave and travel back to Allentown. He, his wife Charlotte, and my young cousins Matt and Stephanie had brought Karen and David back home from a weeklong visit. I was playing in the park when I was called in to say goodbye. Karen felt blue and wanted to follow them to the beltway.

We had a ritual at the Bellers' that when our family or friends left from visiting us, we would escort them out of the neighborhood and all the way to the beltway. Baltimore is completely surrounded by a highway system referred to as a beltway because it makes a belt around the city. Main roads dissect the beltway, like spokes on a wheel, and run all the way to the inner city. Some of these roads were exits and elaborate on and off ramps were built called clover-leafs. If you viewed them from a spaceship, their name would make perfect sense.

Our whole family piled in the big blue bus, and my uncle followed us up the big hill towards Alda Drive. We followed Alda to the end and made a right onto Joppa and then a left at Harford towards the beltway. As we approached the cloverleaf, my father put on his right blinker to let my uncle know to take the on-ramp. As we drove past it, my uncle followed us instead, totally missing the exit.

We all burst out laughing as they followed us down the next on-ramp and up the next off-ramp to the other side of Harford Road and then down the next on-ramp. This was where they needed to be, so we all waved goodbye as my dad signaled with his left blinker for them to merge onto the beltway. We shot up the off-ramp and they followed us once again. We were all howling at this point while looking out the back window and waving madly. My Uncle Bruce was really playing it up, like he was genuinely confused, as we started to ride the cloverleaf a second time. Down the on-ramp, up the off-ramp and back down the on-ramp, we lead the train. Karen said it reminded her of one of the patterns on her Spirograph.

Finally, Uncle Bruce and his car load of Allentown Bellers merged onto the beltway and headed home. At that moment I realized that it doesn't matter how old you get, brothers still like to have fun. It was a special moment. Nowadays, whenever I am feeling depressed or ashamed, and when I am in need of laughter or craving some time with my siblings, I think about these moments.

BROKEN THINGS

In the **Way Back Machine** things don't break that easily. We don't just play with Tonka Trucks; we ride Tonka Trucks.

Now, they are made out of sucked plastic and could maybe support Paris Hilton's dog. Manufacturers used metal and steel to make the things we used as consumers. If they used plastic, it was reinforced somehow.

I remember, for no other reason than being bored and stupid, that Fitz and I tried to destroy our Wizzzers. Wizzzers were hard, rubber gyroscopic spinning tops that generated speed by being rubbed on the floor. The faster you rubbed, the faster they spun, making a loud whizzing noise as they went. Two of them would do battle and bang off of each other until one went down. Fitz and I had another idea though; we each amped up our Wizzzers as fast as we could and then we placed them into our hair. Doing this would cause them to stop on a dime and would create a huge and painful hair knot in the process. *Oh, what fun!* We could only perform that trick twice as the extraction process was long and difficult.

All of the odd, discarded things you see people picking up at yard sales on The History Channel are things we grew up using. They remained intact and unbroken. There were even commercials on television where gorillas beat the hell out of American Tourister luggage; they couldn't break it. I admired the account executive that developed that idea. On the other hand, things fell apart pretty easily around me. I concluded that it had to have been a Bellerism.

Once while cutting the grass, a wheel fell right off the lawnmower. I didn't even run over the metal top to the septic system my father had warned me about. When he taught me how to cut the grass, he was very specific. He explained that wheel tracks needed to overlap and that the spent grass was always expelled into the grass you hadn't cut yet. Squares or rectangles were carved out of the yard, and the track was always clockwise.

Our septic system had a metal cap which you could barely see as its top slightly towered above the lawn, so I was instructed to be very cautious and not run over it. I never did that, but I did run over a rake, a hubcap and a two-by-four. Those things would never hurt our powerful lawnmower. I thought my father was going to kill me when its wheel fell off, though. I felt pretty worried, so my mother told him that I found the rake. Lucky me. He didn't get that upset after all.

Sometime during the next week, nevertheless, I took our brand new electric hedge trimmer and cut right through the grounding wire for the television antennae. I immediately thought that lightning was going to strike the house and burn it down. Sadly for me, the lightning I experienced was named Dad. We visited the basement for some hand to ass bonding.

I didn't know what the big deal was. All that lightning wire would do was transfer the one million volts of electricity from the antennae, down the wire to the grounding rod and safely disperse it into the ground. I fixed it with some aluminum foil, and, just to cover my bases, I buried eight big plastic army men and an old metal roller skate next to the grounding rod to see if they would melt or come to life. Unfortunately for the world of science, lightning never ever struck our house. Bummer.

Our father had rules on just about everything. They weren't written rules or even unwritten rules. They were things he expected us to know through common sense, like not sticking your tongue in the toaster or poking yourself in the eye with a screwdriver.

He had taken Karen, David and me on a camping trip to Codorus State Park so my mother could have some downtime. In the middle of the trip, he drove us to a convenience store to pick up some supplies; and by supplies, I mean beer. Codorus is a state park in "Pennsyltucky," as our father called it, and they didn't allow alcohol there, so he referred to beer as "no-nos." If he sent you for a no-no, you came back with a yes-yes.

While he was inside the store, Karen was holding his new transistor radio. She was about to break Common Sense Rule Number One: Practice proper retraction. An ambulance went by, which quickly drew our attention as most loud noises and bright blinking lights do. As we turned back, I noticed that Karen was crying uncontrollably. I had recently learned that Karen was extremely sensitive when I noticed her sobbing at the end of the movie *Godspell.* I figured that she saw someone in the ambulance and was upset by it until I saw what she was holding in her hand.

Karen, reacting to the sound of the rushing ambulance, placed her flat palm on top of the radio antennae and tried to collapse it, but instead, it snapped in half. Karen neglected to lower the antennae from the bottom, one section at a time, clearly a breach of etiquette which we all had been taught *ad nauseam.* I instantly felt horrible for her. My dad had a wonderful way with Karen and didn't slaughter her, but the no-no's were flowing freely later that evening to the sound of a static filled Oriole game.

When my parents felt that I had finally figured out how to tell time, I was given a Timex wristwatch. I swear I wore it twice before tripping on some loose gravel in front of the Beachs' house on Oakdale Avenue and falling onto the street. I didn't skin my knees or rip my pants or even chip a tooth, but I sure broke the face of the watch. *What are the odds, seriously, like a bazillion to one?* It shattered right over the place where the date showed through, and even that was cracked. I was toast and had nobody to blame but myself. I thought long and hard and in the end ... I blamed Fitz.

Every now and then, a perfect thing happens and nature gives you a gift. When you discover the gift, you want to keep it a secret, while at the same time, you want everybody to know about it. I guess that is how the guy felt who discovered dipping lobster in melted butter.

In the woods, right next to the tunnel, a single tree had fallen over and wedged itself into the fork of another tree. A twenty-foot piece of the tree was hanging parallel to the ground, about twelve feet in the air. If you climbed the first tree and made your way out near the end of the fallen tree, you felt like you were sitting and balancing on a huge spring. Shifting your weight made the whole tree bounce up and down and created a fun ride.

Keith Hudson, who rarely made an appearance away from his continuing "Smoke on The Water" electric guitar serenade, was right in the middle of the excitement. Six kids had climbed up onto the tree and their weight had brought the top of the fallen tree closer to the ground. Keith had jumped up and grabbed the tree with his hands and was spring boarding it up and down. The tree was bouncing so high that Keith had left the ground by a good five feet. He had created a giant teeter-totter and was currently supplying all the entertainment to about twenty-two neighborhood kids. He was holding the tree directly above his head and laughing just as hard as everybody else. I had to wait my turn due to the fact that I weighed as much as four of the kids who were already on the tree. I watched the tree going up and down and then all of a sudden ... *CRACK!*

Right where Keith was holding the tree, the weight finally gave way; it snapped in half, landing on top of Keith's head. Kids who were happily riding the tree tumbled out of the sky and landed all over the place. Other kids hanging in the upright tree, waiting their turn, also tumbled to the ground. Keith was hammered about a foot into the earth and just stood there holding his head.

After digging himself out, he ran around in circles, screaming a concerto of cuss words. Then, I started laughing and I laughed long and hard. There must have been fifteen kids involved in the incident. They were all holding an appendage while moaning and giggling. I had broken a lot of things in my lifetime, but never before had I broken a tree.

One day, when I was fourteen, I was literally caught in the middle of an argument between my parents. I didn't know what to do, or who to side with, so I got in trouble with both of them and had to run away from home. I had witnessed two neighborhood kids running away before, and it looked interesting. When they were six years old, Joey Orla and Brucie Green had decided to run away and had announced to everyone exactly what time they were departing.

Laden with suitcases, the pair walked up Uxbridge Road, followed by one of their mothers' cars. Illuminated by headlights, they passed my house and waved goodbye to me as I watched. They made it all the way to the top of Missing Pine Park before heading home. I'm sure they felt their mission was a success.

My journey turned out a little different. It all started when my mom had gone food shopping while my dad was at work. I didn't know why, but he called us every half hour, demanding that no one use the phone until he had spoken with her.

My mom finally returned and was struggling up the sidewalk with two bags of heavy groceries when the phone rang. I knew I had to get the door for my mom, but at the same time, I had also been given strict instructions to answer the call. I stood there, frozen at the door, in my indecisiveness, as the phone rang again. I moved left and then right and then I finally went for the phone. It had rung three times by the time I had picked it up; my father had immediately questioned my tardiness. All at once, my mother was banging on the glass storm door. She had seen me standing there only seconds earlier and was wondering where I had gone.

As I attempted to explain the situation to my dad, my mom loudly and furiously banged again. This time, however, she had smashed her arm right through the glass door. It made a loud, crashing sound and was followed by a scream and lots of expletives. I dropped the phone and ran to the door. My mom was bleeding and screaming at me as she ran past. Groceries and glass were everywhere. I started to pick them up when I remembered that my dad was still on the line. I hurried back to the phone and picked it up to hear an argument already in progress. He was yelling at me, wanting to know what was going on. Then my mom started yelling at me for not getting the door. I was, in fact, living my last day on Earth.

My dad continued to ask me a million questions while my mom began to call me all kinds of unsavory things. I finally had had enough! I handed her the phone, I grabbed my jacket and I walked out the back door.

Six hours later, Karen found me in the woods behind the Flanagans' house. My mom sent her to find me, and when I told her I had run away, she asked if she could join me. I eventually made my way home, ending my six-hour adventure. In hindsight, I should have waited at the door for my mother. Lesson learned: Always follow the food.

NEIGHBORS

Certain characteristic traits stick out in my mind when I think of old friends. For instance, Richard Travers and his family had an interesting way of eating donuts. Once while Richard and I were playing, we went inside for a snack; his mom pulled out a box of cream-filled donuts. We both plopped down at the table, drooling with anticipation, while his mom placed a donut and a spoon in front of each of us. I thanked her and grabbed for my donut when I noticed the spoon. I remember thinking "What the hell is the spoon for?"

Just then, Richard picked up his spoon and started spooning the cream out of the middle of the donut and eating it. *Who does that?* I took a bite out of mine, and they both stared at me like I had just insulted their heritage. I think about that every time I eat a cream-filled donut. Actually, I just did that yesterday.

The Lamantias had a swing in their basement. Upon hearing that, one would think it was a rope or a tire swing. Nope, it was a double-chained swing set type of swing that their dad bolted right to the basement rafters. That was pretty cool for a basement, but the coolness stopped when you went upstairs; all their furniture was covered in plastic. I sat on the couch one time, wearing shorts, and my bare leg fused right to it.

One day, Fitz and I walked across the street from my house and decided to stand next to a big mud puddle. It was left over from a bread truck that had parked there, during a rainstorm. I was standing there talking to Fitz, when, all of a sudden, the puddle exploded. Muddy water dripped off my face; the shock took my breath away. I tried to figure out why Fitz would drop a huge rock in the puddle we were standing next to, but when I squinted at him, he, too, was wiping mud from his face and obviously hadn't done it.

My ears helped me follow a quick cackle of laughter to the park where Joe Suess was standing, behind a tree, BB gun in hand. He pointed and fired and the puddle splashed again. He wasn't shooting at the puddle; he was shooting at us. Fortunately, we were slightly out of range. *What a knucklehead!* After we chased him down and gave him a pink belly, the three of us spent the next hour shooting at the flagpole from about thirty yards away. I am happy to report that everyone's eyeballs remained intact.

Joe lived on Oak Summit and had an older brother named Jackie. The pair of them were always smiling. Jackie loved to play football and seemed to always want to be the quarterback. During one game, he threw twelve touchdown passes to me, a Missing Pine Park record. I'm sure one of the Flanagans had earned it originally, but I can't remember which one.

I ran into Jackie years later at the University of Maryland, Baltimore County, or UMBC, where he was studying for his doctorate. We had a nice time reminiscing, and when I got in my car to drive away, I realized that I might've just spoken to the future Dr. Suess.

Once, after a snowstorm, I had been walking around outside, witnessing the peaceful blanket that covered the ground. As I moved through our backyard, I spied Mr. Ed Chadman in his backyard with Rusty, their Irish setter. The dog was pretty nice, when others were around that is, but tried to eat me when I was left alone with him. Mr. Ed called me over to him for some reason, so I cautiously walked through Mr. Herman's yard to the fence line and started talking with Mr. Ed (Insert horse joke here).

During our brief conversation, I spotted a single wire that weaved in and out along the horizontal pole on top of the fence. As we stood there talking, I casually reached out with my wet glove and leaned on the fence. Something strange had happened, at that exact second, which caused me to instantly wet my pants. A crazy force had rifled through my body, enabling me to speak in tongues. I tried to say, "What is happening to me?" However, it came out as, "Train garden moo goo crusty slipper." If you hadn't already guessed, I was being electrocuted. In order to keep Rusty in the yard, Mr. Ed had rigged up his own electric fence. I assumed he called me over to see if it was working. It was. This was the second time I had witnessed his electrical handiwork.

One Christmas, he decided to cover every peak and outline of his house in blue, medium-based Christmas lights. There must have been a thousand of them. In the *Way Back Machine* most people decorate their front door and a few windows, so to see an abundance of lights on one house is a rarity.

Perceiving his display as a challenge, Mr. Hudson, the electrician on the other side of us, put up even more lights on his house. Not to be outdone, on the following day, Mr. Chadman added a couple more strands, and then the party had really begun. Each man tried to top the other, so, every couple of days, more and more lights were added by both of the neighborhood's illuminators.

Mr. Chadman outlined every window and door, and even the pitch of his roof, in blue lights. He also made a giant frame out of wood in the shape of a star and covered it with blue lights. It looked pretty awesome, actually, and could be seen from Bethlehem. Some guys wearing Burger King crowns had even shown up and left a can of myrrh.

Mr. Hudson added so many lights that he had to climb the pole between our houses in the middle of the night to access more electricity. He eventually ran out of decorating room, so he ran a strand from his house to the other neighbor's house. I think he won the Christmas light contest, but Mr. Chadman ended up winning the prize and the attention.

One evening, when Mr. Chadman switched on his lights, he noticed that a few were missing. However, what made this crime so prolific was that they were missing from the very tip-top of his roof. He climbed up and replaced them, but the next day they went missing again. Hudson!

Rumors were flying that Mr. Hudson was climbing onto Mr. Chadman's roof and stealing his light bulbs. Can you imagine? What a scandal! I stopped by the Chadmans after dinner one night to drop off some homework for his daughter, Tonya, who currently had the plague, and he invited me in.

He exhibited a schoolboy giddy attitude as he took me through the house to his sunroom. This room had a glass wall which faced the backyard. He didn't turn the lights on, so I sat down in the dark. He owned a huge reel-to-reel tape recorder, which sat on a shelf. I noticed its reels moving very slowly. He told me to sit quietly and listen, so I did. He was chuckling as he advised me that he had figured out exactly who had been stealing his lights and had set a trap in order to catch them in the act.

He had positioned a microphone on his back fence, and presently some whispers were being recorded from his backyard. Their yard backed up to the Graysons' who had a fort near the fence. The whispers got louder, and within a few minutes you could hear people climbing the fence. We couldn't see them at all but figured out where they were by the sounds being picked up from the high-powered microphone. They made their way down the hill and were positioning themselves around the yard in various hiding places. Like a strike force team, they maneuvered through the yard with military precision. Their goal was to scale the shed, which backed to the roof, climb up to the top and steal a couple of the coveted blue light bulbs.

Unbeknownst to the guerillas, Mr. Chadman was prepared and booby-trapped the yard. Earlier in the day he hung two big spotlights in his tree. He cut an extension cord and cleverly attached both ends to a clothespin. When the pin would close, the wires would touch and the light would come on. Between the clothespin ends, he set a little piece of cardboard that was tied to a long piece of fishing line. The fishing line was strung across the ground and acted as a trip-wire. When someone tripped over the line, it would pull out the cardboard and the clothespin would close to illuminate the yard.

We waited only a few minutes and then ... *whoosh!* The whole yard lit up. I expected to see Mr. Hudson and some other grown-ups, but that wasn't the case at all. There, frozen in their tracks, stood about five of my good friends. Nobody moved for a few seconds as pupils dilated, and then, like Road Runners, they all bolted. Mr. Chadman laughed for ten straight minutes. He was very cool that way. No wonder my father enjoyed his company so much.

LIDSVILLE

One morning, during the summer before my senior year, I woke to find that it was pouring outside. And it was the Fourth of July no less. It looked absolutely miserable outside; the thought of seeing fireworks ran far from my mind. My mother had recently become a nurse and had to work until eight at night. Jan was gone, Karen was going to Bernadette's, but I have no recollection of David's whereabouts. Around noon, Greg Hoffman called me, and together we commiserated about the sucky day. I asked my dad if he could come over; he shook his head, yes, while watching *Password Plus* on the TV.

My dad owned that show. He always got the answers right, every one! I used to swear he had previously seen every episode, either that, or the producers were mailing him the answers. I sat with him, in amazement, for about an hour until Greg showed up.

He had swung by Slater's house and picked him up along the way. They had also picked up two cases of beer. In the *Way Back Machine* the drinking age is eighteen, so beer is always present. We go to Joppy's at Satyr Hill Shopping Center on Monday evenings for dollar pitcher night.

It was a great place to hang out and also where I had seen, for the first time, Jimmy Leininger do his Elvis impression. Jimmy was a year older than us and would randomly show up at various places, to jump up on a table and belt out an Elvis song. He had developed quite a following and word quickly spread of his talents and upcoming venues.

Out of nowhere, at nine fifty-seven, about one hundred fifty people would show up at Burger King, expecting to see Jimmy. At exactly ten sharp, Jimmy would walk out of the bathroom, climb on a table, perform an Elvis number and then depart. In unison, fifty people would yell, "Elvis has left the building" and then everyone would vacate the premises. Fast food managers were left, totally puzzled, with the untold myth of record-breaking French fries sales blowing unfulfilled in the breeze through the exit door.

I didn't collect Elvis memorabilia, but I did collect hats. My collection was unique and vast, and my bedroom wall was littered with them hanging on display. When Greg and Mark showed up, I was sporting a safari hat. I looked like the guy from *Laugh-in* who carried an emu under his arm. Remember him? Greg just happened to be wearing his iconic straw hat with its see-through green visor. Mark felt left out, so he went into my room and grabbed an army helmet. He loved army helmets as they matched his army jacket, which he had worn on a daily basis.

My father put on his blue Northside softball cap, and the famous Fourth of July Lidsville Party was born. Lidsville was the fictitious town where the living hat characters resided in the Saturday morning TV show, *H.R. Pufnstuf.*

As the beer flowed, the phone started to ring off its hook. It seemed that many other people were also sitting around in the pouring rain, wondering what to do, so we set up a phone chain. We'd call someone and give them two names to call, and so on. An hour later, thirty people were walking around the house, all wearing hats. The rain didn't let up, but no one cared, especially my father. He was having the time of his life and making new friends.

One vision had seared itself into my brain forever, as I was looking out the kitchen window. My father and three of my baseball friends were grilling in the rain. They were all huddled together with their sides to the house, watching my dad cook hot dogs. He was holding a ginormous, bright-yellow umbrella over everybody. And, by ginormous, I mean the same big beach umbrella that a family of seven could lay under. You know the one with the tassels hanging down and everything, right? Kevin Landers was wearing a tri-cornered patriot's hat. He was standing to my dad's left and was regaling everybody with an animated and funny story. The smoke from the grill was billowing up into the rainy sky. It was a glorious sight. The party continued into the evening.

By seven-thirty that evening, the rain had finally stopped, and a cold front had moved in. About fifteen of us were sitting on the living room floor in a big herd, watching television. It had been a long day, and we were completely wiped out but still wearing our hats, of course. My father, on the other hand, was just getting cranked up.

He ran the big grill in the yard all day long and had just fired up the hibachi on the back porch. My mother was coming home soon, so he wanted to have something ready for her to eat which screamed Fourth of July. He also wanted to squelch any issues she might have with our impromptu party, so, while waiting for her, he enjoyed some wine, as well.

He put on his baseball jacket and went out onto the porch to check the grill. Mrs. Joan Chadman was also out in her yard, two houses away. Our back porch light was on, so she could clearly see my father while he hunched over the hibachi. We could all hear their conversation as she began with, "Hey, Beller, aren't you chilly in those shorts?"

There was a brief pause, and then my father yelled back in a somewhat slurred manner, "There's no chili in my shorts!" The whole living room burst out laughing. People were wiping tears from their eyes as he bellowed, "I just checked again, and there is no chili in my shorts!"

Needless to say, my father was feeling no pain. It added to his jocularity.

When my mother finally came home, she was in a very pleasant mood for having a house full of hat-wearing knuckleheads. She grabbed her hot dog and her wine, and still wearing her nurse's hat, went up to the Graysons' to retrieve Karen. They were having their own party, so my father eventually joined them too, and my parents stayed for a few hours. By midnight, everyone had left, and I was too tired to go upstairs, so I pulled out the sofa bed and instantly fell asleep. I don't remember my parents coming home, but I do remember dreaming of constant laughter.

My father had a great way of waking a person up in the morning. He would gently tap you on your toe until you woke up. There were no sudden movements or screaming, and it was a wonderful way to start any day. I stretched my arms and rubbed my eyes and slowly sat up. My father, appearing very stoic, was sitting in his favorite chair, watching me. After a few minutes he spoke, in a very deep voice, "Did you have a good time yesterday?"

I sat straight up with my back to the couch, smiled and said, "Yes, yes I did." He paused and then slowly took a deep breath and responded, "Did I have a good time yesterday?" Chuckling, I replied, "Oh, you had a great time yesterday." He turned his head and smiled.

My dad was all about the hair of the dog, and on occasion, would walk into the bathroom with a beer. He called it "The Experiment." There was no need for an experiment today, and life was good. The next week Jim O'Neil was having a party, and the word-of-mouth invites were running rampant. I received a phone call with an invitation from one of its planners. After I said I could come, they paused and then asked me if I could bring my dad.

RED DOG

Remember how cool it felt, as a wide-eyed youth, to make a new discovery? The first time I had heard Boston's "More Than a Feeling" on the radio, I couldn't wait to tell everybody about them. I felt like they were my band, which was a feeling that continued with me decades after they'd become so famous. My discoveries were always special to me whether they were positive or negative.

When I was very young, I spied something tempting in our kitchen cabinet. I wanted it and couldn't wait to get at it. I waited until my mother had left the room; as soon as that happened, I climbed upon a chair and jumped up to the counter so I could reach it. Standing on my tiptoes, I stretched as high as I was able to and pulled out the desired box. The box was deep dark brown and had white letters spelling out Hershey. Inside the coveted cardboard carton there were several individually wrapped pieces of chocolate. *Yum!* I unwrapped one and took a big bite of the thick, fragrant, chocolate square. I expected my taste buds to scream with joy but was presented instead with a yucky bitter taste. I had discovered unsweetened baking chocolate, a very bad discovery indeed. My tongue will never forget that god-awful memory.

The aim of my discoveries wasn't just limited to one or two of my senses. My ability to make darn good sound effects was derived from my keen observation of noises. Comedian Rich Little and his impersonations had intrigued me. I liked how he had also perfected mannerisms of the people he imitated along with the impression of their voice, so I attempted that with sound effects. Many times, I turned heads with a jarring impression of a skidding car. In fact, one time while in the backseat of our car, I had faked skidding so well that I had caused my mother to jam on her brakes, believing another car was about to slam into us. If a group of my buddies and I were crossing the street, a well-timed skid sound effect would have kids running in all directions, with soiled britches I might add.

My strong suit was supplying the sounds for a fake fight. It sounded so real that people were surprised not to see blood spillage. It takes at least two to fake a fight, so I trained my little brother David to play along. I had developed three different fight sound effects. The first one was a stomach punch, the second was a face slap and the third was a direct shot to the face, which perfectly resembled Rocky punching raw meat. They each had a distinct sound, so I taught my brother how to react to each one as well. We would practice routines like Broadway dancers. Right before my mother would enter the room, my plan was set into motion. I would say to David something like "Okay, I'm going to throw one stomach punch, followed by a left and right face slap, then another stomach punch and, finally, a shot to the face." I guaranteed David that her reaction would be priceless. My mom would hear a fake verbal altercation as she entered the room, and then the choreographed number would begin.

What I didn't plan on, one particular day, was David's reaction after our fake fight. The routine was perfect and every fake punch and fake sound triggered a fake reaction from David. My mom screamed as David went down, and she started beating me about the shoulders and head. I kept telling her that it was hoax and that he wasn't really hurt. David, however, remained on the ground and rolled around and moaned while holding his "pitiful" face. I ended up being sent to my room, and he ended up eating ice cream. That day, I discovered my little brother was a sly one.

A very cool discovery came via my father when he showed up one evening with something called a citizens band radio. He kept the CB in his car and talked to total strangers while driving. Overnight, my dad had become a trucker. What a concept! It truly revolutionized our lives, and, in my mind, was the precursor to chatting on the Internet. Think about it. You are in a store, surrounded by people who you wouldn't give the time of day to, but, as soon as you get in your car, you are saying things like, "Breaker one-nine, anyone got their ears on?" Talking to total strangers within a one to two mile radius became a daily occurrence. The beltway had become a big chat room, and your email address was known as your handle. My handle was Red Dog because that was the color of the last dog that bit me.

A whole new vernacular took over my life. I no longer called law enforcement personnel the police, but bears. VW bugs became known as pregnant roller skates, and the car behind us was our back door. As we drove, we put the hammer down, and, thanks to musical artist CW McCall, everyone was looking to be in a convoy. Without CB's, Burt Reynolds would not be a household name.

My dad was on his way to work one day, heading north on Belair Road, when he saw a policeman sitting in his car on the side of the road, taking radar. Deciding to be a good citizen, he picked up his CB and reported, "Breaker one-nine, whoever has their ears on, there is a smokey taking radar on Belair Road by the Friendly's. Check your speed." My dad hung up his mic and waited for a response. A few seconds later, he got his response all right; he heard "Big Mouth." It was the cop! My dad was so proud of that verbal altercation.

My favorite discovery involved my personal ties to outer space. I have always been interested in NASA and used to own model replicas of every Mercury, Gemini and Apollo rocket. The very moment I was born, Astronaut Alan Shepard blasted into space, becoming the first American to circumnavigate the earth. It was on May fifth, 1961. My mother remembers watching it on the TV in her hospital room. Eight years later, my father woke me up to watch a man walk on the moon. His name was Neil. I was excited to read about him in my *Weekly Reader* at Carney Elementary and when I learned of his first name, I couldn't have been prouder.

If I had been smarter, I would have used the ***Way Back Machine*** to take my dad's new toy back to 1969 and ask Neil Armstrong, "Hey spaceman, you got your ears on?"

SPEED BUMP

During my last year at Parkville Senior High, the seniors had the opportunity to go on a ride-along with the Baltimore County Police. We were paired up by our public issues teacher, Mr. Montgomery, and scheduled to ride with an actual policeman during his shift. My partner was Greg Hoffman, and we were one of the first to be scheduled, so there was no precedent about ride-alongs to discuss with other students.

Prior to this, our teacher had informed us of his past desire to join the police force. At the time, the county had height restrictions, so he didn't qualify. That was totally plausible, because he was definitely vertically challenged. In any event, I was very excited about the ride-along program.

Greg and I prepared handsomely and dressed to the nines. Each of us was sporting a gun holster; I even wore bullets crisscrossing my chest like a Mexican *bandito*. I also donned my official Stetson cowboy hat on which I pinned my sixth grade safety badge. When we strolled into the Parkville Police Station and presented ourselves, the desk sergeant didn't know what to say to us. When we told him why we were there, he stared at us, in utter amazement, and hesitantly made the call for a ride-along officer.

Greg was a photographer for the yearbook, so while we waited for the officer to come and pick us up, we staged some shots for the senior slide show. I have a very strong memory of seeing a wanted notice on a bulletin board with a white plastic knife from Burger King sticking into a man's forehead. We photographed the standard police station shots, including my mug shot, me standing inside a holding cell, and the desk sergeant eating a donut.

After fifteen minutes a straight-faced, no-nonsense, policeman headed right for us. His name was Officer Bill Winters. He didn't seem amused at all by our appearance. He didn't smile as we shook hands but turned and escorted us to his police cruiser. I had never been inside a squad car, so I jumped in the backseat with extreme enthusiasm. Greg rode shotgun. When Greg slammed his door, my door popped open. Good thing I wasn't a hardened criminal. We pulled out in extreme silence, and I knew we were in for a long evening. We cruised around Parkville for a while and then pulled off of Harford Road into the alley next to Sunny Surplus.

I loved Sunnys and used to shop there for odd work shirts with names already stitched on them. For years and years, I had a forest green electrician's shirt with the name Clyde sewn on a patch over the left breast. Every time I needed electrical supplies I would wear it to Commerce Electric in Timonium and pretend I just walked off a big jobsite. They always treated me right, and I received a twenty percent discount.

Officer Winters got out of his patrol car, ticket book in hand, to check on the parking meters out front and ordered us to stay put. When he left, Greg and I complained about how much of a bummer this guy was. I was really hoping for a cool experience, and this was utterly uncool. He definitely wasn't from 7-Adam-12.

When he returned, he scribbled a few notes in his ticket book in silence and then turned to talk to us. He asked us why we were doing this and if we wanted to be law enforcement officers one day. Greg and I choked our way through a politically correct, polite response. He then asked me to hand him this odd-looking, wooden box that was sitting on the floor of the backseat next to the shotgun. I handled it like it was filled with grenades. My imagination saw it as some sort of torture device used to calm down rowdy criminals.

It measured eighteen inches long and three inches wide, and there was a piece sticking out of the bottom that resembled the handle of a wooden paint stirrer. He turned it over in his hand gently and asked us if we knew what it was. My guess was a nun chuck holder, and Greg predicted cyanide container. He responded, "No," to both guesses and then paused briefly to admire it. At that instant, he took it by its handle and began to shake it violently. A high-pitched sound filled the car *"glubble glubble glubble glubble."* "It's a turkey caller!" he quipped. Greg and I looked at each other in total, wide-eyed bewilderment. Someone had body snatched Officer Winters and replaced him with this cool guy who was whaling on a turkey caller in the alley next to Sunny Surplus.

Immediately, his demeanor changed. He was funny and talkative and started to tell us awesome police stories. We drove around some more and participated in real, honest-to-goodness police work. As we were approaching Old Harford road from Taylor Avenue, a car drove by with one headlight. He didn't notice it, but when I pointed it out to him, he flipped on his siren and pulled the guy right over. As he walked to the car adjusting his hat, he looked pretty badass. He just wanted to scare the kid, so he gave him a warning. We loved that.

We did other cop stuff too. We went through a fast food joint to order free food. We even met another cop in the Tall Cedars of Lebanon's parking lot. They did the park-next-to-each-other-so-they-could-talk-through-the- windows bit that we all have seen. He told the other cop that we were in high school and on assignment. When the other cop shone his spotlight on me in the backseat with my cowboy hat and safety badge, he cracked up.

The best part of the night was when we met Mr. Montgomery back at school. Greg took pictures of Officer Winters frisking and cuffing our vertically challenged teacher against his police car as I covered him with my drawn, fake service revolver. He was so mad when Greg slipped that photo into the senior slide show. Priceless!

We crossed paths with Officer Winters a few months later, but he never knew it. Greg and I were doing a patio job for his Aunt Judy's neighbor, near Johns Hopkins University. We needed two and a half yards of cement, so we borrowed my mom's 1971 Chevrolet Impala and drove to a concrete mixing yard near Golden Ring Mall. This place catered to residential consumers as well as professional cement truck drivers.

They mixed the cement, poured it into a huge container on wheels and attached it to the bumper of the car. That much cement weighs a ton, and driving it around was pretty scary. Greg's family also owned a 1971 Impala. Those cars were invincible; I mean, they were built like tanks. Its front bumper even came to a point. Greg and I had been known to compare their speed differentials and get-up-and-go power in a simultaneous manner that may or may not have been legal.

We took the beltway to Perring Parkway and headed down towards the city to our job site. We had a limited time before the cement set up and turned to concrete, and every bump we hit caused a little to spill out. The top was open by design, and it felt like we were pulling along a hot tub full of a thick liquid.

I was getting nervous, and as we approached the light at Taylor Avenue, we were cruising at a steady fifty miles an hour. All of a sudden, the light turned yellow on us. I found myself in that brief middle ground of having to make a quick decision to either stop or gun it. Hesitation and wavering were eating up precious time; I decided to stop. I applied the brakes slowly, but the light was approaching fast.

The heavy weight was pushing us forward, and because of the opening in the top of the container, I had to draw out my stop as long as I could. Greg was breaking with his feet in the passenger seat too, but it didn't matter; the car was not stopping. I applied the brakes harder, and, finally, the car came to a stop, right at the light, with a forceful jerk. Greg and I immediately turned around, just in time to see a wave of cement flying out of the tub and disappearing out of site. Seconds later, another wave flew out. The sound of it hitting the highway resembled a thousand dogs yacking at the same time. Greg and I displayed the *uh-oh* face to each other.

There was nothing we could do. We had no way of getting the wet cement off the street and didn't have the time it would take to do it anyway. There were no cars around, so we prayed for the light to change so we could get the hell out of there. I knew there was cement all over the back of my mother's car and I desperately wanted to remove it, so when the light changed, we were off like a shot.

As we drove away, we noticed we had left a six-foot long, five-inch high speed bump right at the light. It was hot outside and it dried in a matter of minutes. For years afterwards, every time I drove on that road, I took the other lane because I knew if I didn't, I would end up airborne. I heard that Officer Bill Winters was the first policeman on the scene of the mysterious speed bump. I can picture him shaking his head as he held his wooden turkey caller. He already had my mug shot, but, to the best of my knowledge, I never ended up on a police station wall with a plastic utensil stuck in my forehead.

CAR WARS

Uxbridge Road was a narrow, dead-end street. There was only one way to enter it, but three ways to exit it. And those were: backing out, maneuvering the basic three-point turn, or going all the way down to the cul-de-sac and turning around. Most neighbors parked in front of their own house, leaving the other side of the street to act as a community parking area. The first four houses didn't possess driveways like the rest, so those occupants always drove down the street to turn around in the small cul-de-sac before parking in front of their house. Apparently, in the **Way Back Machine** no one has mastered the skill of reverse.

Mr. Herman C Bell III tired quickly of driving all the way down the street and developed a shortcut. He would drive past the Chadmans' house and make a break-neck and drastic, left-hand, three-point turn. On many occasions I thought he was headed right for the stream. All the kids hanging out in the park when he'd come could be seen making bets on when he'd finally take a dive. (Think Five O'clock Charlie from *M*A*S*H*.)

One February morning, I walked out of my house to catch the bus and noticed the front of Mr. Herman's Chevy LUV truck, complete with front-end damage and tall grass stuck in its grill. Success! I couldn't wait to tell everybody. The best thing was that it would happen again, two more times.

Mr. Green's car tried to back itself into the stream once, but not intentionally. The big swing set in the park was across from Brucie Green's house; one day, a small group of us were hanging out there when his father came home. Their house was also on a grade, and their driveway was positioned uphill. As he got out of his car and started to walk towards the house, his car started to roll backwards. Trying to get his attention, we began screaming out his name as we scattered from the swing set, but he didn't hear us. Well, maybe he *did* hear me. I wasn't his favorite person ever since I threw a dart into the side of his swimming pool.

In my defense, we were playing darts in Brucie's backyard. The dartboard was attached to a tree, and it was my turn. I had a great arm and even better aim. When I threw a dart, it usually took some effort removing it from wherever it was stuck. I was in mid-throw when someone ran in front of me, so it was either the pool or the side of Frankie Henson's head. I opted for the pool. You'd think I would have been awarded hero status, but, no, it was banishment for me.

He finally heard my screams and ran to get his car. It made it down the driveway and across the street, but did not make it into the stream. My friends were a little angry with me because they really wanted to witness some carnage that day. I'm sure they were thinking that nothing cool ever happens on Uxbridge Road. They were wrong.

As we lived in the third house down the street, if we were doing something wrong and we noticed our father drive by, we knew we had at least twenty-three seconds, as he was turning around, to change our evil ways and pretend to read a book by the time he walked through the door. It usually worked, but years later, I found out the hard way that my father could see through the walls of the house with an extremely rare form of peripheral vision. He always knew exactly what we were up to.

A few months later, I was sitting in the house when I glimpsed something dashing by the front window. I hurried to the front door and stood in awe as I witnessed an eighteen-wheeler backing down Uxbridge Road. I scurried outside and watched a masterful display of truck driving as a massive vehicle, with ALPO painted on its side, parallel parked at the bottom of our street. I ran back inside the house to tell my dad what had just happened. He merely smiled and said, "That is my Uncle David." *Uncle who?* I had never heard him mention his Uncle David. Minutes later, a small man with a heavy Pennsylvania Dutch accent was knocking on our front door.

As he and my dad caught up, I made my way down the street to investigate the spectacle up close. Every kid in the neighborhood was out there. I was asked a million questions, only because he walked into my house. It was the only time I had ever seen anything or anyone back down Uxbridge Road.

One year later, I took driver's education classes. Paul Flanagan and I were in the same class and drove together with our instructor to Bel Air to take our test. I will never forget, for as long as I live, that on the way to Bel Air, our instructor passed a truck going up a hill, with a solid yellow line, on a blind curve. *Hello?* She broke like nine driving laws within five hundred feet!

The test was a breeze, and I was now driving. I shared my mom's car, the Impala. The car could be described as a land yacht. Things fell off it all the time, but it kept right on driving. The front seat may as well have been a sofa. Someone had broken off the key in the ignition, so losing the car keys made no difference at my house, unless someone had locked the door, that is.

When my mother got home, she would immediately park in front of the house and then when she left, she would drive all the way down Uxbridge and turn around. One night, she asked me to turn the car around and wait for her.

It was late fall, the time around seven-thirty, so it was dark out when I drove very slowly down our road. Mr. Andy Gable, who walked his dog every night, waved to me as I drove by. When I reached the bottom of the street, I started to apply the brakes so I could make the slow left- hand turn around the cul-de-sac. Something strange happened. The brake pedal went right to the floor. *What?* I was only going eight miles an hour, but it could have been a hundred, as I slammed through the wooden fence and into the big pine tree in the front yard of the Williams' house.

The next part of the incident all seemed to happen in slo-mo and without sound. I got out of the car and turned around to see Mr. Gable running towards me. He was waving his arms to see if I was okay. Mrs. Williams had opened the front door and was standing on the porch, talking on the phone. She wore a look on her face which said, "Why did you ride through my fence?" The pine tree was still moving back and forth, and pine needles were slowly falling on the hood of the car. Mr. Gable was still waving at me as he moved closer. I could hear him now. He was saying, "Stop it ... get away." I was very confused by his words until I realized he was talking to the German Shepard who was chewing on the back of my thigh. I didn't even notice the dog was there. Sadly, none of my friends were available to witness the event nor the subsequent tetanus shot. It's true. Nothing cool ever happened on Uxbridge Road.

HUSKY & STARCH

My first real job, other than babysitting, was as a cook at English's Chicken and Steak House on Joppa Road. I loved working there and met some good friends. Larry Merrifield and Gregg Curtis immediately come to mind. Larry was a year older, while Gregg was a year younger, and together we hazed every other employee who worked there, anonymously of course.

On the way to work one day, I had the new song by Foreigner stuck in my head. It was called "Cold as Ice," and it had me pondering about the ice used for the drinks at English's. It was this fine crushed ice that could also double for making snowballs. My hazing thinking ability allowed me to fill a couple of empty five-gallon pickle buckets with ice and store them on the landing, over the back door, awaiting the busboy to take out the trash. It was amazing how many times it snowed in the middle of August.

The chicken was delivered to us, already battered, and came in huge boxes. After the boxes were emptied, they were stacked up before being taken out to the dumpster and subsequently broken down. If you could carry five boxes at once, you were really somebody, however, you had to walk to the dumpster blind because the stack measured about seven feet high. There's nothing funnier than seeing someone carrying five empty boxes of battered chicken to a dumpster while it is raining down crushed ice on him. If you hit the top box perfectly, they would implode in all directions; the carrier would usually end up covered with batter. No one had ever gotten hurt. Well, maybe their ego had stung a bit. Larry was a dishwasher and could bus twenty tables simultaneously.

He used to share with us all the bizarre eating habits that some of the patrons had. I remember seeing him walk into the kitchen, holding a steak bone, which had been gnawed so precisely that it resembled a perfect

T-shaped ancient artifact. He held it up and said, "You ever wonder why it's called a T-bone?"

Together we discovered that the breaker box for the Hobart dishwasher was located in the kitchen. By turning it off, a rookie dishwasher would wonder what was wrong and walk into the kitchen to ask for assistance. We would tell him to clean out its drain at the bottom of the unit. When he would lift up the doors and lean in, we would throw the breaker. Upon hearing the scream, we would rush back, looking all concerned, to find a soaking wet employee. "Oh, look, you fixed it."

Joe O'Donnell was my supervisor; he had taught me that trick. I used it endlessly. I also remember Joe telling me, in the most enthusiastic way imaginable, about something amazing he had experienced while taking a parachuting class at Towson State University. He declared in a Shakespearean-type way that when he pulled the ripcord, it was like "God himself lifted him up with the palm of his hand and set him gently on the earth." I have always wanted to jump out of a perfectly good airplane just to experience what Joe had.

One night, I was out changing the letters on the sign when I saw a white Chevy Impala drive by. Upon closer examination, I spotted three of my friends driving my car. Word had gotten out about the broken key in the ignition, so people borrowed it like it was the community bicycle. Here I was working, and my friends were out joy riding with my mother's car. I sensed that trouble would soon be on my horizon.

One cold night before Thanksgiving, Gregg Curtis and I were driving down Northwind Road towards Fergeson Road when I decided to live out a fantasy. There was a small farm there, which still had corn growing in its front field. I had recently seen an episode of *Starsky and Hutch* where they showed an awesome chase scene involving a taxicab in a cornfield. They were riding around blindly, playing a great game of cat and mouse. I vowed that I would definitely try it one day, and that day had arrived. Gregg had no idea what was happening, as I turned left off the road and into the field without prior discussion. As stalks of corn broke and bounced off the windshield, he soon found out. "Woo-hoo!"

We were flying through the field and laughing like a bunch of idiots as we mowed down the brown cornstalks. In a moment of sudden clarity, Gregg pondered aloud the possibility of there being a big piece of machinery sitting in the field somewhere. We would never see it until we were wearing it. The last thing I needed was a reaper for a hood ornament.

Gregg started throwing unopened beer cans out the window in a panic, so I decided it was time to leave. In an instant, however, the car went from going thirty miles an hour to zero. We had bottomed out in a field of mud. When we got out of the car and surveyed the scene, we discovered that all four tires were partially submerged, and the bottom of the car was almost touching the ground. *Holy shit!* They didn't teach field extraction in driver's ed, so we were on our own.

It was almost eleven o'clock, and the cold was starting to bite as we jogged a few miles to Kevin Harper's house. I hadn't seen him since he had thrown all our laundry in the swimming pool, but I believed that he or his brother, Bryan, would help us. Sadly though, no one was home. My angst was peaking now as we each stole an armful of split firewood from their porch and ran back to the car. As I ran, I learned how powerful anxiety was. It was either that or it was my fear of the wrath of Dad.

When we finally reached the car, I started to shove firewood under the back wheels to gain some traction. I was wearing maroon corduroy pants and a matching rugby shirt. In the **Way Back Machine** corduroy pants are all the rage and come in every color of the rainbow. Even though it was cold and I was wearing cords, I was sweating like a champ.

I positioned myself under the bumper near the driver's side so I could coach Gregg through the extraction. I figured with all the adrenaline pumping inside me, I was a bit stronger so I could lift the car right out of the mud. Gregg didn't drive yet, but I told him to gently give it some gas while I pushed the car. "Okay, ready, go." Suddenly, pieces of muddy firewood soared past my face, like javelins, as Gregg gunned it. I soon learned that Gregg didn't understand what "a little gas" meant. I was officially covered in cold, wet mud and ground up cornstalks.

We found ourselves in a bad state, and Gregg knew it. He did the only thing a friend in his position would do. He left. Gregg had a midnight curfew and lived near St. Ursula's, which was at least three miles away, so he bolted. *Um, hello?* Gregg didn't hear me and took off for home. Next, I did the only thing I could do; I knocked on some strangers' door and asked them to use their phone. As I peered through the remaining stalks of corn, I noticed there was only one house on Northwind with their lights on, so I headed for it.

The family who lived there seemed very nice; however, I am pretty sure that I was the only person who had ever knocked on their door at midnight to ask to use their phone. Their whole family came to the door but wouldn't let me in due to the five pounds of mud I was wearing. From their point of view, even without a hockey mask and scary background music, I'm sure that I had set the perfect horror movie scene.

I walked around the back of their house, and they handed me the phone out through the kitchen window. I instructed them to dial my dad and waited very impatiently. The silence was deafening on his end of the phone as I spun a yarn about being chased into the field by a crazed jeep, full of bullies. When he let out a long breath, I knew I was a dead man. I had heard my father breathe at me on many occasions, but this one seemed different. This one meant my life, as I knew it, was over.

I handed back the phone and walked around front, shivering, to wait for my father. By the time I reached the front of the house, a car was leaving the driveway. To make matters worse, the very nice father of the family heard my story and jumped into his car to go and find Gregg. Gregg had no idea about the story I had invented, so I was pretty sure that upon his return, this other father was going to end me too.

I made my way through the muddy cornfield back to the car and continued to wait for my father. He showed up fifteen minutes later with Mr. Hudson and his work truck. *Oh, for Lord's sake, he had to wake up Mr. Hudson!* He was the third father who was going to kill me.

He had a winch on the front of his truck, and he let out all of it, but it wouldn't reach the car. He backed his truck into the field, about ten feet, and then the unbelievable happened. He got stuck! *Could it get any worse?* I couldn't believe the farmer didn't come out with a shotgun. If he had, I'm sure my father would have held me still for him.

Mr. Hudson called for help; ten minutes later a tow truck showed up. This guy had a very bright yellow light on top of his truck, and it lit up the whole circus. Finally, he pulled Mr. Hudson's truck out which pulled me out. If I had managed to get out of the first ditch, I would have found five or six others, as it was literally a mud bog. Through the whole event, my father was very nice to me. He didn't yell, he didn't chastise me and he didn't embarrass me. He didn't have to; for the first time ever, it was my mother's job.

She was standing at the front door as I walked up the long sidewalk. I was expecting a worried or concerned look, but all I saw was the face of a seething woman. When I walked in through the front door, all muddy and cold with a hint of demoralization hovering above my head, she smacked me a few times and started to berate me with questions. Then the inconceivable occurred. She held out her hand, and I was forced to turn over my two-month old driver's license. She told me I would get it back when I'd turned eighteen. She was serious.

For months she held onto it, until she needed something. "Here is your license. Go and pick up your sister." "Here is your license. We need a gallon of milk."

That was all I heard until spring. She would hand me my license, and upon my return, I had to hand it right back. And there you have it. My horizon had been met.

One Saturday night in early February, Larry and I decided to go bowling at Colt Lanes off of Providence Road. As we were leaving my father proposed, "If you bowl a two hundred game, I'll give you your license back."

"Seriously?"

"Sure, I have faith in your poor bowling abilities."

It was on!

I had never bowled a two hundred game in my life. The best game I had ever bowled was a one hundred eighty-two. My father was an excellent bowler and the best player in his league with an average around two hundred seventy. Unfortunately, my mother was on his team and the worst player in the league with an average of twelve. They were both very proud of the last place trophies that they'd won and excitedly displayed the horse's ass statues on the bookshelf.

I was very focused on my game, so I only drank one beer. For the first game, I bowled a one hundred forty-two, followed by a one hundred sixty-one. Larry was laughing at me, thinking I was surely doomed. In the *Way Back Machine* there are no electronic bowling scoreboards or animated characters that tell you when you bowled a spare. We have to keep track of our own score on a giant piece of paper, so if someone tells you there will be no math in bowling, they are lying. Determined to get my license back, I decided to not bowl the final game, but to make up my own score instead, and, lo and behold, I bowled a two hundred two.

Now, my father was the smartest man I had ever met and wasn't going to buy that score without a witness. Larry held absolutely no credibility due to his involvement in the driver's license caper, so I took the score sheet to the front desk where the manager signed it and made an announcement to the entire bowling alley over the PA system that I had bowled a two hundred two. I must have had one hundred witnesses now.

When I walked through the door with Larry, my father was sitting in his chair, and with a grin, said, "So?"

I was beaming as I handed him the score sheet and responded, "A two hundred two, read it and weep." My father just laughed and said, "What do you take me for?"

Larry spoke his piece in my defense, leaving for home soon after, and I pleaded my case, telling my dad the whole story. In any event, I went to bed with a two hundred two and dreamt of getting my license back.

In the morning I awoke, and hanging on the refrigerator was my bowling sheet. There was a circle drawn around the fifth frame with a note that said "Hey idiot, when you were cheating, you added wrong." *What? I paid money to sit there and cheat and because of an addition error, only ended up with a one hundred ninety seven. How stupid could I be?* Damn, I hate math!

LUNCH

I will never forget the day that my mother decided to tell my friends an embarrassing story about me as an infant. I was expecting the cute-as-a-bug type of story, but before I knew it, she blurted out that once I took the contents of my dirty diaper and pushed it through the window screen. *Okay, didn't need to have that out there.*

Besides her limited filter, she had many wonderful qualities. She was a great cook, loved to laugh and had a good heart. It might have been difficult to see it at times while she was reaming me out for not re-filling the ice cube trays, but she was extremely sensitive.

I remember it like it was only yesterday when she walked into the house, crying, after finding out that George Wallace had been shot. It happened ten days after my eleventh birthday, and she was yelling, "They're going to kill them all! What is going on in the world?"

I had known who George Wallace was and felt ashamed that he had been shot in Maryland. I tried to cheer her up by making her laugh, but she was really upset and stayed in her room all night.

I couldn't understand why that man, Arthur Bremer, the gunman, shot him in public. He had to know that he'd get caught. What makes someone turn into a whack job and get so insanely involved in politics? Why didn't he just speak his mind? I decided to speak my own mind, and, six months later, David Thomas and I campaigned for Richard Nixon at Carney Elementary School. We stood outside for about an hour and as voters approached, we chanted, "Nixon, Nixon he's our man; McGovern belongs in the garbage can." I really liked the nickname Tricky Dick; it didn't take much to get me rolling.

The evening Wallace was shot was the very first time I packed my own lunch for school. I really enjoyed it, and it became my chore for a while. I also made Karen's lunch and then, years later, David's. I took great care in making lunches and handled their contents with kid gloves.

Once, when I was running late, I threw my books and lunch bag on the sofa and ran to my room to get something I had forgotten. My mom screamed at me because she had taken so much time to make sure I had whole potato chips in my lunch, and by tossing it on the couch, I likely had broken them. At that very moment I began to understand the loving care with which she had treated us.

I created a great sandwich assembly line, which allowed me to make all three at the same time. It was rare, but occasionally the wrong thing ended up in the wrong bag, and I would certainly hear it when my siblings got home from school. When you are seven and expecting to eat bologna and cheese and bite into tuna fish, it can totally ruin your day.

When I was in high school and very busy, my dad made lunches for a brief period. Once while sitting with my friends, I opened up my bag to find a sandwich, neatly wrapped in a baggie. The pretzels, though, were just strewn about the bottom of my brown paper lunch bag. That night, I explained to my dad that the pretzels needed to be placed in a baggie too. He shook his head in acknowledgement, and I went off to bed.

The next day, I pulled out my sandwich, and jammed inside the same baggie with it were the pretzels. I guess he didn't take too kindly to my criticism.

My mom had been a chunky kid growing up, so she knew how I felt growing up overweight. When I hit the tenth grade, I finally decided it was time to do something about my weight problem. I had friends who were girls, but had no girlfriends. They all used to tell me that I had a great personality and that I was funny, which is girl-code for you are too fat to date.

My mother signed me up for an outfit called Diet Workshop. They met once a week in Loch Raven, and I was the only male in the whole place. On the first night, I got weighed-in and noticed that the room was filled with middle-aged women. Weighing-in in front of total strangers was a big motivator. It literally scared the weight off of me. The diet required that you made your own food from recipes that they sold. My mother and I cooked together and made a whole week's worth of meals and froze them. After the first week I lost ten pounds and was ecstatic. The next week, I only lost two pounds and felt a little defeated. I felt better, though, after my instructor explained that two pounds is equivalent to eight sticks of butter. Imagine that!

The diet had some cool things about it, like the requirement to eat four hot dogs for dinner. *What? I love hot dogs.* You couldn't eat bread, but who cared? Four hot dogs! Lunch was an experiment, and on the bus one day, when some older kid stole my lunch and started to go through it, they promptly handed it back when they found rice cakes. In four months I had lost fifty-three and a half pounds and literally felt like a new person.

I think my mom was more excited than I was. She called friends and relatives and let everybody know. I couldn't thank her enough. She helped me do wonders for my esteem. At Thanksgiving that year, when I walked in through the door of my grandparents', I felt like the king of the castle, and I owed it all to my mom. Moments later, nevertheless, she reminded everyone that I pushed the contents of my diaper through the window screen.

RALPH

For as long as I can remember, I had been called "Little Neil." *Barf.* It was one of the side effects of sharing a name with my father. Ever since I could walk, I hung out at Carney Elementary while my dad played softball. As I grew up, I became their official score keeper, and during practice sometimes they'd let me shag balls. Near the end of every practice, Mr. Herman C Bell III would call out, "Little Neil!" I would hustle in, grab a bat and hit a few. I looked forward to that all week.

When I look back at the critical learning points in my life, it was these men who had taught me the basics. And by basics, I mean how to cuss, fight, smoke and drink. You know, the standard staples for any growing boy.

When I reached high school, I certainly wasn't little, but my father's friends still referred to me as Little Neil. I imagine if I'd run into them today, they'd do the same. My dad played for his work's softball team as well. After seeing me play at a company picnic, some of his co-workers asked me to play for the team too.

For the first time in my life, I was playing softball with my dad. He played left field and I played left center. In softball, as opposed to baseball, there are four outfielders; that fourth guy usually roams all over the place in the outfield. That was my role.

There was an incident where during a pop-up, another outfielder yelled, "Neil!" and we both thought the other one would catch it. The ball landed right between us, and so, from that moment on, his work softball friends called me "Ralph." The whole thing was an inside joke about the way I dressed. One of the guys asked who I thought I was, and I said, "Ralph Lauren."

We weren't very good, having won only half of our games, but at seventeen years old, I had a great time playing with these men. The Korvette's team certainly couldn't compete with Mr. Herman's Northside team. I thought I could rally a team that could. I gathered a bunch of my friends and challenged Northside to a game to be held at Carney's field number two; they reluctantly agreed. On the outside they talked up a storm and declared they would slay us, but on the inside they were scared shitless. After all, they were no spring chickens. I mean, they *were* in their forties!

During the winter months, Northside would also get together to play football in the outfield of field number two, and occasionally Larry and I would play, as well. I remember that Larry had once been guarding my dad on a very muddy day. He went long on three consecutive plays, and when he slowly walked back to the line, I heard Larry quip, "I think you have one more in you," which brought forth laughter from everyone.

At the time, Mr. Herman was about one hundred twenty-nine years old, so even though we only played touch football, he insisted on wearing my yellow racing helmet for protection. Several years earlier, he had been injured at work and spent some time in the hospital. I remember it being very serious, and there was even talk of death. When he finally came home from the hospital, my dad made a big sign and planted it in his front yard. It said "Guzzlers Gulch welcomes the return of its number one citizen, Herman 'Champ' Bell III." My mom took a picture of my dad standing next to it, wearing a nurse's hat with an enema bag hanging over his shoulder.

The football banter would be racy at times, but I was pretty good at dishing it back. For all my life, I had watched these guys play softball, and now they were attempting football. The outcome was hilarious. They were dropping like flies. I mean, they would call for a timeout just to have a cigarette.

In late May, I selected my teammates from school. We all met for the young bucks versus the old geezers game at Carney Elementary. Most of the guys I picked played varsity baseball at Parkville, but there were some ringers as well. Even Greg Hoffman showed up, and to him, the soft in softball was just another four-letter word. Greg only played full contact sports, and due to his size and quantity of facial hair, he looked like a Greek Olympian. He had tried to play catcher with his lacrosse stick, but they objected after seeing him fire bullets to second.

The old men gave a good fight, but we promptly kicked their asses. My dad was impressed but didn't like losing to a bunch of kids. For a brief moment, I was king of the hill and my kingdom was vast. I would have loved discussing the game over a beer, but that never happened. One of my life's deepest regrets was never having the opportunity to sit down, one on one, with my dad and have a beer.

While he and his friends went off to the Bucket of Blood to soak their wounds, we went to Burger King. After all, we felt like royalty.

TINKERING

It's a well-known fact that taking things apart to see how they work is genetically embedded in boys. Tinkertoys were invented precisely for that reason. Mothers across America got together in 1914 and demanded that toy companies develop an alternative option for their children who were sticking their tongues in electrical outlets. Putting things together directly correlates with taking things apart. The latter is where I excelled.

I had always been intrigued by anything mechanical. For one of my first chores, my father gave me the hateful task of weeding. I need to go on record right here and say that I detest weeding. In fact, I hate weeding more than splinters and hangnails combined. Furthermore, on my top ten hate scale, it is just below burning the roof of your mouth on pizza.

When I was very young, my father would hand me the red-handled grass clippers every Saturday and send me out into the yard. The clippers resembled a giant pair of scissors and looked like they could cut a small dog right in half. This was strictly a marketing ploy and done on purpose, because our clippers couldn't cut Jell-O.

I would squat down as low to the ground as possible and hold those heavy, metal babies with both hands, squeezing with all my might. All that I was able to do was bend the grass over and wedge it inside the dull garden tool, causing it to malfunction. Eventually, I would yank the grass right out of the ground and then pull out each blade individually until the clippers worked again. I swear that weeds in the *Way Back Machine* are made out of rebar.

We had a small, wooden sandbox in the middle of the backyard that my dad made out of two by fours. It had become invaded with tall weeds, so I was given the task of removing them while he cut the grass. The job was daunting and was slowly making me want to stick *my* tongue in an electric outlet. I had just about had it when my father came by with the push mower. Due to the loud noise created by the mower, he hand gestured me to get up and move out of the way. He went right over the sandbox with one swipe of our blue lawn mower and cut down every single weed. That was ten minutes I would never get back!

When I was fifteen, I became interested in car engines. Every year, my mother would lose the heat in her car. She would walk in the house shivering and could not figure out what the problem was. After doing some investigating, I figured out that there was a problem with the thermostat. It sat in the radiator hose, surrounded by a gasket, and would occasionally lock up. In the *Way Back Machine* car engines are spacious; you can physically climb inside one while you work on it.

One day, as I was about to replace the thermostat, I heard a voice over my shoulder. It belonged to Scott Sullivan. He commented that he saw me open the hood and had wondered if I needed a hand. That was just another reason why I treasure the memories of the people of Carney, especially those who lived around Missing Pine Park. As the sun went down, we took things apart, we fixed them and we put them back together again. The only thing I gave Scott was a dirty handshake.

I took Electronics in high school and learned how circuits worked. I also learned how anal-retentive one could be when it came to organizing tools. Our teacher hung every tool on a giant pegboard and then traced around them. When you used a tool, there was an outline of exactly where it should go when you were done with it. I wanted to do that inside our kitchen cabinets because I couldn't find anything. It was a free for all when it came to unloading the dishwasher.

The electronics classroom had also housed an enormous amount of rubber bands, located in a big bowl on the teacher's desk. One day during the lecture portion of the class, I sat in the second row and tied about a hundred of them together. Paul Merson sat right in front of me and partially blocked the teacher, so, naturally, I used him as my test subject. Paul was a rather large boy; I believe he was also the front four for the football team.

Classroom chairs in the *Way Back Machine* look exactly like they do now. They have small, high, oval-shaped backs with two thin, silver poles that attach to its seat. I tied one end of the rubber band to the pole and the other end to one of Paul's belt loops.

I sat there laughing to myself in anticipation, wondering what was going to happen when the bell rang. Before I could finish my thought, I heard *"RING, RING!"* Paul stood up and walked out of the room. I cringed at the thought of these rubber bands snapping and whipping me, so I got up and moved out of the way PDQ. Paul must have been walking quite a distance because the rubber bands had stretched to the door and around the corner. I knew they were going to snap at any second, making the moment very tense. Then, the unbelievable happened. The chair shot across the room and out through the door.

OMG! I lost my breath laughing, and my eyes were watering so badly I had to fall back into another chair. I would have loved to witness that chair as it shot down the hallway to Paul. A few minutes later, he walked back into the classroom carrying the chair in his arms, and asked me to untie him. I apologized to him for my tinkering. It was a good thing he was a nice guy because he could have killed me. Twice.

A few weeks later, my father called me into the dining room and told me to go to work. Stacked on the dining room table were fifteen to twenty stereo receivers. He was allowed to buy them from work on the cheap because they didn't work. I don't know if they had fallen off a forklift or if they had been returned by customers, but no matter; he had subsequently offered me a business proposition. For every one I fixed and sold, we would split the profit right down the middle. Deal!

I used one or two for parts and had completely repaired about twelve altogether. I placed an ad in the *Penny Saver* and sold them all. Gregg Curtis brought over his sister's boyfriend who bought the last one. I was excited about our venture and asked my dad to go back to work and break some more electronics.

CURTAINS

As I grew older, the things I did to have fun as a kid still appealed to me. Once during a little snowstorm, I was spending the night at Buddy and Tony's house. We attempted the ol' hand-in-the-lukewarm-water trick on their cousin Michael. He claimed that he was going to stay up all night with us playing cards, but fell asleep long before midnight.

I had only heard of the trick and had never seen it in action, but the theory behind it made sense in my mind. Whenever I had washed my hands in warm water, I surely had to pee. Since, I had no problem whatsoever wetting the bed, the trick definitely would have been lost on me. It didn't work on Michael, so we turned to the next best sleepover trick, which was, of course, igniting flatulence. We gave out nicknames like Mushroom Cloud, Blue Flame and Sphincter Boy. I swear some of my friends could light an entire birthday cake.

I loved the snow and, to this day, I can't wait to play in it. I remember feeling so excited to hear about the possibility of white in the forecast. I would stay up all night, parked by my window, waiting for the first flake to arrive. The Hudsons' lamppost was the perfect object to stare at and observe the snow dance around in the glow. Mornings following snowstorms are magical, especially when every single limb of every single tree turns sparkling white overnight. Snow can be cleansing and calming and create wonderful holiday sentiments.

A surprise snowfall has always been my favorite kind. One Sunday when I was nine and a half, my parents dropped me off at Perring Plaza Cinemas to watch *Tarzan* with Fitz. The sun was setting and nighttime was on its way. When the movie had ended, about two hours later, three inches of snow lay on the ground. Bonus!

On February eighteenth of 1979, I awoke to the sounds of weatherman extraordinaire Marty Bass, of Channel 13, delivering his weather forecast. He was talking about a fast-moving front that was on its way and said that we would see a dusting to two inches sometime during the day. *Music to my ears.* I jumped to my feet, eagerly getting ready for the dusting. It was a Sunday, and my thought process was that if it snowed later on, we might have to go to school two hours late the next day.

Receiving good news from your weatherman is like hearing from an old friend. His forecast can change your mood and your plans. About an hour later Greg Hoffman showed up. I had asked him to help clean out our basement, not because of his work ethic, but because of his special relationship with dumpsters.

Since it was Sunday and going to the dump was a hassle, Greg and I would load the car with junk and cruise behind Mars Shopping Center where all the dumpsters were stationed. I would drive at a slow pace, and Greg would open the passenger window and sit on the door. As we passed by a dumpster, he would start heaving whatever we had into the closest bin. It worked like a charm, and by the end of a perfect run, we would have hit at least twelve different dumpsters without ever stopping the car. In the *Way Back Machine* security cameras don't exist. If they had, they would have also captured other types of dumpster footage in the main parking lot.

Greg called it dumpster surfing. We would chain a dumpster with wheels to the bumper of the car and pull the huge trash can around while someone surfed on top of it. When this got old, we would try to break the shopping cart train record. One lucky person would push a shopping cart with someone kneeling in the cart. That person was leaning over the front, holding a second cart in front of him with another person in that one. This was replicated until we had a whole train. I think the best we did was fourteen shopping carts. Those trains are hard to push.

Greg and I gathered a mess of crap from the basement and came upstairs. As I turned the corner at the top of the stairs, I caught sight of our picture window where evidently we were having a blizzard. *Holy whiteout, Batman!* I couldn't believe how hard it was snowing. In an instant the whole yard was white and Greg's car was covered. From the television I heard Marty Bass update his forecast to a two to four inch wintry mix. He explained that the front had stalled and more moisture was making itself known. Greg and I looked at each other and carried the junk back downstairs.

My mother asked Greg to stay for lunch, like she had a choice. She was a little miffed at Greg and Mark after the time she had asked them for advice on how to handle my sister Karen. They were very smart students and had a good reputation, so when Karen was caught hooking a few classes at Pine Grove Junior High, my mom asked them to go and talk some sense into her. Greg and Mark marched right into Karen's room and shut the door. When they came out fifteen minutes later, they informed my mom that everything was going to be okay.

They had, in fact, *not* changed Karen's mind about hooking class; they simply taught her how to do it without getting caught. I'm sure she loved having two crazy mentors, but when my mom found out the truth, she was not happy.

As Greg and I grabbed a couple of sleds to head over to the park, we heard Marty Bass update his snow totals from four to eight inches. *What the hell, Marty?* To his credit, if you jumped in the **Way Back Machine** there is nothing called Doppler and satellites don't track every falling flake. I am pretty sure that weathermen are merely looking out the window and reporting on what they see. Nonetheless, my guess was that they'd call a friend in Cleveland and ask what the weather was doing there, and then add twenty-four hours. I didn't care.

It was snowing so hard and fast that sledding was difficult, so after a few hours we headed back home. Upon re-entering the house, Marty was currently talking about ten to twelve inches which made it pretty obvious that Greg was going nowhere. *Thanks, Marty!* What do two high school seniors do when snowed in? Well, they make dinner of course. Greg and I cooked a feast, and the whole family ate like meat -eating heathens as the snow piled up.

Around seven thirty in the evening, we headed out into the deluge to see what fun we could have. Greg was sporting a couple of pairs of my socks and some other odd clothing articles to brace for the North Pole excursion. We walked up the big hill with a left turn on Oak Summit and a right on Joppa Road.

We ended up in a neighborhood behind Carney Elementary. Parts of it were still under development, construction materials left all over the place. You could tell that this dusting, which was now well over a foot and a half, had caught many people off guard.

Greg and I came upon a gigantic piece of corrugated, black drainpipe. Standing next to it reminded me of the very pipe I walked through one thousand times, called the tunnel. For no other reason than to see the tracks it left in the snow, Greg and I started pushing the twenty foot-long piece of ridged pipe. It was not easy, and we struggled driving it through the deep, heavy snow. The trail we were leaving was very cool, but I wasn't sure the struggle was worth it. It felt like we were pushing it uphill. Additionally, the blinding snow and height of the pipe made it impossible to see where we were going.

All of a sudden, though, it had become easier to maneuver, so we picked up speed. Having said that, we went from shoving to walking to running and then falling as we crested a hill, and it took off on its own. We both got up and looked at each other, in horror, as we realized that this pipe was now heading down a street we didn't even know existed.

The further it rolled away from us, the more of the neighborhood we could see. I clenched my teeth as this runaway pipe missed two parked cars and took out a mailbox. *Holy crap!*

In tandem, Greg and I took off running and we didn't stop until we reached Second Avenue and Avondale. When we got there, we turned right and started for Joppa. It was trash night, so earlier in the day everyone had put their garbage at the curb. Every couple of houses had a spent Christmas tree lying on the curb as well.

As Greg and I trekked on, he casually picked up one of the trashcans and set it in the middle of the street. When we reached the next house, I did the same. Greg crossed the street, laughing, and as we strolled, we decided to put everybody's trashcans in the middle of Avondale. Fortunately, there was nobody else outside. We knew that eventually the snowplow would have a field day with this and were quite amused with ourselves. Looking behind us through the streetlights, you could see trashcans and bags all over Avondale.

By now, my hood had fallen over my face. As I grabbed another bag of trash, out of nowhere Greg ran right past me, darted across a short front yard and scaled a fence. I stood there, staring and wondering where he was going, when I heard "What are you doing?"

I looked in front of me, and about twenty feet away, standing behind his opened driver's door, was a policeman. *Where'd he come from?* You would think that Greg would've warned me as he sprinted by, but no; he left me there to fend for myself. Lucky for me, his tracks were easy to follow, so before you could say Iditarod, I scaled the fence and tracked his footsteps up a hill and onto field number two of Carney.

I found him in the woods between field one and field two, and we decided it was time to head home.

When we reached Alda Drive, it was still snowing pretty hard. The Christmas trees out for pickup were covered with snow and resembled a mountain range. Halfway down the street, Greg picked one up and started dragging it. When I inquired why he was leaving such a trail, he informed me it was a present for Slater.

Mark had a pretty big porch, and an old Christmas tree would be lonely, so I grabbed one too. Not to be outdone, Greg grabbed another, and I did the same. After placing the four trees on Mark's porch, it just didn't seem like enough, so we headed off and grabbed some more. Before we were done, there was a dead forest on Mark Slater's porch.

There were at least twenty snow-covered trees, all standing upright and leaning against his front door.

The next morning, his father had to crawl out the basement because their front door wouldn't open. We didn't leave a calling card, but somehow they knew who had left them the presents. The one positive thing that came out of our snowy adventure was that the Christmas tree truck only had to make one stop on Alda Drive.

The snow stayed for a while, so the next week, Larry and I took off in his Plymphrison car to go sledding. Larry drove a white Rambler, but I always called it the Plymphrison car. That was how his nephew had pronounced their family car, a Plymouth Horizon. His nephew also introduced me to Stretch Armstrong. *Loved that doll.*

So, Larry and I were driving and *Bam! Bam! Bam!* A barrage of snowballs riddled the side of his car and scared the hell out of us. Two years earlier, *we* would have been the ones throwing snowballs at cars, but now we were all grown up and mature. Yeah, right!

The flooring of Larry's car was vinyl, so we pulled over and filled up the front of the car with snow and decided to get them at their own game. As we drove around, I made dozens of snowballs and created a whole ammo bunker on the floor. It was hilarious to throw snowballs from a moving car; occasionally, we would pull over and battle for a few minutes before taking off again. We were even hitting passing cars. They had no idea what was happening, which made it even funnier.

After the initial hit, Larry and I went looking for the kids who started it all and found one walking on the side of Joppa Road. He was minding his own business, walking down the street right toward us. I didn't want to hurt him, so throwing a snowball was out of the question. By the time we had reached him, we were going thirty miles an hour, so I simply handed him a snowball out the window. It exploded when it hit his chest, and Larry and I laughed so hard we cried. I think I even spotted.

Two years later while living in Pasadena, Maryland, I had visited Greg at his family's farm in Glen Arm. Greg's family lived in an old farmhouse that was quaint and at least one hundred years old. We had been out partying at The Barn, and I was driving him home, when it started snowing. Greg talked me into staying at his house, so I curled up on his living room couch and prepared to slumber. Fifteen minutes after he went up to his room, I sat up in a panic.

The last time I had spent the night, Greg's dad had woken me up in the morning by poking my forehead with his giant finger. Greg's dad was Paul "The Bear" Hoffman who played professional basketball for six years. He was an all-star and was even the general manager of the Baltimore Bullets. In the *Way Back Machine* the Washington Wizards are called the Baltimore Bullets.

His fingers were huge and they felt like vulpine hammers when he poked you. I decided it would be best if I left. *If I sneak out of the house now, no one would even know I'd been there.* I walked to the front door but noticed the inside door was locked with an eyehook latch. There would be no way I could leave the farmhouse and lock the front door, so I opted for the window.

The couch I had been on backed up to a front window. I couldn't climb out the normal way and close it properly, so I put my hands on the floor and pushed myself out, feet first. My thought was that I could close the window with my hands right before I got out. When I was about three quarters of the way out, my feet touched what I thought was the ground. Unfortunately for me, it was actually two closed, wooden doors that led to the basement. Since they were angled and dusted with snow, when I put my weight on them, my feet shot out, causing me to fly out the window. It all happened so fast that, without thinking, I grabbed the closest thing I could find to stop my fall. The next thing I knew, I was sitting in the front yard, holding their curtains. I had pulled both of them right off the wall and into the yard. This was not good. This was, in fact, very bad. I knew I'd be in big trouble if I got caught, so I jumped into my car and drove home.

The next morning, Greg was abruptly awakened with a giant finger thumping on his forehead. His father was berating him as to why the window was open and what the hell the curtains were doing in the front yard. "Beller!"

THE BEST WORST DATE EVER!

I was seventeen years old when I saw *It's a Wonderful Life* by Frank Capra, for the first time. I had found it while channel surfing on a Saturday afternoon, so I decided to check it out. Two hours later, I was lying on the couch, crying at how much the film had moved me. My favorite line from the movie was delivered by a T-shirt wearing, old man on his front porch who said, "Aw, youth is wasted on the wrong people." He was right.

I was smitten with this girl from work and had wanted to ask her out but, until now, hadn't developed the nerve. She was a blonde-haired, blue-eyed beauty who resembled Princess Diana. Her name was Darcy.

I was somewhat unsure of myself but normally could talk to anyone. I struggled with confidence in her presence. Unfortunately, around her I had developed fumble-mouth. Her smile made me queasy, and her laugh was a joy to my ears. Before I had lost weight, some girls at school nicknamed me Pooh Bear; she just called me Bear. I really liked her.

Her sister Maria also worked at English's, and when I prompted her about Darcy, she told me that her sister liked me and that I should ask her out. Needless to say, I was beside myself. Well, not anymore because I had lost fifty-three pounds, but I now had gained the nerve plus some affirmation that she wouldn't laugh in my face. I decided to ask her out.

A few days later, we were both working together, and at an opportune time, I went for it. It was quite romantic next to stacks of dirty dishes and cases of lettuce in the dish room, so, while donning my red and white vertical striped work shirt and floppy chef hat, I asked Darcy to go to the movies on Saturday night. When she accepted, I smiled, asked for her address, and prepared for the most awesome date in my short dating history.

There was a lot to prepare for, and it all started with finding transportation. At that time, we had two family cars, the white Impala and the family Truckster. After the blue Volkswagen had met its demise, my dad purchased a brown-paneled station wagon. It was a sad day when we buried the big blue bus; we practically lived in that thing. My dad drove it until it literally died. I used to like riding in the way back.

Over the years, it had been slowly falling apart. The windows didn't go up or down, the doorknobs were broken and all the knobs were missing from its front panel. On many occasions, I was awoken from a deep, early morning slumber in order to push that beast down the street.

It had a bad starter, so with all my might I would push the bus down Uxbridge Road until my dad popped the clutch, and it would come to life. To combat this problem, he would park on hills or ramps or anywhere weightlifters were working out. When it had finally died, we left it at the Volkswagen garage next to The Rite Spot because we couldn't find its title. It sat there for twelve years, disappearing part by part.

I politely asked my dad if he could drive the white Impala to work on Saturday so I could use the wagon for my date. Saturday was his fourteen-hour day, so I knew he would never be home in time for my departure. The Impala was an okay car but a little on the ugly side for a first date.

The Champ starring little Ricky Schroeder was playing at the Senator Theatre, and I had heard it was a real tearjerker, so, by design, I chose that movie. I mean, she couldn't hate me if she was *zub-zubbing* over Ricky. Everything was going to plan, and I was very excited to see Darcy and myself wearing something other than her waitress outfit and my chicken suit.

When the big day arrived, I woke up and practiced the clever tidbits of information and conversation that I was going to lay on her. She would surely be impressed with my knowledge of stupid things, like how many dimples were on a golf ball (three hundred ninety-two), and my comedic approach to life.

While I was ironing my favorite shirt, I glanced out the front window and spied the Impala in front of our house. It didn't register at first, but when it finally did, I was angry. I immediately called my dad at work and asked him why he didn't leave the wagon. His simple retort of "Oh, I forgot" said it all.

Steve Martin had a whole comedy routine about how saying "I forgot" could get you out of so many jams. "I forgot armed robbery was illegal." In any event my dad wasn't coming home, so I was forced to drive the Impala to pick up Darcy. Anxiety, enter stage left.

When I went to her house, I parked two blocks away so nobody could see the rusty holes in the side of the car. She looked beautiful, and I acted very charming to her very nice parents, so the evening started off well. If the date would have ended right there, I would have been happy. In retrospect, it should have.

Parking was at a premium around the Senator, so I found a space on a residential side street, and we went to the movies. To my dismay, *The Champ* was sold out. *Damn.* Quickly, we chose *The Villain*, a comedy starring Kirk Douglas and Arnold Schwarzenegger. The movie was pretty lame, but the Woody Woodpecker cartoon saved our movie experience.

I was scared to death with bad nerves throughout the movie and even asked permission to put my arm around her. *Who does that?* I wanted to kiss her in the worst way and thought about my game plan for after the movie. It was very cold as we walked to the car. I helped her through the neighborhood and opened the car door for her. It was just as cold inside the car, so I started it up and turned the heat on high. Secretly, I hoped the thermostat didn't fail.

Darcy told me she was freezing and that she had a sure fire way in which to warm up. My mind was racing with wonderful scenes of warm embraces when the cold air had suddenly been shattered by the sound of her screaming.

"AAAAAAAAAAH!" I jumped back in shock, which made her laugh. She went on to explain to me that screaming at the top of her lungs actually warmed her up. I guess it made her blood circulate faster and heat up her extremities, but it sure scared the bejesus out of me.

She screamed a couple of more times, and then I pulled the car out. I drove about a hundred feet when a different noise filled the air. It was the loudest rumbling noise I had ever heard. We both looked around for the helicopter which was surely landing on the roof of my car but saw nothing. I noticed a space ahead, so I pulled over and turned off the car. The noise stopped. *Oh, for God's sake, what now?* I asked her as politely as I could to stay in the car while I went outside and looked under it. To my horror, the muffler had broken in half, and the tail pipe was lying on the ground. *This is a joke, right? I waited patiently for months to ask her out, and this is what I get?* I shoved the tailpipe back into the muffler, clapped the rust off my hands and got back in the car. I was so embarrassed I could hardly look at her.

When she asked what it was, I simply said I wasn't sure and apprehensively started the car. I drove another hundred feet and it happened again. I was mortified. I quickly pulled over and turned off the car. Neighbors were looking out their windows, trying to determine if a NASCAR event was taking place. I told her it was the muffler and, sadly, got out again to try to fix it.

In the trunk I found some twine and decided to tie it up. Oh, sure, hindsight would tell you that a red-hot muffler would burn through twine in a heartbeat, but at that moment I had never heard of hindsight. All I knew was that I had a wonderful girl named Darcy sitting next to me, and my car was falling apart. I cursed my father, under my breath, for putting me in this situation and continued to tie up the muffler. It lasted all of three minutes. This time when I pulled out, we were at an intersection when it fell off. *Oh my god!* I apologized to Darcy as we drove through the intersection and pulled over, yet again, in another residential area.

I could tell that she was aware of my utter embarrassment as she decided to try making idle conversation. We small-talked for a few minutes, and she giggled a little, telling me that someday we would laugh about this. I disagreed. My embarrassment was slowly turning to anger as I left the car's warm interior again and crawled under the car onto the frigid ground. After a few minutes, Darcy got out of the car and sat on the curb across the street so she could see me and we could talk. It was very nice of her, but my rage was getting to its seething point. It officially reached boiling a few minutes later when a police car showed up.

The officer had been out cruising the neighborhood when she saw my legs sticking out from under the car and was concerned for my safety. I was hoping she would just shoot me and end the nightmare, but she decided to turn on her spotlight and the bubble gum machine on her roof so all the neighbors could come out and share in my misery.

Darcy was playfully talking to the cop as I melted my wallabies, trying to hold the muffler up. I had a burn on my forearm and my fingers were raw. I could hear the two of them laughing, and I imagined they were laughing at me. There was a puddle in the street; I watched the red and blue lights reflect in it as I tied up the muffler again.

We thanked the cop and got in the car. I was a mess. I had wanted to impress her so badly and kiss her even more, but now anything positive that could happen would have the word pity written all over it. Before this night, whenever I heard her sweet voice, I wanted to spend hours getting to know her better. Now, all I wanted her to do was silence it. It wasn't her fault; she was merely becoming a sidebar in the terrible happening, and I just wanted to take her home.

This time, I had made it to Joppa Road and was coming down the hill towards Goucher Boulevard, praying that the worst was behind me. I was wrong. Peering in my rear-view mirror, I could see that I was rooster tailing a fountain of sparks down Joppa Road. Cars were passing me and pointing behind me like I didn't know I had set the street on fire. Darcy was busy chatting about school, but I wasn't listening. As she was a student at our high school's archrival Perry Hall, I should have known this date was cursed long ago by the anti-dating-from-a-different-high- school gods. I tried to ignore the loud conga band I was driving and finally pulled into Eudowood Shopping Center, parking against the curb, under a light.

Darcy had suddenly turned into Chatty Cathy, which I figured was just her way of handling this extremely awkward situation. If we hadn't been in the *Way Back Machine,* I'm sure she would have been texting her ass off and asking her friends to come and rescue her. We only lived five miles from the Senator Theatre, but it was taking us two hours to get home. I was getting concerned because she had a midnight curfew and I didn't want her parents thinking I had lost my charm. She already knew that.

It was during this pit stop that I realized the twine was burning through and I needed something stronger. I walked about the parking lot and saw an old clothes hanger. The light finally went off. I could wire it up quickly, but I had to wait for the muffler to change from the molten orange color it was back to a lovely shade of brown rust before starting.

The parking lot was empty with the exception of one car whose owner was obviously working late. We both chuckled a little bit at the event, but I was still getting angrier by the minute. *I'm going to have to quit my job and possibly move because every time I look at her beautiful face, all I am going to see is a replay of this horrible night.*

After twenty minutes, I crawled under the car and wired up the muffler. When I got back inside the car with my melted footwear and charred fingers, I turned to her and apologized one more time. I told her that I had looked forward to our night and that I couldn't believe what was happening. I really felt like crying. She smiled in a soothing-I -understand kind of way and momentarily made me feel better. That is why I liked her.

I started the car and put it in drive when a massive bang shook us right out of our seats. We both jumped out just in time to see the back passenger tire totally deflate to the ground.

"Look how fast it's going down," she loudly announced.

"Oh my god. Shut up!" I yelled.

I felt terrible for barking, but I had just snapped! I couldn't believe my eyes. A date this bad couldn't be scripted; hell, it couldn't be duplicated. The amount of negativity needed to create such a nightmare could only be generated from the devil himself. I kicked the car and laughed like an evil scientist. I was officially done.

Just then, I noticed someone walking toward the lone car in the parking lot and I flagged him down. I begged him to ride us to the McDonald's down the street so I could call someone to come and get us. He reluctantly agreed and we officially abandoned the car.

Being a guy, he could read the horror on my face but didn't ask what had happened. His entire backseat was filled with marketing crap, but I didn't care and climbed in and sat on top of it. I would have ridden in the trunk with a dead body to end this date. Darcy sat in the passenger seat and was as pleasant as she could be.

At McDonald's I saw a friend and asked him to drive us to my house. As we pulled onto Uxbridge Road, I saw the family Truckster. I needed to get Darcy home, so we both walked into my house. While we walked up the steps, I was thinking about how selfish I had been about the car. If my father had taken it, all this would have happened to him, and he had enough pressure to deal with.

When we walked in through the front door, my father was sitting in his chair. Upon seeing Darcy, he jumped right up and greeted her. I'm sure he was as intoxicated by her smile as I was. He looked at me and said, "What the hell happened to you?"

"It's a very long story. I'll tell you later, but I need your car to drive Darcy home."

I couldn't wait for Darcy to get out of the car. I liked her so much, but there was no way to recover from such a horrific evening. I walked her to the door, apologized again and left without a kiss. *What a freaking disaster.*

My father laughed as I told him the whole story. I'm sure it was funny and someday I would laugh, but it was definitely too soon.

Early the next morning, my dad and I took the wagon to go and retrieve the car. While I was getting the spare out of the trunk, my father found something on the windshield. For a second I thought it was a kind note from Darcy, thanking me for a wonderful evening. It was a fifty-dollar ticket for parking in a fire lane. My father chuckled as he handed it to me. Youth wasn't wasted on anybody that night.

POLICY 2474B

In Mr. Saturn's class I sat in the front row, next to Mike Roman. I had known Mike since Carney Elementary School, and he was a good guy. We had history class right after lunch, and it interfered with his naptime. Mr. Saturn was also my homeroom teacher. He had been at Parkville for a very long time, so he was super-efficient at his retorts, as he had been practicing them for years. Unfortunately, he spoke in a monotone voice that could easily aid the sleepy into slumber. (Think Bueller.) Almost every day, Mike would put his head down on his desk, and the class would be treated to the same dialogue. "Mr. Roman, are you sick? Do you need to see the nurse?"

"No."

"Then pick your head up and pay attention, please."

"Okay."

Every Friday, we had a five-question quiz on current events, and the instructions were always the same. "Take out a piece of paper, tear it down the middle, and share it with your neighbor. Put your name and class in the upper right-hand corner and number it from one to five."

Then he would ask us five questions like why someone said this or why someone did that. We were then instructed to turn in our quizzes up the row, placing ours on the top. When they all reached the front row, they were passed to the left, placing each stack on top of the next. After grading them he would hand them back the same way. Pure efficiency.

On one Monday, when our teacher returned the graded quizzes to us, Mike was absent, so I placed his quiz on his desk and passed the rest of the stack back. I couldn't help myself but explore further after seeing the big red "E" on Mike's quiz. I leaned over to inspect his mistakes, and what I read cracked me up. He had numbered his paper from one through five, just as instructed, but here were his answers:

1. Because
2. Because
3. Because
4. Because
5. Because of the wonderful things he does.

I was still laughing when I got in trouble for sharing his "answers" with some of the students near me, but comedy *that* wonderful needed to be shared.

I love a good practical joke. Doesn't everybody? Of course, since I was an overachiever, I was inclined to push the envelope. Perry Hall was hosting Parkville in a big football game, and I came up with a grand idea. I convinced a couple of friends of mine from English's to travel to our archrival's field and leave a little present. My plan was to get some black and gold spray paint and write on their track "Parkville is #1." *Just some simple, elegant graffiti, no harm in that, right?*

In Baltimore County, most high school football fields were located in the middle of their track. I know this because I hated to run track, so I usually hung a left and threw up in a football field. Black and gold were our school colors, and I thought they would look wonderful displayed in front of the Perry Hall Gator fans. I didn't want to make a mess of it; I wanted to create a work of art, so I recruited Michael Fridley. Mike was an amazing artist and was more than willing to play with us.

Years earlier, Mike and I shared a very boring class. He was sitting next to me, and we hadn't met yet. Out of nowhere, I heard the sound of a vintage World War II mortar going off and I quickly looked up to see Mike making the sound. *Holy crap, I found someone else who loved to make sound effects!* I fired my own mortar back at him, followed by a short, sustained, B-52 bombing run. Before you knew it, we were in a full-blown sound effects war. The best thing was that nobody else in the class knew where it was coming from. In the **Way Back Machine**, you are allowed to make simulated-automatic gunfire noises with your mouth in class and not get suspended or expelled. Mike and I became instant friends.

On the night before the big game, four of us met at English's and drove over there in one car. I don't want to use their real names in case they've become priests or something, so I'll say it was Kevin

Witts and Brian Richardson. Wait a minute. It was Kevin and Brian. Okay, let's say it was Tom Williams and Marty Meehan. No, wait again. They were involved in another practical joke, the one involving the fictitious sports team.

I remember Joe O'Donnell telling me that when he graduated from Parkville, a group of guys had taken a team picture of a fake rugby team and tried to get it in the yearbook. I took that idea a step further and created the varsity water polo team.

We had a complete roster, managers, schedules that hung in every homeroom, and even a teacher as our coach. We had chosen Larry Saunders because he was a biology teacher and looked like he hadn't exercised in thirty years. We even made fake morning announcements that were read to the whole school with highlights of fake games. We didn't have a swimming pool, so all our games were away games. We would show up at parties with wet hair, and some of us carried swim fins around school to make it look like we practiced. We told everybody our home pool was at Essex Community College.

The night before each match, we would all meet at someone's house to go over the highlights so everybody was on the same page. We even had fake injuries, and that is what led to our quiet demise. Tom was faking an arm injury and wore a sling around school for two days. When he tried to get out of badminton, the gym teachers, who definitely knew we had no water polo team, called foul, and we were all busted. We ended our season undefeated.

On Thursday evening, the night before the football game, we snuck onto the track and made our way over to the Gator's home side. Mike, being an artist, had visions of grandeur and started to make a "P" that was six-lanes wide.

"Dude, what are you doing? That P is huge!"

"I want them to be able to see it from the stands."

"You can see that from Skylab!"

It took three cans of gold spray paint just to fill in the P. It looked just like our school's varsity letter and was awesome. We took about half an hour to finish the rest, and when completed, the whole thing was about forty yards long. It was our first and only attempt at tagging, and I think we exceeded our expectations. It was a win! Now all we had to do was keep our mouths shut until game time. That was a loss!

Unable to keep our secret, we told everybody to wait and see what we did over at Perry Hall. Needless to say, a ton of people showed up to check it out. When I got there, I saw various banners and signs promoting Perry Hall all over the school. Some were hanging on the brick walls of the school and some were attached to the white pylons that rimmed the road leading to the track. I had never seen such a display of school spirit. When I made my way to the track, our artwork was covered with a giant tarp. I hadn't counted on that. I was walking around to our side of the field when I ran into Darcy. She was a card-carrying Gator and not too happy about the vandalism. *Vandalism?*

She told me that while she was in gym class, she found some empty spray cans of black and gold paint. I looked down at the recently painted tips of my tennis shoes and told her how shocked I was that someone would do that. Apparently, while we were tastefully painting the track, another group of knuckleheads were painting all kinds of vulgarity on the school. When we started to tell people that we couldn't wait for them to see what we did, we had inadvertently taken credit for all of it. Oops!

We won the game in the last six seconds, and as our principal, Mr. Phillips, used to say, "Parkville's banner is flying high today." He said that during Monday's morning announcements and immediately followed with, "However, because of a few individuals, our flag has been lowered to half-staff." Homeroom people started glancing in my direction, and I immediately figured that I might be called to the office during the course of the day.

When the bell rang, I went to first period, and Mr. Phillips was waiting for me. That was the first time in my life when I thought it unfortunate to be the only person in the school named Neil. He had my name and everybody else's initials. The story was that the football coach of Perry Hall heard some of us bragging about painting the track and the school. *Really? The football coach?* Someone had turned us in; no one knows who ratted, but speculation had been fierce, and our Student Council Association President, Guy Therien, was thrown under the bus. To combat this allegation, Guy took out an ad in the senior edition of the final newspaper, which simply stated, "Neil, I didn't do it. Guy." It was 1979, and that ad cost about five bucks, which was a lot of money, so naturally I believed him.

The principal was in his first year and said that he had to make an example out of me. *Like I had never heard that before.* I was expelled from school and was told that a letter would be sent to my home. I would also have to attend a hearing with the Board of Education to see if I could come back to school. *Great.*

I feigned a quick illness and stayed home for two days in hopes of intercepting the mail. When it arrived, I discovered that I had been charged by the Department of Recreation for violating Policy 2474B. My crime was for producing disruptive behavior, but also included in that policy was defaming recreational property, creating carnage in an inhumane manner, and blowing things up. It sounded a lot worse than it was, and some people thought it was even worse than that.

There were rumors of undercover narcs in our school, and some people thought my suspension was the result of drugs. Some even thought I *was* the narc. Totally silly, I know, because I was the delinquent athlete, not the druggie.

The third day home, I received a sympathy card in the mail, which was signed by all my friends. Someone had even offered their legal services. My sister Jan was suspicious, so I told her what happened and she laughed. "They do that all the time; I don't know what the big deal is. My class did that to Dulaney High School." Knowing that made me feel better. She was so awesome about it that she decided to tell my mom for me.

I stood at the bottom of the stairs and listened while Jan and my mom talked in my parents' bedroom. It sounded like two teachers from Charlie Brown because all I heard was "Wa wah wa waa wa wa," and then I heard "WAH!" and the door opened.

Needless to say, my mom was a tad upset. She smacked me around a bit and then walked me by my ear to the telephone and made me call my dad at work. Beating me with a club or kicking my shins repeatedly with pointy shoes would have been better. My father breathed at me, but deep down inside I thought he was only doing that for effect. I convinced myself he was probably jealous. The next day, my hearing information showed up, and my father and I had a date on Friday. The week flew by with Dick Van Dyke re-runs and ABC after school specials, but my anxiety was peaking.

On Friday morning, my dad drove me to the Board of Education in Timonium, and we sat next to each other at the south end of a very,

very long table. A couple of staunch-looking people sat at the north end and, lastly, the president of the board came in and sat down at the head of the table.

He started off by thanking us for coming and then launched into a diatribe explaining how seeing the graffiti at Loch Raven's dam on his daily drive to work makes him sick. I looked at my dad and gulped. He simply smiled as if to say everything would be all right. The next thing the board members did was read some notes that all my teachers wrote about me. Thank God they all loved me, except one. I'm not going to mention the teacher's name, but if I did, it would be Mrs. Dunhaven.

The secretary announced a fine of two hundred dollars, which was only a portion of the cost to sandblast the track at Perry Hall. I agreed to the fine. I gave my regrets. And we left. When we reached the car, my father started giggling and said, "That wasn't too bad." I'm sure he was reflecting on all the bad stuff he did as a kid and saw this as a rite of passage. We bonded in a way that only fathers and sons understand.

Mike's meeting was after mine, so I waited a while before calling him. Truth be told, I didn't want to talk to his parents. I was pretty sure they would blame me, and I had enough grief in my own house. I learned that most of the other painters in both crews turned themselves in so I didn't have to take the fall alone. Admirable friends.

Altogether, Mike and I had to pay four hundred dollars to have the track sandblasted. We had until March first to pay it, and since that was a few months off, we went back to school and enjoyed our short, celebrity stint as high school rebels.

Never to be outdone, we decided to have a little fun with our mode of payment as well. Mike and I went to the bank and got four hundred one-dollar bills and locked them in a Blues Brothers style briefcase. We confiscated two white rifles from the marching band room and asked two bystanders to escort us to the principal's office. One of our guardsmen was Kevin Witts.

We sent in Greg Hoffman ahead of time to chitchat with Mr. Phillips. Since he was a yearbook photographer, Greg would surely capture the Kodak moment. We had a tape recorder playing the "Peter Gunn Theme" and walked in behind the rifle guard. The principal was in shock and sat there smiling. He had totally forgotten about the fine.

MISSING PINE PARK

We opened the case and dumped four hundred one-dollar bills on his desk. It was hilarious.

We also constructed a referendum in scroll-form, which we read aloud. The first line started "We, the people of the Perry Hall Art Committee, do hereby apologize for the unfortunate misplacement of our spray paint." We had previously gone over to Perry Hall and had the janitors who were assigned to clean up everything sign our scroll too.

I visited Parkville a year later for a pep rally and upon entering I noticed graffiti on the walls of the school, describing Parkville's sucking ability. When Mr. Phillips saw me he said, "See what you started!" I still have flashbacks and get a little excited every time I shake a can of spray paint.

LEATHER

Near the end of my senior year of high school, I remember getting off the school bus and walking home. I was thinking about how much I loved baseball. We had just lost the state championship game to Winston Churchill High School the week before, and I was still grieving about it. Our third baseman, Kevin Landers, was robbed of a grand slam by this tiny leftfielder named Bobo Kirpatrick. He did make an amazing catch, but who names their kid Bobo?

For my whole life, I had secretly wanted to be a professional baseball player. Okay, it really wasn't a secret; I told everyone I met. My prized possession was a catcher's mitt that my father had given me on my previous birthday. I loved it. One of my favorite things in life was the smell of a baseball glove. If they made a Yankee Candle that smelled like my catcher's mitt, I would buy it.

My dad loved baseball and together we could always talk about it. We discussed strategies, the un-written rules, and the reason it is considered a gentleman's game. Most kids pick their uniform number based on their favorite player, like number five for Brooks Robinson, or number seven for Mickey Mantle. I chose the number one because that was the number on my father's back. When Karen started playing softball, she chose the number one as well. She was also a catcher, and a good one at that.

While we watched the game on TV, my dad used to tell me stories about his youth. They played in the street. *I wonder if he ever had the opportunity to play on bright green grass.* Our lawn was a combination of weeds, burnt areas and dog excrement.

He knew I would get nervous when he would watch me play, so he stopped coming to games, or so I thought. One day, I saw him leaning against a tree way down the left field line, near the parking lot. He would watch in secret.

I found out after the fact that during our state championship game, he kept calling the janitor of Dundalk Community College, asking him to run outside to check on the score. I don't know how he pulled that off, unless he started breathing at him. To this day, when I see a newly trimmed baseball field, I think about my dad. Kevin Costner, who starred in three baseball movies, totally nailed the father-son sentiment with the ending of *Field of Dreams*. I tear up every time I see it as does every other person who played catch with their father.

As high school was ending, my mind had been teetering back and forth between my awesome past and my uncertain future. I was new experiencing many of those clichés I had always heard about, like stopping to smell the roses and life happening way too fast.

While walking, I was reminiscing about all the fun I had growing up in the neighborhood. I was still laughing as I walked past Missing Pine Park, but then my smile slowly faded. I stopped and concentrated at the small field that I played in for a good portion of my life.

When did I grow up? How did it happen so fast? I found myself feeling jealous of the little kids I saw playing. I couldn't remember the last time I had played there. I longed for the days of having no responsibilities, of riding my bike with no purpose or direction, and of using a brown paper bag to collect the doggie land mines I'd set afire on someone's porch. I had the greatest impulse to knock on Fitz's door and run.

The last time I saw him, we had removed every label off every can in his pantry. He might have received a significant punishment for that. I sat on the edge of the tunnel and thought about how much my life was about to change.

As I looked down at the stream, I was reminded of the day that my brother David was standing on this exact spot. He was watching Eddie

Chadman throw huge rocks into the stream below. It had recently rained, and the deep water was creating giant splashes for David and Eddie to enjoy.

David decided he wanted to try one too, but when he threw it he went right over with it and created the biggest splash of the day. Mr. Herman had been driving by when he witnessed David's sudden disappearance from the tunnel. As he was very familiar with the stream, he stopped to lend a hand.

When David crawled out of the stream, Mr. Herman carried him to our house and placed him on the dining room table, soaking wet. When I asked David what had happened, he said that he forgot to let go. He wasn't hurt too badly, just scared. Being scared is part of life. I was scared. I actually hated the feeling that I was growing up.

As I glanced down at the stream again, it seemed like just yesterday I was looking for crayfish. Crayfish are tiny little lobsters that live under rocks in water six to seven inches deep. There is an art to catching them, and if you weren't extremely patient, you would go home empty. The first method was the scoop. This worked well for stationary minnows but could surprise a crayfish as well. You had to lean over and wait patiently, making sure not to let your sweat drip into the water. Focusing your eyes on the prize, you would slowly move your outstretched, cupped hands together. After surrounding the prey, you would quickly scoop him up along with some sand or small stones. At the time, I felt like I was on the *Deadliest Catch*.

Another way was the swamp people method, where you grabbed the middle of the crayfish with your thumb and forefinger. You could then pick them up while they snapped their tiny claws at you. The biggest crayfish I had ever caught was a five-inch Jenny Run Giant.

Once, I caught a fish almost six inches long. I ran home with him in my hands to get a container and couldn't find one. If you couldn't prove your feat through visual means, then you were lying, and I had to show Fitz for proper size verification. Thinking quickly, I emptied a bag of bread on the counter and put in the fish. I normally had dealings with empty bread bags in the winter. My mom would put them on my feet to help slide my rubber boots over three pairs of socks. It was quite the struggle.

I had to run back to the stream to fill it with stream water before he died. When I finally showed Fitz, we had to wait for all the soggy

Wonder Bread chunks to settle to the bottom of the fish bag for verification purposes. For convenience, his name was already on the side of the bag: Schmidt. He was a blue ribbon fish.

I sat on the tunnel until the junior high bus pulled away. Andy Locke and Brucie Green were walking down Uxbridge, and when they saw me, they asked if I wanted to play catch. I smiled and thought it was just what the doctor ordered.

We started playing three-way catch, and before long more kids showed up. Soon, we had a huge game of rundown going and laughter filled the air. I was still in my school clothes and clearly the oldest person there, but I didn't care. We laughed and played until dinner. I smelled my glove as I put it away that night, thinking I might never use it again.

THE LAST HURRAH

Most of my friends were gearing up for college, but it wasn't in my plans. No mindless, drunken toga parties for me, though, as I had recently secured my very first full-time job. I was going to be an employee of the Black and Decker Company in Hampstead, Maryland and was scheduled to start the Monday after Senior Week. I would be working in their electronics department. Because I could earn ten percent more money, I chose to be on the night shift. Clearly, I had crossed an invisible barrier; which transformed me into an adult. It must have been during a recent bender. The fact that I had not been able to control my laughter after seeing a kid walk into a pole meant, however, that I was still bordering on immaturity.

Senior Week is when high school graduates head to Ocean City, Maryland to spend a week on their own, without adult supervision, and pretend they have scruples. I elected to bunk up with the Perry Hall art committee, along with the addition of Mike Reider and Jeff Ficek. Mike was a musical standout and the student leader of the orchestra; Jeff was a fellow baseball player.

We stayed on Fourth Street and had an excellent game plan. We divided up the rooms and agreed to meet back at the apartment every night for dinner. Each person was in charge of setting the table and preparing a tasty meal to share. The first night, we had an amicable time and chatted like a normal family. The second night was spaghetti night, and when Kevin Witts served it with his hands, the party was over. Let me rephrase that; the party was just beginning. He grabbed a handful of cooked noodles, dipped them in the sauce, and slammed them on a plate. Can you say food fight?

We were very excited about our housemates; in the apartment next door were a group of beautiful girls from Perry Hall. They were acquaintances of Darcy and her friend Diane whom I had met one night at English's. Diane and I were both awarded for having the best sense of humor in our respective classes, so I was sure that the hi-jinx would be outstanding. So far, there were a few jokes back and forth but nothing to write home about. That would soon change.

My girlfriend was staying several blocks away, so I wasn't around that much, but when I was, it was nothing but jocularity for my roomies and me. We discovered we had a new thing called cable television. I was in awe that we could sit in our living room eating pints of ice cream with flat wooden spoons while watching *The End* starring Burt Reynolds. If this is what life was like after high school, then I was all in.

Frid brought his whole stereo, and I brought the newly released albums *Don't Look Back* by Boston and *Breakfast in America* by Supertramp. We had many other albums, but those two were popular that week and played nonstop.

One night after dinner, we took all kinds of odd-shaped cooking implements to the beach and constructed a sand castle for the ages. We used pots and pans and trashcans and even Tupperware. Some of our neighbors thought we went off to do our dishes. It was truly awesome. As a matter of fact, it was so awesome that the boardwalk police had even visited it as well. They were concerned with the bag of beer cans I was also carrying until I explained that I was majoring in ancient engineering in college and needed them to build a pyramid in our apartment. I proudly declared that it was suitable for a king. They followed me back to witness its construction.

We saved the best prank for our last day in O.C. Since the ladies next door were so quiet, we decided "to help" them make some noise. That same night, everybody in Ocean City seemed to be having a party, which made for a very long and interesting evening. We stayed up all night and, at five-thirty in the morning, launched our clever plan. Very quietly, we carried two three-foot speakers next door and positioned them at each end of the girls' apartment. We put baby oil and suntan lotion all over their hallway tile floor and spread peanut butter on all the doorknobs.

We had to traverse sleeping and passed out bodies all over their place as we made our way back to our living room.

At six on the dot, Mike turned on the stereo and needled up "Black Dog" by Led Zeppelin. We immediately started laughing in anticipation; however, nothing prepared us for the chaos of sound that ensued. We heard crashes and screams and bangs and grunts. It sounded like a bit from *Fibber McGee and Molly's* closet.

I should go on record and say that no one was injured or harmed in the making of that moment, and no lawsuits were filed. Later in the day, before we had all departed, the Perry Hall girls came over to say goodbye and bring us a present. They were so graceful and kind to us that I started to feel really badly. The bunch of us chatted, hugged goodbye and wished each other well. Next thing you know, we hear all the girls laughing together as they proceeded to open up their bag and dump out onto the floor all of our underwear. Surprise!

Apparently, on the first night of our stay, they had stolen every pair of underwear we owned. The only problem with their plan was that we didn't even notice. I wore my swimming trunks every day and the rest of the guys probably went commando. By the middle of the week, I guess the girls were so grossed out that they stopped coming around. *Doh!*

Two days later, I started my new job. Even though I was donning clean underwear, I hated the night shift. I never knew when to sleep or which meal to eat. My digestive system got all screwed up. I'm not even kidding on the latter. The only thing I can remember eating was cheese. It's a well-known fact that too much cheese can act as ass cement. I think a whole month went by before I had what my mother referred to as "a proper BM."

At Black and Decker I worked on an assembly line and ran a spot welder. If you threw a power saw against the wall, a big chunk, called a core, would fall out. I made them by the hundreds. It was so noisy that I would sing at the top of my lungs without anyone hearing me. I taped a song sheet to my spot welder and performed a concert every night. That was the only way I could make it through the shift. I had become a power-saw-singing-minion. At lunch one night, I spoke to a man who had worked for Black and Decker for fifty years. *Fifty years? That's almost half a century!*

When I would get home in the morning, I would try to stay awake as long as I could. Every day, I slipped into a coma by nine-thirty. While my friends partied all summer, I worked. By August, I was spent. How anybody could work anywhere for fifty years in a row was beside me. *Do you know how many concerts I would have to sing?*

A week later, my dad took a phone call that changed my life. I had been offered a scholarship to go to college and play baseball. *What?* He sat me down, told me the decision was mine to make and suggested I weigh all my options. It took me all of two seconds to choose. I went to my room and grabbed my glove. Lying on my bed, throwing a baseball up and down, and grinning from ear to ear, I thanked God for the opportunity to fulfill my lifelong dream. Then I got up and had a proper BM.

MY FAVORITE TOY

I sat on the edge of my bed, slowly wrapping Saran Wrap around my thighs and waist. I was out of shape and needed to get ready for college baseball fast, so I built my own sweat suit. I started running. Halfway around the block, I collapsed in Buck Spot's front yard. The sweatshirt, sweatpants and Saran Wrap did their job perfectly. I'd have been fine if it hadn't been ninety-seven degrees outside.

College seemed like the thirteenth grade to me at times and at other times, more like an episode of *Cops*. I attended C.C.B., or The Community College of Baltimore. The multi-ethnic campus was located on Liberty Road, very close to Mondawmin Mall and The Baltimore Zoo. In November of that same year, fifty-two Americans were kidnapped in Iran and held hostage for four hundred forty-four days. There was a heavy Iranian presence on campus, so, naturally, the Iranian students took some heat for the event.

We had an amazing baseball team and cruised through fall ball in preparation for our spring season. Every night after college, I would put on my spikes and do wind sprints in the park. I had never been so excited.

As it turned out, my daily concerts at Black and Decker had helped me greatly. My sister Jan married John that September, and I sang a duet at their wedding with my friend Kathy Insley. It was the first wedding I had ever attended, and I was in awe of the whole process.

I remember hearing two of their friends talking at the bar about the house band and betting on what their first song would be. One of them put his money on Jim Croce and, sure enough, the very first song played was "Bad, Bad Leroy Brown." Too funny!

It was great to see our extended family show up for the event. Aunts, uncles and cousins traveled from Pennsylvania, and I even met my Uncle Russell from Boston for the very first time. He was one of my dad's three brothers; I couldn't believe how much he reminded me of my dad. They had the same laugh and mannerisms. I really enjoyed getting to know him.

Everyone wore a tux or a nice dress, and the bride looked beautiful, of course. The next day, everyone visited our house to hang out before driving home. My dad was very complimentary of all of us and spent a lot of the time bragging about his children. He didn't gush at us all that much, so it warmed my heart to hear him go on about us to his brothers.

I had also heard some great stories that day about my dad and his youthful antics. One in particular stuck in my memory. My dad took weeks and weeks to build a huge model airplane out of balsa wood and tissue paper. When he had finished, he didn't know what to do with it. He lived miles from a field and his entire neighborhood stood upon the concrete streets of downtown Allentown. Without a viable solution, he poured lighter fluid on it, lit it on fire, and threw it down the alley, right into a traffic cop. *Can you imagine?* At least I got it naturally.

Not to be outdone, I needed to impress my dad's brothers, so I chimed in with some of my recent antics. After leaving Black and Decker, I landed a job at Toys "R" Us at Eudowood Plaza. I hadn't been back there since the big scary Santa episode when I was a tyke, so I sucked it up and went inside. I had the pleasure of wearing an orange vest with a giraffe on its back. The only uniform exception made was on Sundays. In the *Way Back Machine* there is a limit to what you can do on Sundays, due to religious standards. Bans are adhered to activities that take place on a day of rest and they are called Blue Laws. In some places they deal with alcohol consumption; no one can sell it on Sundays. In other places they ban shopping, which obviously affects us at the toy store.

We were limited as to the number of employees allowed to work on the Sabbath, so on Sundays some people had to wear their winter coats the whole time they worked. If shoppers came inside the store, the employees had to act like they were shoppers too. Silly, I know, but we did whatever we could to sell another game of Chutes and Ladders.

I worked the game wall which was the very first aisle upon entering the store. This meant that I had to be an authority on everything we sold, because everyone who arrived would ask me where the item they sought after was. When this would happen, I pretended like I knew and sent everyone to aisle twelve. I didn't even know what was in aisle twelve, but that is where I sent everyone.

I quickly learned that if you had an interest in doing a psychological study of humans, instead of taking a college class, all you really needed to do was get a part time job at a toy store during Christmastime. Toy stores are giant petri dishes of psychotic visitors with wayward personalities.

In the *Way Back Machine* Target and Walmart don't exist, so people have to venture to an actual toy store to purchase toys. On top of that, people rip off the shrink-wrapping of a brand new game to see if it contains all its pieces and then put it back on the shelf and grab another one.

I would screw with their heads and innocently inquire, "What if this one doesn't have all the pieces?" They would stand there, puzzled, and then open up that one too.

Due to this bizarre behavior, the management of Toys "R" Us came up with an ingenious plan. Inside the stock room of every store, they installed a large shrink-wrap machine. It was awesome. I would simply take an opened box and place it in between two sheets of clear plastic. With a long, heated iron, I would seal all four ends together and with some quick hits from a massive blow dryer, shrink the plastic tightly onto the box. It would look brand new and be placed right back on the shelf. I could happily shrink-wrap thirty boxes of

Hungry Hungry Hippos in a heartbeat. My predicament, however, was that I couldn't stop there.

Close by stood a series of cubbies where employees would store their personal items. I would shrink-wrap everything inside them: tennis shoes, lunches, and purses. I even took the telephone off the wall, shrink-wrapped it firmly, and promptly hung it back up. Moments later, I would call that extension from a nearby station and watch another employee struggle to answer it. Friends from school, Nora Murphy and Mike Fridley, worked there too and eventually learned not to leave anything lying around. One night, I dumped out Nora's purse on the table and painstakingly shrink-wrapped each individual thing inside it, from her chewing gum to her keys.

Mike Fridley and I were in charge of building bicycles in the springtime. The storerooms wrapped all the way around the store and in some places were just as big as the show room. After building a bike, it needed to be tested, so we would ride up and down the aisles of the storeroom at breakneck speed.

Mike jumped onto a red Radio Flyer wagon, and I tied its handle to the seat of my bike and took off. He was steering for a while with the wagon handle until my erratic driving ripped it from his hands. The look on his face as I swung around corners was fantastic but soon turned to fear as we slammed right into a tower of boxed Nerf footballs. We were ideal employees!

On one afternoon later in the year, I came to work directly after registering for the draft. President Carter had signed Proclamation 4771 in order to prepare the nation for a draft of combat troops. The Soviets had just invaded Afghanistan; I was not very excited about going to war.

One dark night as I was walking through the Tonka truck aisle, I heard the familiar static of the beginning of an announcement over the intercom. Seconds later, I heard "Ladies and gentlemen, may I have your attention for a very important announcement? The United States has just..." I immediately fell to the ground. I knew the manager was going to end with "declared war on the Soviet Union" and I would be on a transport ship in the morning. My imagination was in hyper-drive, conjuring up horrible scenarios, when she finished her sentence "... beat the Russians in ice hockey!" *Oh, my god!* It was the Olympics, not war. I went straight to her locker and shrink-wrapped every last one of her belongings.

THE BAD DAY

One October afternoon in 1979, I was in the basement working on my fielder's glove at the workbench. I formed this tool out of a dry cleaner's hanger that allowed me to re-thread my glove. I used rawhide bootlaces and soaked them in warm water so they were pliable. I had it down to an art and could lace up a whole glove in the time it took to watch an episode of *Get Smart*. Would you believe half an episode of *Get Smart*?

I was just about done when I heard a strange noise upstairs. Someone had come in the front door, which was normal, but this time their entrance was accompanied by an odd noise. It was a wail; someone was crying. It didn't sound like the typical "I fell off my bike" moan or even the whine associated with tripping up the stairs and smashing your face on the concrete steps. This was different.

I had heard everyone in my house cry, except my dad. He did tear up a little watching *Rocky* at the movies in Golden Ring Mall, but only for a second. I will never forget him wiping his eyes.

I ran upstairs and found my mother, and she was literally wailing. I didn't know what to do, so I tried to make her laugh, but she was having none of that. I asked her what happened, and she struggled to tell me. Glancing out the window, I saw that the car was intact, so I knew she hadn't wrapped it around the mailbox. I questioned her about her job, then her relatives, then the house payment, but received no response.

"Mom, what is the matter?

What is going on? Please calm down and talk to me." She looked at me and I immediately knew I was about to learn something bad.

"Daddy has cancer."

A few weeks earlier my dad had been walking and stepped off the curb without knowing it. I have done that before while walking down the stairs where I thought I was at the bottom, but there was still one more step. The jolt threw me forward into the front door.

For my dad, it caused him to slip and stutter step. The unusual action jammed his spine, and he had been in a lot of pain ever since. Of course, being my dad, he never told anybody he was in pain; he just stopped using the stairs, and started sleeping on the couch. When he couldn't take it anymore, my mom took him to Union Memorial Hospital. As a family, we were totally kept in the dark.

This just added to his bad month. Recently, he had been let go from E.J. Korvettes after many, many years. It was his life. He was qualified to do many other things, but he stayed there, slowly climbing, the corporate ladder, to support our family. Korvettes had been purchased by a French company, and to cut costs, they decided to clean house. A slash of the pen and he was gone.

For the first time in my life, my dad was unemployed. He was very positive and every morning he sat at the dining room table, looking through the help wanted ads. I started to get worried after a few weeks. It was out of the norm to see him around the house, say on a Tuesday.

My parents used to do this little romantic thing where they would call each other in sick once every six months. They would hang out all day and just relax. They both had good jobs and had plenty of sick days, but now that was over. There was one job that he really wanted to do but knew he couldn't support our family on the entry-level income, so he let it pass.

The job was a writer for a police magazine. My father could write the hell out of anything. When I had been asked to write a poem for the high school yearbook, my father got very excited for me. He knew I was a decent poet, but I told him I was unsure what to write about. Without thinking, he immediately suggested school spirit. I decided to sleep on it. When I awoke the next morning, there was a note on the refrigerator.

It was written on an envelope, and the note said "How about something like this?" He had written a poem called "Knight with a K." The entire poem was about school spirit, and every stanza ended with a word that had a silent first letter. He included words like psychology, gnome, herb, and czar. It was amazing and beautiful and brought tears to my eyes. He wrote it with a pen, and there wasn't one scratch mark or edit. For a hundred dollars I couldn't think of one word that started with a silent letter much less twelve of them. He was a bona-fide wordsmith and made it look so easy.

I ended up writing a poem called "Reunion" which was about attending the funeral of a high school friend. I know, real uplifting stuff right? It was printed in the senior addition to the school newspaper and had girls crying all over homeroom.

My father eventually took a job selling, of all things, life insurance. He took some classes and read a lot of material, familiarizing himself with his new craft. He was just starting to make appointments with some prospects, when he got sick. He bought policies for all of us kids and only sold a few others before ending up in the hospital. I remember looking at Karen and David and wondering how we would explain this to them.

The cancer had started in his lungs, obviously from smoking, and it quickly spread throughout his body. I was in my first year of college and playing fall baseball and couldn't visit him for a few days. The day I was going to finally visit him in the hospital, his new business cards arrived, so I took them with me. I thought they might cheer him up. I was wrong. It really depressed him because he thought he would never get to use them.

It was strange to see him in hospital garb. When you think of your parents, you picture them wearing the clothes you have seen many times. The old, white, torn sweatshirt he wore on Sundays, the army jacket he used when he painted the house, his blue Northside softball shirt, these were normal, everyday attire for my dad.

Sitting up in a strange bed, wearing a print gown with little fish on it that tied in the back was not one of my visuals of him, and it was hard to digest. I wasn't sure what to say when I saw him.

When I walked in, he perked up and immediately pointed out a bounty of hospital food items he was hoarding for Karen and David. That was a classic Dad move. Here he was, in the hospital with cancer, and he was worrying about others.

I was very uneasy and wanted answers. Cancer is such a bad word, and I had not met any survivors. He looked the same and didn't seem different at all. The conversation started out pleasant, and then I ruined it.

"You want a pudding or Jell-O?"

"No, thanks I'm good ... how much time did they give you?"

"What?" He looked at me and laughed, "What the hell kind of a question is that? I'm going to beat this thing."

That was all I needed to hear. My father was the strongest man I had ever met, both physically and mentally. If anyone could beat cancer, it would be my dad. There was no question in my mind.

"I'll have the pudding."

THE MAGIC

On a typical Beller Christmas Eve, our house was decorated with homemade decorations, like paper chains and snowflakes we cut out ourselves. On Christmas mornings, however, we awoke to find a completely different, magical scene. A glistening, six-foot tall Christmas tree stood proudly in front of the picture window, fake snow sprayed in the corners of its glass. Lights were twinkling and presents were stacked all over the living room. There wasn't a doubt in my mind that Santa had been there. I mean, who else could have done all that? If it had been my parents, they would've had to have stayed up all night. That would be crazy! As it turned out, my parents were card-carrying members of crazy.

With my father in the hospital, the house was very sad and dreary. I would go and visit him right after my college classes, and, by the time I got home, Karen and David were already in bed. My mom would sometimes take them for a visit earlier in the day, when they got home from school, but they usually just waited until the weekend. There was no more laughter in the house.

A few years earlier, after Jan graduated from nursing school, my mom decided she wanted to become a nurse. My dad had no problem with it and helped her with papers and study regimens. Every night, he and I would sit at the table and write out what seemed like an endless array of drug cards. Drug cards were individual index cards labeled with the name of a particular drug and all of its uses, side effects and treatments. This helped my mom study in a more efficient manner. When we were done with all those cards, *I* could have taken and passed the test.

Since my mom and sister were nurses, they were well-aware of the severity of my dad's cancer and handled it accordingly. Karen was thirteen and David was ten when he was diagnosed, and I believe all they realized was that dad was sick. I was a realist, but totally in denial. I couldn't remember one time that my dad even had the flu; it seemed that he was never sick. It was hard for everybody.

I found myself having small-talk conversations with him that I might've had with a stranger on an elevator. We talked about the weather, the bad-tasting hospital food, the latest sitcom and college baseball. He wanted to know everything about what I was experiencing as a college catcher and yearned to come to a game. I shared with him the locker room antics, a description of each player, and, especially, the details on how we learned to play like a team. His closed-mouth smile announced his approval.

You can't imagine the generosity of people when you are dealing with such an event. Everyone was wonderful and caring. Reverend Crossland (yes, that was his real name) stopped by from Linden Heights United Methodist Church just to talk and pray with us. When he left the house, we found a check from the church on the kitchen counter.

November dragged by, and in early December, my mother took a note from the movie *Mame* and decided we needed a little Christmas. She informed us that Santa wouldn't mind if we got our own tree this year and decorated it. She wanted the kids to be a little distracted.

We bought a big tree, put it up, and, together as a family, decorated it with every ornament we owned. We were creatures of habit, so decorating the house was always a non-adventure. We removed each ornament from the big box marked "X-mas Decor" and placed it where it belonged, immediately knowing exactly where its location should be.

The gold bells went on the crooked nail on the back door, the big, red half-burned candle went in the middle of the coffee table, the boots that seven-year-old Jan made out of orange juice cans, paper mache and cotton went on the shelf, and David's paper plate ornament hung right in the middle of the tree. That particular ornament was a family favorite. He painted a paper plate yellow, glued a Christmas card to its middle, and presented it to our mom. It had been the focal point of the tree ever since. The house was pretty but just didn't feel the same.

Karen and I always had a tradition of sleeping one night under the Christmas tree. We loved to look up into the litany of colored lights and watch how the ornaments glistened. We had never done that *before* Christmas, so we got out our blankets and pillows and changed our tradition. Again, it felt different.

It was very important to my parents that we go through this as a family. They wanted life for Karen and David to be as close to normal as possible. Our house was anything but normal, so I guess they meant for us to just to be our crazy selves.

If that meant friends spending the night, then so be it. It was hard to try to fake normal when the world as we knew it was changing so drastically.

We also wanted our dad to feel some normalcy, which is almost impossible to do in a hospital. One night, we dressed David up as Santa Claus and all went to the hospital to visit him. I can picture David walking down the hallway in a Santa suit with a beard and everything as nurses smiled with gratitude. He looked great. Jan and John went in first with my mother and then Karen and I preceded the small Santa. My dad's eyes lit up as he entered the room, and to impress Santa, Dad immediately proclaimed that he had been a good boy.

Etched into my mind is the picture of a small Santa Claus sitting on my father's lap. Unfortunately, we didn't get one picture of the jolly young elf's visit, but everyone in the room still carries that holiday image with them.

A week later, I walked in our front door, after everyone had fallen asleep, and was immediately startled. To my surprise, a reindeer was staring me down. Our neighbor, Kim Bell, was an elementary school teacher, and when she told her class about our predicament, they found it in their young hearts to do something to help us.

The reindeer was a box mounted on four wooden legs and stood about three feet high. A reindeer's head, complete with a red nose and antlers, was sticking out of the front of the box. Trailing the box by colorful reigns was another box on skis acting as a sleigh. Both of the boxes were filled with food. On the side of the sleigh was a sign which read "Get Better Mr. Beller, From Miss Bell's Class." I stood there and cried.

People amazed me. Just when I was at the point where I was getting pretty pissed off at God for dealing us this hand, someone's random act of kindness would set me straight. I always wondered if I had that in me.

In preparation for our dad's return from his last hospital stay, we made a huge banner, with the help of Mike Fridley, and plastered it across the front of the house. It was bright yellow and could be seen for miles. Mike was good at art projects for mass viewing. We all made a big scene for him as the enormous banner hung in the background, announcing in huge, capital letters "WELCOME HOME DAD!" He really enjoyed it.

A few days later, he had to go back to the hospital for some tests. When the ambulance brought him home this time, he had a different driver. Coming down Appleton Avenue, the new driver saw the sign and told my dad, "You should see this. They have something big happening." My dad told him to make some noise to impress us, so he blasted the siren and woke the neighborhood. When they opened the back door to pull him out, it seemed like a ghost town. We were all at school. Nobody was home to greet him. Later that night, my dad told me the story, and we laughed about it. Three days later, he was back in the hospital again.

By the time Christmas Eve arrived, the tree was dead. Every time someone walked through the room, pine needles rained down onto the wrapped presents below. It sounded like a never-ending bag of rice leaking onto wax paper. We visited my dad earlier at the hospital, and after a small family get-together at the house, and everyone went to bed. I, however, sat down to watch television and waited for Santa Claus.

At 12:30AM, I stood up, walked over to our skeleton of a tree, and started to remove every ornament, placing them on the coffee table. The removal of the colorful light strands came next. I quietly placed them all on the couch. Out through the front door, I dragged the tree, now completely vacant of ornaments and Christmas spirit, and dropped it in our yard. Earlier in the evening, while everyone was eating dinner, I had snuck out to procure a new Christmas tree. I bought it at George's Market on Harford Road, only moments before it closed. He charged me thirty-eight bucks and helped me tie it to the roof of my Vega. I hid it next to Mr. Herman's shed.

It took me about a half an hour to vacuum up the remainder of the first tree. My mom used to vacuum while we were sleeping all the time, so no one stirred as I worked. When everything was cleaned up, I brought in the new tree and decorated it, trying to remember where each ornament was previously placed. I felt very excited as I scurried around the house, and, surprisingly, not tired at all. I couldn't wait to see the little ones' faces when they came out in the morning. *So this is what Christmas was all about.* I finally understood. The feeling was wonderful. Knowing that tomorrow morning Karen and David and even my mom would think that something magical happened gave me the energy to stay up all night. I admired my parents for all the years they'd brought me the magic of Christmas. Before I could experience that, however, I had to drag the old tree's carcass past the park and into the woods.

The next morning, as David and Karen were busy opening presents, I noticed that my mom seemed to simply be sitting there wishing my father could have joined us. Then, all of a sudden, Karen said, "Look at the tree. Santa brought us a new tree!" I watched my mother as she looked up. She looked harder, and then, placing her hands over her mouth, she gasped and immediately started crying.

She looked at me and mouthed, "Did you do that?"

"It was Santa," I said.

Later that afternoon, when I walked in my father's hospital room, he just smiled and said, "Hey there, Santa." Then, he gave me a very welcoming, approving smile. The torch had been passed.

A week later, I was at a New Year's Eve party that I didn't really want to attend, but my dad insisted that I go. I had a bad record when it came to New Year's and was still scarred by a party I attended at Therese Cromwell's house. At midnight, I ruined her mother's best pot with a hammer.

When I called my dad at midnight to wish him a Happy New Year, he was alone, which has stuck with me ever since. Everybody looks ahead and says, "It's going to be a great year!" I always look back and say, "What a shitty year that was." I mean, the Baltimore Orioles did lose to the Pittsburgh Pirates in the World Series *again*. To this day, I dislike New Year's Eve.

After hospital stays at Hopkins and Church Home, my father came home for good. We took turns sitting up at night talking with him and feeding him ring bologna. He even asked me to shave him. I was scared to death, as I didn't want to accidentally slit his throat. He never lost his sense of humor and used to laugh like crazy as we watched *WKRP in Cincinnati*. He loved Dr. Johnny Fever.

When my turn came to sit up with him, he lapsed into a coma. I sat there holding his hand all night while talking to him. I thanked him for flying my kite in his work clothes, I thanked him for sharing his humorous approach to life with me, and I thanked him for teaching me the game of baseball.

MISSING PINE PARK

My father passed away on March 29, 1980. He was forty-five years old. He died in a hospital bed in our living room with my mom was sleeping next to him in a rented cot. At 4:02 in the morning, she woke me up and told me that he had just taken his last breath. Jan and John came over. They told Karen and David that Daddy had gone to heaven. I couldn't face them.

Later that day, our neighbor, Mrs. Dorothy Bell, told me that at precisely 4AM, something had woken her up. She rolled over, looked out the window, and saw a light shoot from our house into the sky. At that moment, a light went out in all of us.

MY HOMECOMING

In 1940 Thomas Wolfe wrote: "Some things will never change. Some things will always be the same. Lean down your ear upon the earth and listen." I could not disagree more.

My whole world had changed. My family split up, and I moved to Pasadena to live with my grandparents. For the first time in my life, I wasn't living in Carney. I had attended three different colleges playing baseball, but my dream of becoming a professional player had never reached fruition. My mother sold our house to Jan and John and moved to Loch Raven to raise Karen and David. I think the community is still reeling from their presence. In actuality, I'm sure it had become a better place. Sadly, the closeness that we all shared had dissolved quickly. I still miss that side of sibling-hood and I felt mad at God for not allowing that to continue.

I was asked to come to a Northside softball function to accept a trophy on behalf of my father. It was engraved with his name and the letters MVP. Other than that and an occasional babysitting gig, I didn't venture back to Carney much at all. I totally lost touch with Buddy, Tony, Fitz and the rest of the neighborhood gang.

Jan had asked me once to come over and entertain their houseguest, Alistair Russell, who was visiting from England. When I drove over, he was kicking around a soccer ball in the park. I introduced myself and then immediately took him to Fort McHenry where I proudly showed him the famous spot where we kicked his country's ass. Afterwards, I presented him with steamed crabs. He thought they were covered in mud and stated, "It looks like something you'd scrape off an old brown shoe." Unfortunately, the restaurant didn't have a garden hose. Our date ended with a viewing of the movie *Stripes*.

Once, when a college friend was trying to get in touch with me, he called information. In the **Way Back Machine,** you can dial 411 from any telephone and an operator helps you find someone. When he asked for Neil Beller, the operator excitedly said, "Neil Beller? I know that dude!" As it turns out, it was Paul Flanagan. He was working for MCI at the time. What are the odds?

In Maryland you could also dial the exchange 936 followed by any four numbers and get the weather forecast. You would hear a recording that would convey to you the weather for Baltimore, Washington, and the surrounding areas.

844 followed by any four numbers would give you the time. No kidding. "At the tone the time will be six thirty-four and twenty seconds, BEEP." A friend of my brother and Nashville resident had asked him if people in Maryland were stupid because they needed a recording to tell them what time it was. There is no short answer.

Nine years after my father died, I had the opportunity to purchase my old house. Jan and John had fixed it up and added a big enclosed, back porch. I was excited to keep it in the family. Besides, I longed to live next door to Mr. Herman C Bell III again, that is, until he called me "Little Neil."

On my first Halloween after moving back, I took a deep breath and walked down to the Chadmans' to attend The Vigilantes' party. Out of respect for my dad, there was an empty chair up against the tailgate of their station wagon. It was leaning right next to the hibachi. The sight of it was touching and made me smile. It also made me tear up.

I stayed about an hour then headed home to see all the trick or-treaters. The kids were so cute and brought back a thousand memories of Halloweens past. One group was jockeying for position, and, as I placed candy in their outstretched bags, I heard a familiar voice say, "Neil?" I looked up to see Michael Flanagan. He was escorting his kids around the neighborhood. It was so good to see him. We spent a few minutes catching up before his kids dragged him from the porch.

I sat down to watch television in between knocks at the door and thought about coming home. *Perhaps Thomas Wolfe was right after all.* I longed to play football in the park with my kids and teach them Tin Can Willie. I wondered if I had inherited the ability to breathe at them in a menacing manner when they would be bad. My mind raced with fond memories and imagery until a loud bang at the door startled me. I grabbed the candy bowl and bent over to greet the youngsters as I opened the glass door. However, nobody was there.

Following a shadow, I looked up Uxbridge Road to see none other than Michael Flanagan running towards Missing Pine Park, laughing hysterically. I had come home. It was good to be back in Carney.

MISSING PINE PARK